ROUTLEDGE LIBRARY EDITIONS: LIBRARY AND INFORMATION SCIENCE

Volume 37

EXPERT SYSTEMS IN REFERENCE SERVICES

EXPERT SYSTEMS IN REFERENCE SERVICES

Edited by
CHRISTINE ROYSDON AND
HOWARD D. WHITE

LONDON AND NEW YORK

First published in 1989 by The Haworth Press, Inc.

This edition first published in 2020
by Routledge
2 Park Square, Milton Park, Abingdon, Oxon OX14 4RN

and by Routledge
52 Vanderbilt Avenue, New York, NY 10017

Routledge is an imprint of the Taylor & Francis Group, an informa business

© 1989 The Haworth Press, Inc.

All rights reserved. No part of this book may be reprinted or reproduced or utilised in any form or by any electronic, mechanical, or other means, now known or hereafter invented, including photocopying and recording, or in any information storage or retrieval system, without permission in writing from the publishers.

Trademark notice: Product or corporate names may be trademarks or registered trademarks, and are used only for identification and explanation without intent to infringe.

British Library Cataloguing in Publication Data
A catalogue record for this book is available from the British Library

ISBN: 978-0-367-34616-4 (Set)
ISBN: 978-0-429-34352-0 (Set) (ebk)
ISBN: 978-0-367-37047-3 (Volume 37) (hbk)
ISBN: 978-0-367-37066-4 (Volume 37) (pbk)
ISBN: 978-0-429-35253-9 (Volume 37) (ebk)

Publisher's Note
The publisher has gone to great lengths to ensure the quality of this reprint but points out that some imperfections in the original copies may be apparent.

Disclaimer
The publisher has made every effort to trace copyright holders and would welcome correspondence from those they have been unable to trace.

Expert Systems in Reference Services

Christine Roysdon
Howard D. White
Editors

The Haworth Press
New York • London

Expert Systems in Reference Services has also been published as *The Reference Librarian*, Number 23.

© 1989 by The Haworth Press, Inc. All rights reserved. No part of this book may be reproduced or utilized in any form or by any means, electronic or mechanical, including photocopying, microfilm and recording, or by any information storage and retrieval system, without permission in writing from the publisher. Printed in the United States of America.

The Haworth Press, Inc., 12 West 32 Street, New York, NY 10001
EUROSPAN/Haworth, 3 Henrietta Street, London WC2E 8LU England

Library of Congress Cataloging-in-Publication Data

Expert systems in reference services / Christine Roysdon, Howard D. White, editors.
    p. cm.
"Has also been published as The Reference librarian, number 23, 1988" – T.p. verso.
Bibliography: p.
ISBN 0-86656-839-5
    1. Expert systems (Computer science) – Library applications. 2. Reference services (Libraries) – Automation. I. Roysdon, Christine. II. White, Howard D.
Z678.93.E93E96 1988
025.5'20285 – dc19   88-39835
                                                                                                                                                  CIP

Expert Systems in Reference Services

CONTENTS

Introduction   xiii
    Christine Roysdon
    Howard D. White

OVERVIEWS

Library Applications of Knowledge-Based Systems   1
    Joseph M. A. Cavanagh

Introduction   1
Expert System Applications   3
Conclusion   14

Augmented Assistance in Online Catalog Subject Searching   21
    Zorana Ercegovac

Introduction   22
Users Need Useful Online "Help": Lessons Learned from Empirical Research   25
Implementation of "Tactics" for Subject Searching in Online Catalogs   29
Directions for Research   35

Knowledge-Based Systems in Information Work: A View of the Future   41
    Irene L. Travis

The New Technologies   44
KBSs as Tools for the Provision of Information Services   47
KBSs and Other Electronic Products as Information Materials   56
Conclusion   58

REFERENCE APPLICATIONS

An Expert System at the Reference Desk: Impressions from Users   61
    Nancy J. Butkovich
    Kathryn L. Taylor
    Sharon H. Dent
    Ann S. Moore

Introduction	62
Course and Student Description	62
Literature Review	63
Hardware and Software	64
The Database	66
User Response	68
Problems	70
Summary and Conclusions	73

The Information Machine: A Microcomputer-Based Reference Service   75
    Jeff Fadell
    Judy E. Myers

The Development Environment and Process	76
The Product	94
Reflections	108

AquaRef: An Expert Advisory System for Reference Support   113
    Deborah Hanfman

Software Selection Criteria	116
Data Analysis Phase	117
System Creation	118
AquaRef Distribution	130
Current Perspectives and Future Outlook	131

Designing a Workstation for Information Seekers   135
    Mary Micco
    Irma Smith

I. Problem Statement	135
II. Converging Technologies	137

III. Background	139
IV. Upgrading Existing Subject Access Tools (Proposed)	145
V. Methodology: Building the System of Subject Access Maps	146
VI. Evaluation	149
VII. Conclusion	150

Simulation of the Reference Process, Part II: REFSIM, an Implementation with Expert System and ICAI Modes — 153
James R. Parrott

Simulation of the Consultation Process in Reference	153
Simulation of the Instructional Process in Reference	154
A Common Knowledge Base for Consultation and Instruction	156
Representing Knowledge About the Reference Process	158
Connections Between Knowledge Base Constituents	159
Natural-Language Parser	160
Reference Interview Frames	161
Librarian and Client Frames	163
Strategy Prescription Rules	164
Databases of Reference Tools, etc.	168
Consultation Mode (Expert System Mode)	170
Simulation-Based Coach	171
Socratic Tutor	172
Conclusions	173

Reference Expert Systems: Humanizing Depersonalized Service — 177
Dana E. Smith

What Is an Expert System?	177
Expert Systems in Reference Work	179
Developing the Reference Expert System	180
Site-Specific Reference Expert System Development	182

**POINTER vs. *Using Government Publications*:
Where's the Advantage?**   **191**
    Karen F. Smith

The Development of POINTER	192
What POINTER Does	193
Subject Searching in POINTER	194
What *Using Government Publications* Does	195
Problems with the Indexing of *Using Government Publications*	196
Conceptual Framework of *Using Government Publications*	197
Point by Point Comparison of the Two Works	197
Advantages and Disadvantages	200

**An Expert System for Microcomputers to Aid Selection
of Online Databases**   **207**
    Rodes Trautman
    Sara von Flittner

Introduction	208
Background of the Online Industry and Artificial Intelligence	208
Project Approach	210
Materials and Methods	212
Results	216
Discussion	231
Summary	235

Introduction

The idea that machine intelligence might be substituted for the memory and searching skill of the reference librarian is not particularly new. For several decades, programs have been developed to teach reference through machine simulation of the reference interview; to offer low-level assistance to users when skilled staff are not available; and to capture and model the decision-making steps involved in negotiating a question and selecting appropriate sources to answer it. Early programs developed on mainframes were interesting experiments in simulation and instruction, but lacked the flexibility, speed, ease of development and alteration, and portability required of a reference program intended for use in an actual library setting. The advent of expert systems that can be mounted on microcomputers has promised to overcome some of these limitations. Fully programmed systems can offer sophisticated natural language interfaces and embed detailed knowledge about sources and users. Through the use of expert systems shells, prototype programs can be developed relatively quickly and modified easily. Systems mounted on microcomputers can be placed where library patrons are mostly likely to use them. Through some systems, users may be linked to several databases or to full text almost transparently. The continuing rationale for developing these programs appears to be twofold: to make the expertise of the reference librarian available in a more consistent and timely fashion; and to reduce the burden of repetitive, predictable questions for the professional.

This issue of *The Reference Librarian* has two aims: to introduce readers to expert systems applications in many areas of library and information science; and to present design and implementation issues encountered by librarians who have developed early systems to address the library reference function.

Joseph Cavanagh opens the issue with a wide-ranging survey of projects of central or tangential interest to reference librarians, including attempts to use knowledge based systems in collection development, the construction of SDI profiles, cataloging and indexing, reference systems, post-search processing and intelligent tutoring. Irene Travis provides a more general overview of knowledge-based systems and their potential for information services, focusing on the potential of knowledge based systems for four problem areas: reference and referral; public access catalogs; improved end-user searching of bibliographic databases with controlled vocabularies; and end-user text searching. She draws an interesting contrast between two well-known early systems: NAL's *Answerman* and the University of London's PLEXUS. Built fairly rapidly with an expert system shell, *Answerman* represents "an attempt to prototype a full online reference service." The development of PLEXUS has entailed long, basic AI research, encompasses a much narrower domain (gardening) than *Answerman*, but offers fine-tuned natural language processing and sophisticated subject access. A similar contrast is presented by two systems described in this issue: *AquaRef*, reviewed by Hanfman, and *Refsim*, developed by James Parrott. *AquaRef*, a descendant of *Answerman*, also uses 1st Class shell software, offers links to bibliographic databases and CD-ROMs and has involved several institutions in the cooperative development of its knowledge bases. In that it has involved more fundamental AI programming, *Refsim* is comparable to the PLEXUS project. However, *Refsim* is distinguished by its broad subject scope — the general reference collection — and by Parrott's attempt to base his system architecture on models of the reference process developed by Robert Taylor, Marcia Bates and others.

Several academic libraries that have developed prototype systems that have already received extensive use by their clientele are represented in this issue. Jeff Fadell and Judy Myers share details of the development process of their *Information Machine*, which has provided some 30,000 users at the University of Houston with basic library information — directions, locations, hours — and limited reference and tutorial assistance. Nancy Butkovich and colleagues at Texas A & M have implemented a prototype system designed for more in-depth questions posed by a defined user group — students enrolled in a technical writing course that has typically made heavy use of reference materials in scientific and technical fields. The authors share practical concerns of interest to novice designers from hardware costs to printer problems, while presenting in detail the advantages and disadvantages of the expert system shell selected for the project. Based on his relatively lengthy experience with a microcomputer-based reference program at Purdue University's undergraduate library, Dana Smith reflects upon the unique opportunities that expert systems offer to libraries. He is concerned that library professionals may be squeezed out of the development area in expert systems and limited to a consumer role. However, he sees continuing opportunities to customize systems to the needs of a local user community and the potential for the incorporation of useful question data, objectively and voluminously collected by well-designed systems, into the library planning process. Another designer of an early microcomputer-based reference system, Karen Smith, compares her automated tool for government documents reference, POINTER, with a recently published two-volume work that presents search strategies for government documents. She contrasts the two products in scope, cost, size, presentation format, and other features. Features of the program that appear to be superior are its potential (if not actual) visibility to users, ease of use, customizing capabilities, and simplicity of updating.

Two papers in this issue examine the failings of systems that we currently offer to users in light of the potential of artificial intelligence to remedy those failings. Zorana Ercegovac looks at the deficiencies of the user interface of current online catalogs, and at possibilities for enhancing OPAC access through, for example, the implementation of Marcia Bates' schema of idea tactics and information search tactics. Mary Micco and Irma Smith describe several projects, proposed and in progress, to enhance subject access to book records and to unify subject access to databases encompassing diverse materials and employing different indexing levels.

Finally, a number of researchers have turned their attention to automating the choice of online databases by end users. Rodes Trautman and Sara von Flittner describe a prototype expert system to be used offline for database selection. Built with the expert system shell GURU, it employs a complex scheme of subject "viewpoints." Knowledge embedded in the program is derived from a number of published and online directories. Internal experts, including the "user modeler," "question clarifier," "evaluator" and "ranker" guide the user to a ranked set of selected databases.

BIBLIOGRAPHIC INTRODUCTION

Contributors to this issue, particularly our review essayists, have included ample bibliographies that will direct readers to a generous selection of literature on knowledge based systems. The purpose of this brief bibliographic essay, therefore, is not to provide a lengthy list of readings, but rather to suggest some useful basic texts, important collections, and sources of guidance in software selection.

Many texts are now available on expert systems. Two that we have found particularly readable are Paul Harmon and David King, *Expert Systems: Artificial Intelligence in Business* (New York: John Wiley, 1985); and Philip Klahr and D. A. Waterman, *Expert Systems: Techniques, Tools and Applications* (Reading, MA: Addison-Wesley, 1986). Both texts present basic concepts of artificial intelligence and expert systems in non-technical terms and describe a number of pioneering systems from medical, scientific and other fields. Briefer introductions are provided by F. Hayes-Roth in a survey article, "Expert Systems," in the recently published *Encyclopedia of Artificial Intelligence* (New York: Wiley, 1987); and by K. Obermeier in his somewhat older review piece "Expert Systems" in the *Encyclopedia of Library and Information Science*, volume 38, supplement 3 (New York: M. Dekker, 1985). Two helpful reviews have appeared in the *Annual Review of Information Science and Technology* (New York: Knowledge Industry Publications). Henry Sowizral surveys the history of expert systems, describes pioneering medical systems, and reviews work on knowledge representation (*ARIST*, 1985, pp. 179-99). Linda Smith's "Artificial Intelligence and Information Retrieval" *ARIST*, 1987, pp. 41-77) examines present and projected relationships between AI and IR, reviews advances in machine learning and user modelling, and discusses applications for expert systems in cataloging, reference and online searching.

Several recent collections and special issues provide "must" reading for the librarian who has read a few basic texts on expert systems and artificial intelligence and wishes to become conversant with the state of the art of library/information applications of knowledge based systems. Rao Aluri and Don Riggs' collection *Expert Systems in Libraries* (Ablex, 1988) contains an overview, articles on reference systems and on intelligent computer-assisted instruction; and pieces on expert systems applications in documents, reference, cataloging and classification, indexing and online searching. *Intelligent Information Systems*, edited by Roy Davies (Chicester: Ellis Horwood, 1986), covers similar territory, but also looks at user modeling and at cognitive science topics related to IIS. The more technical *Informatics 8, Advances in Intelligent Retrieval*, (London: Aslib, 1985) addresses automatic book classification, linguistic methods in information retrieval systems, user models, natural language retrieval and other topics related to intelligent information systems architecture. A collection of papers also entitled *Expert Systems in Libraries*, edited by Forbes Gibb (London: Taylor Graham, 1986) presents an overview of expert systems, an article on the PLEXUS system and several pieces focusing on classification and cataloging concerns. Two recent issues of *Information Processing and Management* have also been devoted to AI topics. "Artificial Intelligence and Information Retrieval," edited by W. Bruce Croft (*IP&M* 23(4), 1987) includes articles on knowledge organization and access; user modeling; and intelligent systems for retrieval. Contributions to the very helpful special issue "Expert Systems and Library Information Science," edited by Harold Borko (*IP&M* 23(2): 1987) address expert systems applications and potential impact in areas including map cataloging, medical information retrieval (CANSEARCH), gardening (PLEXUS), image retrieval and library education.

We are happy to add this issue to the growing body of literature on expert systems applications in libraries.

Christine Roysdon
Howard D. White

OVERVIEWS

Library Applications of Knowledge-Based Systems

Joseph M. A. Cavanagh

SUMMARY. Computer-based systems capable of performing a variety of tasks which are regarded as requiring intelligence are finding their way into library operations and services. This paper identifies a broad range of library applications for expert systems. Descriptions of developments include systems for document selection, cataloging, classification, reference, retrieval, and instruction. It may be time for the library profession to consider the effects of expert systems on job structuring and content.

INTRODUCTION

Davis has described the evolution of artificial intelligence from implementation of a small set of domain-independent problem solving methods to the more recent focus on the accumulation, representation, and use of task-specific knowledge in what he refers to as knowledge-based systems; the term expert system is avoided.[1] Davis emphasizes the separation of the knowledge base from the reasoning rules which act on it, the inference engine, and points out

---

The author is Library Systems Planning Officer, Melville Library, State University of New York, Stony Brook, NY 11794-3300.

© 1989 by The Haworth Press, Inc. All rights reserved.

that a single inference engine can address a variety of problems if an appropriate new knowledge base is substituted for each domain. He states that, "the most important consequence of the distinction is that it enables the system to make multiple different uses of the same knowledge, facilitating explanation, knowledge acquisition, and tutoring" (p.959). Expert systems have been described as computer programs "working in complex knowledge-intensive domains with a performance matching that of human experts."[2] There is no shortage of knowledge-based systems in the world at large. A recent work lists more than 1,000 systems in 24 categories covering manufacturing, business, and professional domains.[3] More than 40 development tools (languages or shells) are reviewed. It is claimed that virtually every known commercial, in-house, and research expert system in the world has been identified.

Obermeier provides a good technical description of expert systems.[4] Gibb offers a more general description of this subfield of Artificial Intelligence and suggests some applications in the field of library and information science.[5] An understandable review of the nature of expert systems and descriptions of specific development efforts in the library arena is provided by Vickery and Brooks.[6]

There is in fact a considerable number of applications for expert systems in libraries. Any activity that can be defined by a set of rules, either general or specific, is a candidate for support by means of computer programs. Such programs often incorporate so-called production rules of the form:

   IF — condition
   THEN — action

One might readily think of cataloging, classification and indexing, and reference retrieval as rule-based processes. Machine aids are possible in other activities also: creating ILL forms for materials identified in online searches and not owned; format recognition of various citation layouts; document selection for acquisition or dissemination; bibliographic instruction; interactive library guiding; assignment of Cutter numbers. An appealing expert application not specifically proposed previously is a "tune recogniser" in which the opening bars or other key phrase or characteristic fragment of a tune could be coded and searched. The basis for such a system exists in the National Tune Index: data entry or inquiry by singing, whistling, or humming is conceivable but not an imminent possibility.[7] To a significant degree, all of the applications mentioned here depend upon judgment and involve decision-making. I have noted elsewhere that the essence of expert systems is the generation of decision rules by humans and the execution of those rules by machines.[8]

EXPERT SYSTEM APPLICATIONS

Document Selection

Acquisition is not generally viewed as a rule-based activity. However, it can be described in terms of rules in a particular instance, specifically Approval Plans. Approval plans are based on a profile of library requirements being matched against descriptions of new publications offered through book jobbers. A similar matching process is the basis of conventional Selective Dissemination of Information (SDI); a profile of a user's subject interests is passed against descriptions of newly published materials. If a described item satisfies the selection rules, the item is accepted. Selection rules can be applied either manually or by machine. Book jobbers' approval programs can be regarded as expert systems; they can be very sophisticated. These programs incorporate bibliographic descriptions and also codes to indicate such things as the level of difficulty of a work, the academic levels to which it is most suited, and the treatment of the subject. Brownson simulated mechanical selection in three areas (popular novels, German literature, and contemporary poetry) and concluded that "the test cases suggest that the efficiency of selectors in libraries of any size would be improved by an effort to shift the burden of selection away from expertise wherever possible."[9] Brownson made admittedly generous assumptions about the accuracy and efficiency of human expertise and still concluded that mechanical selection strategies were at least competitive in all cases and more than competitive in some cases. The simulation of expert selection on a substantial scale has been accomplished by Leon Raney.[10] The simulation involved profiling a medium-sized academic library into the domestic approval program of a major book jobber. Raney was able to conclude that the approval program could be programmed in such a way that its preselections closely coincided with the current pattern of acquisitions at the participating library. Under an operational program about 84% of titles pre-selected by the plan would have been judged appropriate by selectors at the participating library. Also, excluding government documents and children's literature, the system would have covered 93% of the 1,971 imprint titles actually acquired by the library through conventional selection and acquisition procedures. Interestingly, on average, new books pre-selected by the approval system would have reached the library approximately three months prior to the time they were actually received under conventional acquisition procedures.

The performance achieved in Raney's simulation is impressive. Presumably, fine tuning of the system for better performance is possible. Raney notes that approval plan profiles emphasize deep non-subject profiling whereas article-level SDI emphasizes deep subject indexing: the approval system studied rarely assigned more than two subject headings to a title while making provision for more than 300 non-subject options. An early effort to use machine aids to alert individuals to new monographs was based on exploitation of the MARC tapes for faculty at Indiana University.[11] A similar type of automated SDI service for books, directed at government agencies, was established in 1970 by the Oklahoma Department of Libraries.[12] Perhaps the most extensive research effort in article-level SDI is the series of studies reported by Swanson.[13] That work includes a proposal for a model retrieval and dissemination system inspired by the fact that so many of the retrieval methods studied were essentially mechanistic. Recently, Pao has offered a comparable proposal.[14]

Other aspects of collection development based in mechanistic procedures are being pursued. An algorithmic approach to journal selection has been taken by He and Pao.[15] Expert system techniques for journal selection at the National Library of Medicine are described by Rada et al.[16] Consideration has been given also to developing an expert system for selecting journals for indexing at the National Agricultural Library.[17]

Cataloging

Cataloging, as a domain for expert systems, has attracted a significant share of the research effort to date. Most of the work has been concerned with bibliographic description and with choosing access points. Fox showed that directed tree-graphs could be used to assign main entries with a high degree of accuracy and to do so automatically.[18] She tested both the Anglo-American cataloging code of 1967 (AACR1) and the ALA code of 1949: the results did not differ significantly between the codes. Simply by virtue of timing, the AACR2 rules have been subjected to intense scrutiny in terms of their amenability to automatic application. Davies and James have reported that rules for determining access points could be restated as production rules.[19] It is Davies' belief that an automatic expert cataloging system capable of carrying out the cognitive tasks performed by a cataloger is possible, but it would not be worthwhile until cataloging codes are rationalized.[20] Such rationalization, he argues, would eliminate reliance on machine intelligence at the search phase to compensate for shortcomings in catalog design. Also, he has noted that a knowledge base derived from AACR2 alone would not suffice to make the entire cataloging process fully automatic. His reasoning is that catalogers utilize heuristics that do not form part of the code.[21] AACR2 has been severely criticized as a vehicle for modelling cataloging activities. Hjerppe and Olander, in particular, have described the lack of hospitality of AACR2 to utilization as a knowledge base for intelligent systems.[22]

According to Davies, the nature of cataloging has less to do with the ability to execute rules and more to do with the ability to recognize the bibliographic conditions which determine the choice of rule.[23] Hjerppe and his colleagues have reached similar conclusions:

> [M]ore important for the design of operational expert systems for cataloging assistance than access to the rule set as a knowledge base, are questions . . . that center on the true expertise of an expert cataloger. . . . How does an expert recognize anomalies, when to apply which rules? . . . How much are the rules used in comparison with, and in cooperation with, refer-

ence to personal examples, earlier cases and their solutions? (p.21)

Description

Davies suggests that expertise in cataloging is worthy of study in its own right. He proposes that semiotics, the theory of signs, be applied so that the title page can be studied from syntactic, semantic, and pragmatic points of view. Using this idea, and considering just the title page, Davies has developed no less than sixty heuristics. He notes that some relate to the title page as a whole but most relate to particular features.[23] Weibel and his associates at OCLC have pursued descriptive cataloging from title pages as a goal for machine intelligence, concentrating on bibliographic description. They report that they have been able to capture a significant portion of the grammar discernible in title pages.[24] Working with a sample of 26 title pages in facsimile and just sixteen rules, 75% of the fields in the sample were correctly identified; fully half of the title pages were correctly analyzed in their entirety. The OCLC system includes rules relating to the layout of information and the meaning of words and phrases encountered in the title page. It is claimed that the output approximates first-level bibliographic description under AACR2. Also focusing on bibliographic description, Jeng has proposed a model expert system for determining title proper from title page data.[25] Jeng introduces the interesting notion of a "consistency enforcer," a module designed to ensure that each decision resulting from automatic processing conforms to cumulated prior experience. I have noted previously that the experience automatic systems have resides in statistics relating to past events, whatever knowledge they possess resides in a thesaurus, dictionary, or other look-up table, and whatever insight they have resides in information combining rules.[26]

Moving to access points, the other aspect of descriptive cataloging, Svenonius and her colleagues have explored the distribution of names in a sample of English language monographs.[27] They found that 93% of the authors, 56% of the editors, 80% of the emanators, and 21% of the illustrators could be identified on the title page through the application of rules. Recently, with support from

OCLC, Svenonius has studied the feasibility of automatically deriving name access points (persons or corporate bodies) from 512 machine-readable title pages. The algorithms tested identified correctly about 93% of personal names and about 80% of the corporate names assigned by the Library of Congress or the National Library of Medicine.[28]

Deriving access points from title pages is one thing, establishing their correct form is another matter. Burger relates concepts from Artificial Intelligence to automated authority control.[29] While authority files exist to validate form of entries, there are other types of validation amenable to machine methods. Several writers have described approaches to quality control in library databases. The flavor of such work is conveyed by a couple of representative papers. Morita has described early efforts to detect and compensate for or correct errors of various kinds in automatic if primitive ways.[30] She also points to the opportunities to manage and improve the quality of library catalogs. In addition to such usual measures as checking the validity of numeric and alphabetic forms, Morita's vision extends to considering artificial intelligence techniques for detecting and correcting spelling errors, and for verifying the appropriateness of assigned headings. The likelihood of a shift from quality control as a post-cataloging activity to a cataloging function is foreseen by Bausser et al.[31] These writers also provide examples of areas where sophisticated techniques might be applied: automatic shelf-listing to detect or prevent duplicate assignment of call numbers; validation of classification sequences to detect inappropriate call numbers; automatic spelling checks; and verification of filing indicators.

Classification and Indexing

There is a fairly long history of attempts at automatic subject indexing. A review of progress in this area has been supplied by Salton.[32] Dillon has achieved some success in automatic back-of-the-book indexing, using a system called FASIT that is extensively rule-driven.[33] The system depends upon the availability of text in machine-readable form and on extensive dictionaries. Garland has reported on an experiment in automatic classification based in title keywords and LC subject headings.[34] She found a relationship between automatically generated clusters of documents and the LC classes of the same documents. Garland envisaged that further work, incorporating other kinds of content words such as those from tables of contents, might lead to a more complete automatic subject classification. There has in fact been some movement in the proposed direction. Enser has pursued the automatic classification of books, taking advantage of the back-of-the-book index, the table of contents, the title, and Dewey Decimal Classification.[35] Independently, Burton has proposed applying expert system techniques to the Dewey Decimal Classification, 19th edition, and amplifying it with title and contents pages and back-of-the-book indexes.[36] He identifies a significant number of problems in the classification of monographs and describes a range of possible solutions.

The Indexing Aid Project at the National Library of Medicine, intended to provide computer-assisted indexing of medical periodicals, is described by Humphrey and Miller.[37] Brenner et al. have disclosed plans for implementing machine-aided indexing at the American Petroleum Institute.[38]

Reference

Attempts to use computers to provide reference assistance are not a recent phenomenon. Some early efforts were quite sophisticated. In 1967, using a symbol and list processing language called COMIT, Weil developed a highly functional system for retrieving works which would best answer biographical reference questions.[39] The system ran experimentally on a batch basis, but it could have been adapted for an online implementation. Weil suggested that her automated advisor could be extended to other information resources such as bibliographies, dictionaries, and atlases, with only slight adjustments to the data structure. Weil's advisor included an output ranking feature, a capability for reformulating the search query when it deemed the search output to be unsatisfactory, and a feature for explaining some of its actions. Weil's system involved fairly difficult coding techniques and it is doubtful that untrained patrons could have used the system effectively, despite her intention that reference librarians "be freed to perform work less easily mechanized." Another early automatic system, REFSEARCH, has been described by Meredith.[40] REFSEARCH was designed for online use in general reference work.

A considerable number of expert systems for reference tasks are currently in development. This writer has summarized some expert systems developments in the domain of reference and referral.[41] A recent listing of development projects includes a system dealing with urban forestry, an advisor on dietary fiber, and a system to advise on how to choose an index in agriculture or biology as a tool to train reference assistants.[17] This list also includes a reference resource in organic chemistry; an extension to assist in searching compounds in Beilstein's *Handbuch der organischen Chemie* is proposed.

Parrott has delineated criteria useful in determining whether or not an expert system might be worth developing for a given task.[42] He discusses the tasks involved in answering requests for factual information and literature searches, and in interpreting bibliographic references and obtaining the corresponding physical items. Parrott then describes the expert systems and the computer-aided instructional modules developed at the University of Waterloo to carry out such tasks. The design, construction and operation of PLEXUS, a prototype referral system in the domain of horticulture, has been described recently by participants in the project.[43,44] This project is noteworthy for its rigorous theoretical underpinnings, its commitment to system evaluation, and its careful reporting. Most extant expert system designs treat a narrow domain, e.g., the Goucher College Biographical Reference Advisor and the POINTER system for advising on federal documents at SUNY-Buffalo.[45,46] I have recently proposed the development of an expert system for general reference, PISCES, to respond to inquiries with citations to preferred information sources or with factual information.[47] Cited reference works would be drawn, in the main, from descriptions of the carefully selected sources utilized in an exemplary library telephone reference operation.[48] The proposed development will attempt to integrate related machine-readable full-text files, where available, with these descriptive records. Walker and James propose a theory in which an expert system would be able to work on "any database in any subject field."[49] Micco and Smith have reported on a project directed towards developing an expert system to "provide subject access to the accumulated knowledge of mankind at least as well as the skilled reference librarian."[50] Given the "half-right" performance reported from many reference measurement tests, a cynic might say that such efforts reflect neither a high ambition nor one that is hard to achieve.[41] Yet the idea has a lot of appeal. Lenat et al. are pursuing an encyclopedic expert system based on the *Encyclopaedia Britannica*.[51] A key design element in that system is a profoundly elaborate user model.

User Models

User models are assuming extreme importance in retrieval systems design. Daniels provides a comprehensive review of recent work in this area.[52] He distinguishes among the user's mental model of the system, the model presented to users by systems designers or trainers, and the system's model of the user; particular attention is paid to the latter model. Brooks et al. have also considered user models in the development of intelligent interfaces.[53] They note that the modelling of users and the construction of problem descriptions, being activities to which human intermediaries devote much time, should be regarded as essential functions in an intelligent interface. Sleeman has described UMFE, a user modelling front-end subsystem.[54] UMFE takes the response from a primary system and recasts it in terms and concepts within the enquirer's intellectual capacities, as established by user responses to a few questions from the system.

Rich has described the important role of user models in GRUNDY, an advisor for recommending novels to library patrons.[55] GRUNDY, armed with responses to specific questions addressed to the user, draws upon a series of stereotypes to construct an initial model of the user. The model includes information about the background and characteristics of the user as well as a record of past interactions with GRUNDY. Brajnik and his colleagues have developed a somewhat similar approach in their Information Retrieval-Natural Language Interface (IR-NLI) system.[56] Rich was able to conclude that the user models developed by GRUNDY contributed significantly to its high success rate in recommending acceptable titles. Until recently there have been few attempts to integrate findings from the behavioral, cognitive, and information sciences in systems design.[57] Certainly, as Brittain has complained, no unified theory has been presented.[58] Among others, Pejtersen has discussed the need to take user behavior into account in the design of retrieval systems.[59] She addresses the optimal design of computer-aided user-system interfaces and the several strategies available to searchers. She also provides an arresting comparison between formal, logical, rule-based classification and what is called intuitive or natural classification based on a resemblance between similar families of classes and patterns of similarities. The work of Pejtersen and her students has led to the development of a new classification scheme for imaginative works (AMP) and the development and testing of several databases which utilize the AMP approach. One of these databases is DANEBASE, another expert system for advising library patrons on the selection of novels; it has a System Suggestion feature.[60] DANEBASE is an experimental system that accesses a database describing a few hundred novels. Users of the system develop a series of dimension, category and feature weights relating to a Model Book of the type being sought. Using the weights developed for just those characteristics highly valued by the searcher, the system calculates a numerical value for each book in the database; this would not be reasonable with databases of even moderate size. The System Suggestion function then retrieves a set of descriptions of books which most closely match the user's Model Book. The user can assess the book descriptions, add or adjust feature ratings, and invoke the System Suggestion module again to produce another list of suggestions based on the revised profile. The authors concluded that the value function permitted users to express a need and to search on a substantial number of features. In contrast, the results indicated that user evaluations of retrieved materials were likely based on a much smaller number of features or interactions among them. This is a well-documented phenomenon in the decision sciences. Consideration of a large number of factors, related in complex ways, is often claimed to underlie human decisions, but a simple linear model incorporating just two or three attributes predicts the human judgment quite closely.[6]

Interfaces

Information retrieval has been the focus of early and enduring efforts to adopt machine methods. Kehoe has reviewed the history of online interfaces in general and development efforts in expert systems for database searching in particular.[61] She notes that an intermediary's expertise often lies with the search system rather than the search subject. Similarly, Paice has observed that the expertise of search intermediaries is centered on the tools and techniques for finding information rather than on the target information itself.[62] One objective in the development of expert search technologies is to relieve end-users of the necessity of learning diverse, elaborate and confusing search system protocols. The problem has been constrained in part by developing facilities directed towards particular databases and particular classes of inquiries. Thus Pollitt has developed CANSEARCH to generate legitimate search statements acceptable to the MEDLINE database.[63] Concepts established in the development of CANSEARCH have led to the notion of a family of "menu-MEDLINE" intermediary systems suited to searching and browsing subject-specific subsets of the MEDLINE database.[64] An expert system is being designed to interact directly with end-users of the *Chemical Abstracts* online, in place of an intermediary.[65] That system apparently deals only with textual representations of information and excludes graphical substructure representations.

There is a need to deal with non-textual forms of data in information systems. An artificial intelligence approach to recovering information from a picture file, together with related descriptive material, is covered by Créhange et al. in their description of the EXPRIM system for retrieving images.[66] There is little evidence of the use of graphic displays in retrieval systems. Micco and Smith have adopted the plan view of a tree structure display in the design of an expert system to assist users in developing search strategies.[67] This helpful representation of thesauri was pioneered by Jan Schuller.[68] Graphic displays and their roles in information retrieval have been discussed at length recently.[69] It seems obvious that the "aerial view" of information and entity relationships will become increasingly important for way-finding in large files. In addition to assisting browsing and navigation, it would seem to be a natural location and anchoring device for Hypertext systems.

Post-Search Processing

Most operating retrieval systems organize output in a manner which is not helpful to users; responses tend to be arranged chronologically rather than by some measure of relevance, and duplicate citations are not filtered out. Some of the problems of massaging retrieval output are now being addressed by intelligent software. SIRE was perhaps the earliest program of this kind.⁷⁰ The software is available for use with microcomputers; it operates on records captured from online searches.⁷¹ Leigh and Paz report on the design and use of a similar system, with full automatic capability, to assess relevance and to rank downloaded abstracts.⁷²

Intelligent Tutoring

Bibliographic instruction has a certain appeal as an application for expert systems techniques. Parrott has included an instructional module in the system under development at the University of Waterloo.⁴² The tutor explains how to use *Index Medicus* for subject searches. In principle, tutorial systems can be independent of the field of instruction. This would be consonant with Davis' observation about the substitutability of databases in expert systems.¹ Thus, intelligent tutoring systems outside of librarianship may be adaptable for instructional purposes. Kochtanek has described a prototype interactive intelligent tutorial for health care professionals.⁷³ The system is directed to training in a variety of computer applications. There are options for testing acquired knowledge and practicing acquired skills, including practice sessions with specific online services. Clancey has written a book describing GUIDON, the remarkably innovative knowledge-based tutoring program that he developed in his dissertation work.⁷⁴ A thorough assessment of the state of the art in Intelligent Computer-Assisted Instruction is provided by Dede.⁷⁵ He notes that people can be trained by computer coaches and tutors to deal with very complex problems, "but the construction of such an instructional system means that an expert system built from its knowledge base can serve as an alternative problem solver." Some years ago, in proposing a fanciful automatic political speech generator with voice input and output, MANIPHESTO,* I suggested the possibility that the system itself might be persuasive enough to be electable!⁷⁶

---

*MANIPHESTO—Machine Augmented, Naturally Intoned, Political Hyperbole Ensuring Successive Terms in Office.

CONCLUSION

By definition, any system that is fully automatic eliminates the human element. The problem of what the British call the "de-skilling" of library tasks, reducing the intellectual content of jobs so that they can be performed by clerks or by systems rather than by professionals, is a looming issue in librarianship. We have seen its effects in cataloging departments as greater reliance has been placed on copy cataloging, and already we can identify serious efforts to automate the cataloging function itself. In addition we can already identify viable systems for delivering some kinds of reference service. It is apparent that two of the key activities in libraries can be supported, in some degree at least, by knowledge-based systems. As expert systems begin to impact library operations and services it will be necessary for the profession to determine just where such systems are appropriate, and to do so objectively yet with sensitivity.

Just as there is no shortage of expert systems in the world at large and as there is no shortage of applications in the library field, so there is no shortage of problems in their design and development. Happily, there are dedicated researchers and developers at work on both the systems and the problems.

REFERENCES

1. Davis, Randall. "Knowledge-Based Systems." *Science* 231(4741): 957-963, 28 February 1986.
2. Jarke, Matthias and Yannis Vassiliou. "Databases and Expert Systems: Opportunities and Architectures for Integration," in *New Applications of Databases* ed. by G. Gardarin and E. Gelenbe. London: Academic Press, 1984. pp. 185-201.
3. Walker T. C. and R. K. Miller. *Expert Systems 1986: An Assessment of Technology and Applications*. Madison, GA: SEAI Technical Publications, 1986.
4. Obermeier, Klaus K. "Expert Systems," in *Encyclopedia of Library and Information Science* ed. by Allen Kent. vol. 38, New York: Marcel Dekker, 1984. pp. 158-176.
5. Gibb, Forbes. "Expert Systems: An Overview," in *Expert Systems in Libraries* ed. by Forbes Gibb. London: Taylor Graham, 1986. pp. 3-21.
6. Vickery, Alina and Helen Brooks. "Expert Systems and their Applications in LIS." *Online Review* 11:149-165. 1987.

7. Rabson, Carolyn and Gustave Rabson. "Hum a Few Bars." *Perspectives in Computing* 5:24-33, 1985.

8. Cavanagh. Joseph M. A. "Intra-Active Retrieval Systems." *Proceedings of the Seventh National Online Meeting*. Medford, NJ: Learned Information, 1986. pp. 59-65.

9. Brownson, Charles W. "Mechanical Selection." *Library Resources & Technical Services* 32:17-29, 1988.

10. Raney, Leon. *An Investigation into the Adaptability of a Domestic Approval Program to the Existing Pattern of Book Selection in a Medium-Sized Academic Library*. PhD Dissertation, Indiana University, October 1972.

11. Studer, William Joseph. *Computer-Based Selective Dissemination of Information (SDI) Service for Faculty Using Library of Congress Machine-readable Catalog (MARC) Records*. PhD Dissertation, Indiana University, September 1968.

12. Bierman, Kenneth John. "An Operating MARC-Based SDI System: Some Preliminary Services and User Reactions." *Proceedings of the ASIS Annual Meeting*, vol. 7. Washington, DC: American Society for Information Science, 1970. pp. 87-89.

13. Swanson, Don R. "Selective Dissemination of Biomedical Information: A Series of Studies and a Model System." *Library Quarterly* 44:189-205, 1974.

14. Pao, Miranda Lee. "Semantic and Pragmatic Retrieval." *Proceedings of the 47th ASIS Annual Meeting*, vol. 21. White Plains, NY: Knowledge Industry Publications, 1984. pp. 134-136.

15. He, Chunpei and Miranda Lee Pao. "A Discipline-Specific Journal Selection Algorithm." *Information Processing & Management* 22:405-416. 1986.

16. Rada, Roy et al. "Computerized Guides to Journal Selection." *Information Technology and Libraries* 6:173-184, 1987.

17. Swab, Joseph N. "NAL's Expert Systems Course Off to a Good Start," *Agricultural Libraries Information Notes* 13:8-9, December 1987.

18. Fox, Ann Martha Sandberg. *The Amenability of a Cataloging Process to Simulation by Automatic Techniques*. PhD Dissertation, University of Illinois at Urbana-Champaign, 1972.

19. Davies, Roy and Brian James. "Towards an Expert System for Cataloguing: Some Experiments Based on AACR2." *Program* 18:283-297, 1984.

20. Davies, Roy. "Cataloguing as a Domain for an Expert System," in *Intelligent Information Systems: Progress and Prospects* ed. by R. Davies. Chichester, England: Ellis Horwood, 1986. pp. 54-77.

21. Davies, Roy. "Expert Systems and Cataloguing: New Wine in Old Bottles?" in *Expert Systems in Libraries* ed. by Forbes Gibb. London: Taylor Graham, 1986. pp. 67-82.

22. Hjerppe, R. and B. Olander. *Artificial Intelligence and Cataloging: Building Expert Systems for Simple Choice of Access Points for Entries; Results and Revelations*. LibLab, Linkoping University, June 1985. Research Report LiU-LIBLAB-R:1985:1.

23. Davies, Roy. "Outlines of the Emerging Paradigm in Cataloguing." *Information Processing & Management* 23:89-98, 1987.

24. Weibel, Stuart, Mike Oskins and Diane Vizine-Goetz. "Automated Title Page Cataloging." *Proceedings of the 50th ASIS Annual Meeting*, vol. 24. Medford, NJ: Learned Information, 1987. pp. 234-240.

25. Jeng, Ling-Hwey. "An Expert System for Determining Title Proper in Descriptive Cataloging: A Conceptual Model." *Cataloging & Classification Quarterly* 7:55-70, Winter 1986.

26. Cavanagh, Joseph M. A. "Impediments to the Adoption of Associative Retrieval Systems—Rationality or Conventional Wisdom?" mimeo, unpublished, December 1972.

27. Svenonius, Elaine, Betty Baughman and Mavis Molto. "Title Page Sanctity? The Distribution of Access Points in a Sample of English Language Monographs." *Cataloging & Classification Quarterly* 6:3-21, Spring 1986.

28. Svenonius, Elaine. "Studies in Automatic Cataloging." *Annual Review of OCLC Research, July 1986-June 1987*. Dublin, OH: OCLC Inc., 1987, pp. 26-27.

29. Burger, Robert H. "Artificial Intelligence and Authority Control." *Library Resources & Technical Services* 28:337-345, 1984.

30. Morita, Ichiko. "Quality Control of Online Catalogs: Automation vs. Human Control." *Energies for Transition: Proceedings of the Fourth National Conference of the Association of College and Research Libraries*. Chicago: Association of College and Research Libraries, 1986. pp. 44-46.

31. Bausser, Jaye, Jinnie Y. Davis and David Gleim. "Error Detection in Bibliographic Records: Can the Computer Do It All?" *Energies for Transition: Proceedings of the Fourth National Conference of the Association of College and Research Libraries*. Chicago: Association of College and Research Libraries, 1986. pp. 27-29.

32. Salton, Gerard. "Another Look at Automatic Text-Retrieval Systems." *Communications of the ACM* 29:648-656, July 1986.

33. Dillon, Martin and Laura K. McDonald, "Fully Automatic Book Indexing." *Journal of Documentation* 39:135-154, 1983.

34. Garland, Kathleen. "An Experiment in Automatic Hierarchical Document Classification." *Information Processing & Management* 19:113-120, 1983.

35. Enser, P. G. B. "Automatic Classification of Book Material Represented by Back-of-the-Book Index." *Journal of Documentation* 41:135-155, 1985.

36. Burton, Paul F. "Expert Systems in Classification," in *Expert Systems in Libraries* ed. by Forbes Gibb. London: Taylor Graham, 1986. pp. 50-66.

37. Humphrey, Susanne M. and Nancy E. Miller. "Knowledge-Based Indexing of the Medical Literature: The Indexing Aid Project." *Journal of the American Society for Information Science* 38:184-196, 1987.

38. Brenner, E. H. et al. "American Petroleum Institute's Machine-Aided Indexing and Searching Project." *Science & Technology Libraries* 5:49-62, 1984.

39. Weil, Cherie B. "Automatic Retrieval of Biographical Reference Works." *Journal of Library Automation* 1:239-249, 1968.

40. Meredith, J. C. "Machine-Assisted Approach to General Reference Materials." *Journal of the American Society for Information Science* 22:176-186, 1971.

41. Cavanagh, Joseph M. A. "The Automated Readers' Advisor: Expert Systems Technology for a Reference Function." *Proceedings of the Seventh National Online Meeting*. Medford, NJ: Learned Information, 1987. pp. 57-65.

42. Parrott, James R. "Expert Systems for Reference Work." *Microcomputers for Information Management* 3:155-171, September 1986.

43. Brooks, H. M. "Expert Systems in Reference Work." in *Expert Systems in Libraries* ed. by Forbes Gibb. London: Taylor Graham, 1986. pp. 36-49.

44. Vickery, Alina et al. "A Reference and Referral System Using Expert System Techniques." *Journal of Documentation* 43:1-23, 1987.

45. Lewand, Robert. "The Goucher College Biographical Reference Advisor: A Case Study in Building an Expert System." *Proceedings of the Third Annual Eastern Small College Computing Conference*. Poughkeepsie, NY: Marist College, 1987. pp. 257-263.

46. Smith, Karen F. "Robot at the Reference Desk?" *College & Research Libraries* 47:486-490, 1986.

47. Cavanagh, Joseph M. A. "Progress and Problems in Expert Systems Development for Reference." *Proceedings of the Mid-Year Meeting of the American Society for Information Science*, Ann Arbor, MI, May 1988 (forthcoming).

48. Neumann, Kathleen M. and Gerald D. Weeks, "Reference Materials in a Telephone Reference Service: A Model for Telereference." *RQ* 20:394-402, Summer 1981.

49. Walker, Geraldene and Joseph W. Janes. "Expert Systems as Search Intermediaries." *Proceedings of the 47th ASIS Annual Meeting*, vol. 21. White Plains, NY: Knowledge Industry Publications, 1984. pp. 103-105.

50. Micco, Mary and Irma Smith. "Knowledge Representation: Subject Analysis." *Library Software Review* 6:82-87, 1987.

51. Lenat, D. B. et al. "KNOESPHERE: Building Expert Systems with Encyclopedic Knowledge." *Proceedings of the Eighth Joint International Conference on Artificial Intelligence*. 1983. pp. 382-384.

52. Daniels, P. J. "Cognitive Models in Information Retrieval—An Evaluative Review." *Journal of Documentation* 42:272-304, 1986.

53. Brooks, H. M., P. J. Daniels and N. J. Belkin, "Problem Descriptions and User Models: Developing an Intelligent Interface for Document Retrieval Systems." *Informatics 8: Advances in Intelligent Retrieval*: Proceedings of a Conference Jointly Sponsored by Aslib, the Aslib Informatics Group and the Information Retrieval Specialist Group of the British Computer Society. London: Aslib, 1985. pp. 191-214.

54. Sleeman, D. "UMFE: A User Modelling Front-End Subsystem." *International Journal of Man-Machine Studies* 23:71-88, 1985.

55. Rich, Elaine. "Users are Individuals: Individualizing User Models," in *Intelligent Information Systems: Progress and Prospects* ed. by R. Davies. Chichester, England: Ellis Horwood, 1986. pp. 184-201.

56. Brajnik, Giorgio, Giovanni Guida and Carlo Tasso, "User Modeling in Intelligent Information Retrieval." *Information Processing & Management* 23:305-320, 1987.

57. Cavanagh, Joseph M. A. "Some Considerations Relating to User-System Interaction in Information Retrieval Systems," in *Information Retrieval: The Users Viewpoint, an Aid to Design* ed. by A. B. Tonik. Philadelphia: International Information Inc., 1967. pp. 119-125.

58. Brittain, J. M. *Information and Its Users*. Bath: Bath University Press, 1970.

59. Pejtersen, A. M. "Design of a Computer-Aided User-System Dialogue Based on an Analysis of Users' Search Behaviour." *Social Science Information Studies* 4:167-183, 1984.

60. Morehead, David R., Annelise M. Pejtersen and William B. Rouse. "The Value of Information and Computer-Aided Information Seeking: Problem Formulation and Application to Fiction Retrieval." *Information Processing & Management* 20:583-601, 1984.

61. Kehoe, Cynthia A. "Interfaces and Expert Systems for Online Retrieval." *Online Review* 9:489-505, 1985.

62. Paice, Chris. "Expert Systems for Information Retrieval?" *Aslib Proceedings* 38:343-353, 1986.

63. Pollitt, Steven. "CANSEARCH: An Expert Systems Approach to Document Retrieval." *Information Processing & Management* 23:119-138, 1987.

64. Pollitt, Steven. *Menu-MEDLINE for Biochemical Genetics*. Bethesda, MD: Lister Hill National Center for Biomedical Communication. Interim Technical Report, July 13, 1987.

65. Smith, Philip J. and Mark Chignell, "Development of an Expert System to Aid in Searches of the *Chemical Abstracts."* *Proceedings of the 47th ASIS Annual Meeting*, vol. 21. White Plains, NY: Knowledge Industry Publications. 1984. pp. 99-102.

66. Créhange, M. et al. "EXPRIM: An Expert System to Aid in Progressive Retrieval from a Pictorial and Descriptive Database," in *New Applications of Data Bases* ed. by G. Gardarin and E. Gelenbe. London: Academic Press, 1984. pp. 43-61.

67. Micco, H. Mary and Irma Smith. "Designing an Expert System for the Reference Function Subject Access to Information." *Proceedings of the 49th ASIS Annual Meeting*, vol. 23. Medford, NJ: Learned Information, 1986. pp. 204-210.

68. Schuller, J. "Manual Systems—TDCK Circular Thesaurus System," in *Storage and Retrieval of Information: A User-Supplier Dialogue* ed. by H. F. Vessey and I. J. Gabelman. AGARD Conference Proceedings No. 39. Neuilly-sur-Seine, France: North Atlantic Treaty Organization, Advisory Group for Aerospace Research and Development, 1968. pp. 99-110.

69. Bertrand-Gastaldy, Suzanne and Colin Davidson. "Improved Design of Graphic Displays in Thesauri—Through Technology and Ergonomics." *Journal of Documentation* 42:225-251, 1986.

70. Noreault, T., M. Koll and M. J. McGill. "Automatic Ranked Output from Boolean Searches in SIRE." *Journal of the American Society for Information Science* 28:333-339, 1977.

71. Koll, Matthew B., Terry Noreault and Michael J. McGill. "Enhanced Retrieval Techniques on a Microcomputer." *Proceedings of the Fifth National Online Meeting*. Medford, NJ: Learned Information, 1984. pp. 165-170.

72. Leigh, William and Noemi Paz. "SORT-AID with RANK: Search Postprocessing Tools for Automating the Determination of Citation Relevance." *Information Technology and Libraries* 5:345-349, 1986.

73. Kochtanek, Thomas R. "A Computer-Based Tutorial Program for Health Care Professionals." *Proceedings of the 47th ASIS Annual Meeting*, vol. 21. White Plains, NY: Knowledge Industry Publications, 1984. pp. 130-133.

74. Clancey, William J. *Knowledge-Based Tutoring*. Cambridge. MA: MIT Press, 1987.

75. Dede, Christopher. "A Review and Synthesis of Recent Research in Intelligent Computer-Assisted Instruction." *International Journal of Man-Machine Studies* 24:329-353, 1986.

76. Cavanagh, J. M. A. "MANIPHESTO: The Ultimate Persuader; The Implications of Some Behavioral Science Findings for Document Selection Systems." Partial transcript of a speech to the Special Interest Group on Automatic Language Processing, 35th ASIS National Meeting, Washington, DC, October 1972.

Augmented Assistance in Online Catalog Subject Searching

Zorana Ercegovac

SUMMARY. Researchers have just begun to acknowledge the importance of incorporating the component of human-computer interaction in the design of online information systems. With the advent of interactive computer systems designed for direct use by the general public, the need has become apparent to design "friendly" user interfaces. In this regard, online public access catalogs, OPACs, are no exception. Recent research studies of OPAC users have found that (i) subject access in online catalogs is coming to be valued at least as much as known item access, and that (ii) OPAC users have a number of serious difficulties with subject searching. Consequently, we need to understand what characterizes human-computer compatibility and to examine various means of assisting the OPAC user at the heart of online searching tasks.

In this article I will first develop an argument that OPAC users need better online assistance modes than what has been achieved in most current systems by reviewing findings from some of the studies in the areas of individual differences and error behavior. Then the concepts of "idea tactics" and "information search tactics" will be explored in terms of incorporating them into online subject searching and providing terminological assistance to the online searcher.

The author is Doctoral Candidate, Graduate School of Library and Information Science, University of California at Los Angeles, Los Angeles, CA 90024.

The author wishes to thank Marcia Bates and Christine Borgman of UCLA for their helpful comments and discussion on various aspects of the earlier versions of this paper. Professor Borko also of UCLA was kind to encourage the author to submit this paper to *The Reference Librarian*. John Richardson of UCLA read this manuscript and provided useful comments. Linda Smith of the University of Illinois provided useful manuscripts in the early stages of this writing.

© 1989 by The Haworth Press, Inc. All rights reserved.

INTRODUCTION

While the concepts of heuristics, inference, and man-machine communication have been recognized as significant in human problem solving in the context of information systems,[1] not until 1984 did we see a chapter of *Annual Review of Information Science and Technology (ARIST)* devoted to some of the current research issues on human-computer interaction.[2] Expert systems may be regarded as computer programs capable of solving difficult problems for most people. Various attempts at experimental and commercial expert systems, reviewed elsewhere,[3] have been conceived as decision support tools rather than replacement of the practitioners in the vastly diverse domains of geological prospecting, molecular genetics, biochemical analysis, engineering, and information retrieval. It follows that these end-users, rarely computer experts, need computer interfaces which would allow them to move effectively through large and complex knowledge-bases and to focus on their technical tasks rather than on the mechanics of operating a system. Interdisciplinary research has just begun to acknowledge the importance of incorporating the component of human-computer interaction early in the design of online information systems, including expert systems.[4-5]

With the advent of interactive computer systems designed for direct use by the general public, the need has become apparent to design "friendly" interfaces. In this regard, online public access catalogs (OPACs) are no exception. Recent research studies of OPAC users have found that (1) subject access in online catalogs is coming to be valued at least as much as known-item access; and that (2) OPAC users have a number of serious difficulties with subject searching.[6] Consequently, researchers need to understand what characterizes human-computer compatibility and to examine various means of assisting the OPAC user at the heart of online searching tasks.

The term "online catalog" or OPAC will be used in this article to reflect a class of retrieval systems which are designed for end users; which replace a variety of existing card catalogs; and which require little or no training on the part of general public.[7] Since the distinction between OPACs and multidatabase bibliographic retrieval systems has begun to break down,[8] approaches to user assistance from both systems will be discussed in this article. Though we do not yet think of OPACs as expert systems, in order to design better user interfaces than those in most current OPACs, a number of proposals for designing "intelligent" interfaces are starting to appear in the literature.[9-11] I³R (*I*ntelligent *I*ntermediary for *I*nformation *R*etrieval) and CANSEARCH represent attempts to integrate concepts of heuristics, inference, and human-computer interaction early in the design of systems.[12-13] For instance, the I³R system is based on domain knowledge from the user model in order to incrementally refine searchers' information needs, and on browsing mechanisms that allow the searcher to navigate through the knowledge-base. The system's explainer module traces the sequence of rules that led to a particular action. Pollitt's front-end expert system, CANSEARCH, is intended for an infrequent computer user who may have a poor model of the Medline capabilities and inadequate mechanical and conceptual searching skills.[13] This prototype intermediary system is data-driven in terms of its basic inference orientation, and menu-driven and touch-selected in terms of its interface style. The system "navigates" the user through a network of Medical Subject Headings, MESH, providing terminological and search formulation assistance.

Most of the attempts to create knowledge-based information retrieval systems to date fall short of incorporating more sophisticated explanatory facilities. "Explainable Expert Systems," EES, in contrast to expert systems with explanations composed from "canned text" or by paraphrasing the system code, require inferring information goals from questions, then applying the appropriate explanation strategy.[14]

The term "end-user" will include primarily the university students who are typically casual library users with little or no familiarity in using computers, computer terminals, or OPACs. A number of detailed discussions on the "casual" users have appeared in various disciplinary areas.[15-16]

The meaning of the "user-computer interface" that will be used here is Moran's: "any part of the computer system that the user comes in contact with—either physically, perceptually, or conceptually."[17] Therefore the user interface encompasses much beyond the display formats and command languages. It includes the work environment along with computing peripheral devices, cognitive abilities, prior computing experience, search mechanics, personal attitudes, "help" features, documentation, and training. A similar view of user interface is proposed by Hildreth.[18]

In this article, online user assistance will be discussed in the "augmentation" mode along the conceptual dimension rather than along the physical or perceptual dimensions. Augmented assistance, in contrast to accelerated assistance, aids the user in the substance of his or her task and not just in quickening the pace of its execution.[19] Examples of accelerated assistance are various front-end processors which attempt to aid searchers in searching online bibliographic databases in a number of useful ways, most commonly with logon/logoff procedures, with database selection based on information in the user's query, with storing searches, downloading the searches, performing selective dissemination of information, providing useful utilities such as text editing and spelling correction programs. Must less assistance is offered after the database has been selected and before the search formulation has been stored. A "missing link" involves some of the most difficult tasks including selection of search terms, and the decision-making important in formulating and modifying search strategies. As online bibliographic databases designed for use by the general public acquire more of the knowledge-based features, the searcher will expect, and rightly so, a continuous qualitative improvement at the level of human-computer interaction.

Alternatively, the searcher may delegate searching tasks to the system, as to an assistant, to be carried out independently. This article will consider human-computer interaction as a joint cognitive performance with an outcome beyond the user's unaided powers.

Both "idea tactics" and "information search tactics" will be proposed in this article as examples of augmented assistance to online subject searching. Bates defines "idea tactics" as mental devices to generate new ideas or solutions to problems in searching. These tactics may be thought of as heuristics or rules of thumb which facilitate search by giving "tips" to help the searcher search online catalogs more effectively.[20] Bates introduced "term tactics" to help online searchers find specific terms within the search formulation.[21]

USERS NEED USEFUL ONLINE "HELP": LESSONS LEARNED FROM EMPIRICAL RESEARCH

Numerous OPAC user studies demonstrated that effective online searches are difficult to achieve both for experienced and inexperienced searchers.[22-23]

Knowing that most OPAC users are casual visitors, some of them permanent novices,[24-25] and that there exists a wide range of individual differences among people's information seeking styles,[26-30] a need to change systems to fit the needs of users or to change users so that they adapt to computer catalogs becomes apparent. In either approach, researchers need to apply psychological research findings in designing user assistance modes, and/or in devising effective training modes.

That OPAC users have a number of difficulties with subject access can be ascertained by studying research findings reported in four separate project reports sponsored by the Council on Library Resources.[31-34] For instance, 43% of the users indicated a problem of "finding correct subject term."[35] Actually, studies by Knapp[36] and Frarey[37] indicate that correspondence of user terms and catalog headings in the first try will be approximately 50%. Bates' experiment, which investigated the degree of match between the students' terms and subject headings assigned by the University of California at Berkeley Library, found that the results were just over 20%, even when credit was given for partial term and partial word matches.[38] In a recent empirical study conducted at Bell Communications Research, investigators found that "there is no one good access term for most objects," both for novices and experts.[39] They found the probability less than 20% that two persons would favor the same term.

The nation-wide CLR-sponsored study of OPAC users and non-users discovered that 46% of the users had a difficulty increasing the result when too little was retrieved, and 27% of the users indicated a problem in reducing the result when too much was retrieved.[40]

Of the improvements sought for subject searching, 45% of the users desired to view related terms, 42% expressed the need to search the table of contents or index, and 24% desired to search by title words.

In order to deal with some of these problems of OPAC users, various "tactics" for assisting the user in his or her subject searching will be explored shortly.

The CLR-sponsored study gathered much data about non-users' attitudes toward OPACs. When non-users of OPACs were asked for reason of not using OPACs, the most common response was, "I have not taken training sessions on how to use it."[41] Furthermore, 64% of non-users with favorable attitudes toward the OPACs felt that it would take less than 30 minutes to learn how to use the online catalog.

The implication here is that people lack motivation to invest as little as 30 minutes in learning how to use OPACs. Therefore it would seem that researchers need to design effective modes that can assist the users in the core processes of database searching while accounting for their personal traits, differences in information-seeking styles, and lack of motivation to learn how to use this relatively new information technology.

User studies provide a rich source of information for learning the information seeking behavior of OPAC users. The studies found that students have difficulty completing even the simplest type of searches. Users have problems with the user assistance facilities at all levels (e.g., syntax, semantics, and logic), and across three techniques commonly employed in online user assistance modes, including suggestive prompts, error messages, and "help" displays.[42-43] The survey data suggest a number of related difficulties people have with physical legibility, overall clarity in the use of labels and headings, arrangement of data on the screen, and overall use of space on screen layouts.[44] Studies have shown, however, that the most critical time for a novice is his or her initial encounter with the online system.[45] Usage analyses have indicated that it is critical that users be successful in their first use of the system. For instance, Tolle and Hah discovered that people ended their searches 15% of the time after an error was made.[46] Borgman found that 26% of subjects at the Stanford University could not meet the minimum criterion performance level required to be included in the study proper.[47]

Paisley investigated the distribution of cognitive styles in individuals and the role of cognitive styles in the performance of information and communication tasks at the human-computer interface.[48] He identified 12 perceptual/cognitive processes between the different loci involving receptor, processor, effector, and long-term memory. The perceptual/cognitive processes are: scanning, fixation, feature extraction, decoding, comparing, deciding, inducing, deducing, retrieving, selecting, transforming, and producing. Among information/communication tasks, Paisley identified those of learning, problem-solving, decision-making, and searching. He proposed a study bounded by cognitive performance variables, information/communication tasks, and a set of cognitive processes. Each cell of the matrix could expand into a detailed analysis of the relationships of one cognitive style to one aspect of the performance of an information/communication task. Such a study would provide a rich source of information in the context of user assistance modes both in terms of the format (e.g., visualization, linear vs. branched presentation, multi-window displays, etc.), and in terms of the content of the displayed prompts, "help" screens, and error messages, at each cell of the matrix.

The fact that online searching is hard is supported by numerous empirical studies in the area of error research.[49-51] For instance, Borgman found from a transaction log of Ohio State University Library's online catalog that an average of 13.3% of all commands involved either typographical or logical errors, and 12.2% of all sessions consisted entirely of errors.[50] This represents a significant portion of users with various sorts of difficulties during the process of searching.

Tolle and Hah discovered an error repeat rate of 8% in searching the CATLINE database.[51] The investigators found that after an error occurs, the most likely activities appear to be a single-term search or a Boolean search (together accounting for 49% of the activity). The study did not analyze the "correctness" of types of actions which led to certain types of errors. Such "qualitative" studies could advance our understanding of the general nature of error-making at the level of human-machine interface. This knowledge could help researchers design friendlier interfaces than those in today's systems, in terms of improving performance and minimizing either the incidence of errors or the effect of errors on the overall searching performance.

The approach taken by Galambos and his colleagues at Yale University to explain causes for errors was based on an information processing model, "Goals, Operators, Methods, and Selection," GOMS, rules developed by Card, Moran and Newell.[52-53] The goals of the users at each point, and the plans for accomplishing those goals, are considered in an attempt to explain the causes for the various types of errors.

In a recent study by Efe, a "let's talk about it," strategy has been proposed and implemented to simulate a desk calculator.[54] This strategy allows one to explore the problem to whatever depth is desired in order to trace the original mismatch in a constructive manner. The prototype system has a goal to report errors, not to fix them. Reed, too, suggests the approach of "constructive" assistance rather than error-prevention strategies in the design of user interfaces.[55]

At a more general level, Norman provides a detailed analysis and classification of human errors based on the model of Activation-Trigger Schema, which assumes that action sequences are controlled by sensorimotor knowledge structures called schemas.[56] Norman analyzes and classifies human errors with the ultimate aim of constructing an analysis of an appropriate form of human-machine interface that optimizes performance and minimizes either the incidence of error or the effect of the error.

I believe that studies like that of Norman can provide useful information that can be explicated into sound design principles and ultimately applied in the design of the OPACs that are sensitive to different personality traits and information needs of the user community.

Before exploring idea and search "tactics" in the following section, I would like to remark on the distinction made between hardware and software design principles. In contrast to design principles for user-interface *hardware*, based on human physiology relatively fixed and well understood, design principles and informal guidance for user-interface *software* are based largely on psychology about which we still have much to learn.[57-59] The distinction may, however, become blurred. For example, display symbol size, CRT raster variables, luminance, and spacing, may be controlled by software, in which case the physiology of the eye should be considered in software design.[60-61]

In contrast to the traditional approach that studied human-computer interface at the physiological level, Cognitive System Engineering, CSE, operates at the level of cognitive functions.[62] Human research, for instance, centered around "knobology"—display of characters, button configuration, tablets, numeric pads, input and output devices, ancillary control devices, and luminance, and to a lesser extent to cognitive aspects of the user interface.[63-64] According to Hollnagel and Woods, traditional psychology sees human information processing as a linear series of fixed processing stages rather than as an adaptive system. The central tenet of CSE is that a human-computer interface needs to be conceived, designed, and analyzed in terms of a cognitive system. The goal of CSE is to improve the functionality of the user interfaces on the whole rather than to replace as many users' functions as possible. In this regard CSE has considerable implications for the design of the various user assistance modes. While engineering psychology has traditionally attempted to produce a match between the system's image of the user and the user characteristics on a physical level, one of the goals of CSE research is to model the system's image and user characteristics on a cognitive level and make the user-computer boundary more symmetrical.

IMPLEMENTATION OF "TACTICS" FOR SUBJECT SEARCHING IN ONLINE CATALOGS

As noted earlier, both "idea tactics" and "information search tactics" will be explored in this section. The tactics may be regarded as underlying mental devices which may help the online searcher when s/he is "stumped" to generate new ideas or tactics to problems in bibliographic searching.[65] Specific names of individual "tactics" are those of Bates.

First let us turn our attention to the concept of idea tactics. These are general "tips" to the searcher that can be wrapped around vari-

Idea Tactics

No studies have been found as yet that investigated the amenability of incorporating some or all of the tactics into a system design in order to facilitate for a more effective online subject searching.

In regard to the amenability of automating some of the tactics, the question arises as to the presentability of individual idea tactics (e.g., "think," "brainstorm," "meditate," etc.) to the user without displaying on a screen actual definitions of each tactic. Surely, it would be of little help to a "stumped" user to be told to THINK, to CHANGE, to JOLT, etc. Neither would we help the user by displaying on a computer screen some of the underlying philosophical underpinnings for each of the tactics. Instead, the system could be programmed to "understand" users' intentions, plans and goals and on the basis of these cognitive components construct user models for a particular information searching problem. For instance, such tactics as THINK and BRAINSTORM come to mind as potentially useful mental devices after the user had been evaluated by the system as being "stumped." The condition of being "stumped" could be embedded into a diagnostic capability of the system and explained on the basis of an information processing model, such as GOMS (Goals, Operations, Methods, and Selection rules) developed by Card, et al.[66] Accordingly, the initial goals of the users at each point, and the plans for accomplishing these goals, are considered in the attempt to conclude whether or not the user is "stumped."

The first three tactics, THINK, BRAINSTORM, and MEDITATE, might be implemented by showing the user samples of searches from the past case history of similar searching problems and how these had been resolved; by focusing on parts or subgoals of the search which appear productive; by demonstrating other parts which need shaping up; and by pinpointing those parts of the search that are contradictory, error prone, and illogical. Such a system, which guides the searcher through a problem-solving process, is represented as a dynamic model with a dynamic memory that is updated with each new experience and reasoning process. A model might be developed to show the boundaries of diagnostic capabilities between the user and a system. In this regard, Cognitive Systems Engineering has considerable implications in the design of augmented user assistance modes.

Various assistance modes wrapped around the "idea tactics" should be based on the design rules for effective user assistance proposed by Norman and based on his analysis of human errors.[67] The sort of system interfaces which automatically infer types of information-searching problems and suggest to the searcher directions in searching and repairs have been reviewed in the literature under different names: user modeling, users' extraction features, and theories of feedback.[68-71] These systems represent efforts to customize searching while accounting for user diversity.

The RESCUE idea tactic has been defined as a way to overcome misjudgments due to the emotional reaction of disappointment and to rescue fruitful possibilities.[72] This tactic might be useful in minimizing fruitless time spent in the process of searching. For instance, Tolle and Hah's study, noted earlier, found a common pattern of making consecutive errors. Once an error was made, another error was made immediately following it 8% of the time. By using "constructive" rather than preventive strategies, this sort of error clustering might be rechanneled into a fruitful strategy, instead of the user's prematurely giving up the whole approach or aborting the session.[73] RESCUE might check for possible productive paths still untried.

The CONSULT idea tactic suggests a symmetrical participation between the user and the computer where the searcher is expected to ask the system as one would consult a colleague for a piece of advice.

Among the tactics which emphasize mental pattern-breaking, the JOLT tactic might be of particular use in that it could suggest that the user restate the problem from another perspective or another discipline; or within the framework of different assumptions, perhaps qualified with different parameters. The system might suggest various possibilities through suggestive prompts or "help" screens, as discussed in the literature.[74]

The CATCH idea tactic has been rarely implemented and to a limited extent only. For instance, some systems are programmed to allow users an infinite number of unproductive trials, letting the user give up the entire search after several unsuccessful trials. Other systems have a control loop built in which allows the user to make only a certain number of errors before the system either aborts the session or suggests to the user to seek alternative paths. Most of us have experienced logging-on sessions where the frustrated user tries unsuccessfully to input a series of identification numbers or passwords according to a rather rigid set of protocols accepted by the computer. Rarely have there been any attempts to provide meaningful in-context messages which tell the user where s/he erred and how to repair those errors.

Of particular interest is the REFRAME idea tactic. It deals with both question negotiation and mental pattern-breaking. Iterative checking with the user during the process of online searching to uncover that frame of reference which has been initially stated seems invaluable.

The idea tactics such as WANDER, FOCUS, DILATE, and CHANGE have more specific implications for the information-searching tasks of browsing, broadening searches, narrowing searches, and a range of possibilities for the terminological assistance modes.

Bates introduced "term tactics" to aid online searchers in the selection and revision of specific terms within the search formulation.[75] Each tactic could be incorporated in an online catalog to assist users in finding right subject terms, to broaden or narrow down their searches, or to browse through an OPAC.

Term Tactics

In the rest of this section I will pay attention to the various decision points involving search term selection, increasing or reducing search strategies, and browsing the online catalog through a more symmetrical pattern of participation between the user and the computer. The "co-orientation theory" provides a useful basis for conceptualizing the information needs of people who can only recognize what they need when they see it, rather than specify it in advance of the search.[76-78] Bates has argued persuasively that effective search formulations almost always contain more variety in terminology than typical end-users and even many intermediaries provide. A growing number of programs has been experimenting with the co-orientation theory.[79-82]

The following is a list of seven tactics, considered important in the design of enhanced online catalogs, that would assist the user in finding the right subject terms. The tactics are:

TRACE — to examine information already found in the search in order to find additional terms to be used in furthering the search.
VARY — to alter or substitute one's terms in any of several ways.
FIX — to try alternate affixes, including prefixes, suffixes, infixes.
REARRANGE — to reverse or rearrange the words in subject terms in any or all reasonable orders.
CONTRARY — to search for the term logically opposite from that describing the desired information.
RESPELL — to search under a different spelling.
RESPACE — to try spacing variants.

While some of these tactics have been partially implemented in existing systems, and some experienced information specialists have incorporated various "tactics" into their own personal styles of searching (many of them not aware that they are actually using some of the "term tactics"), there have not been, to my knowledge, attempts to formally implement tactics into the design of subject searching of online databases or online catalogs. In fact, I have come to believe that each of the tactics offers enough material for empirical research — that each could be expanded into a research study.

The TRACE tactic could be "zoomed" into a variety of design and implementation possibilities. For instance, in terms of systems design, the TRACE tactic could mean to trace and expand each of the subject-rich fields within a retrieved and displayed record on a screen. Consider topical subject headings, cross references, personal and corporate names as subjects, corporate names with subject terms in them (e.g., National Center for Vital & Health Statistics), free text (e.g., titles, series titles, title-added entries), and classification numbers. Each of the bibliographic records in OPACs is machine-readable, allowing for easy access to most of the tagged fields. In terms of implementation, TRACE could be wrapped around "constructive" strategies and other useful message and explanation facilities, using some of the available display technologies. The mouse device might be programmed to zoom some of the fruitful areas and project a wider view of any of the subject-rich fields. The use of multiple screens, touch panels, and hierarchical menu displays with highlighting have been already proposed in the literature.[83-84]

We in the field of librarianship attempt to understand the inner workings of the library catalog, why things are as they are, and how to make catalogs work better. The library user off the street, indeed, a faculty member, has no awareness of some of the principles that have become sacred since the time of Panizzi and Cutter and which have provided the theoretical foundation of our catalogs. Knowledge of some of the principles (e.g., the principles of specific entry, common usage, uniform headings) helps us a great deal in understanding the inner working of library catalogs, and the reasons these principles were introduced in the first place. The REARRANGE tactic might in a transparent manner help the searcher understand some of these principles and rules underlying the Library of Congress Subject Headings, LCSH, more efficiently than it has been possible so far. It should be possible to rearrange automatically a sequence of subject terms so that the sequence fits the pattern of LCSH (e.g., History, Military, but Social Conditions; History — anecdotes, facetiae, satire, etc.).

The extent to which OPACs are tolerant of spelling variants, spacing, capitalization, and so forth, should be improved by the RESPELL program and the RESPACE program. For instance, a spelling program might check individual terms against an entry vocabulary for variations in spelling.

The FIX tactic might be left more to the user than to the system. The system could be written to spot a problem and, by means of suggestive prompts and error messages, display various options the user might consider in repairing the problem.

The VARY tactic is another powerful way to guide the user in any of many ways to alter and substitute subject terms. A number of authors have suggested various ways to provide terminological assistance by means of "searching vocabularies," "enhanced thesauri," and "post-controlled vocabularies."[85-87] At the implementation level, the VARY tactic has been, to a certain extent, implemented in the CITE prototype OPAC at the National Library of Medicine, PaperChase, and BRS TERM database.[88-89]

I believe that tactics such as SUPER, SUB, RELATE, and NEIGHBOR could be expanded to provide valuable guidance to those who, according to user studies, have difficulties broadening or narrowing their searches. Those who expressed the desire to explore online catalogs should be able to see alternatives to terms they could come up with.

DIRECTIONS FOR RESEARCH

Since people lack the motivation to invest as little as thirty minutes in learning how to use OPACs, we need to devise effective ways to assist searchers in their decisions.

Learning behavior is less well understood than expert performance. The theoretical underpinnings of the Keystroke-Level Model provide a useful and accurate account of the time performance of expert users.[90] We have no similar account of why some computer systems are easier for novices to learn than for experts. More research is needed in investigating predictors of learning and using OPACs.

Furthermore, we need to set and optimize boundaries among decision points for which various assistance modes appear most suitable and productive. For instance, we need to identify productive scenarios for those processes and tasks which can be usefully mediated by the computer, and those that can be most efficiently operated on by the user. We might consider various decision points involving database selection, search term selection, broadening/narrowing search strategy, and so forth, and suggest a specific range of possibilities for assisting the user at each decision point. Would the user be best served if we delegate the process of reformulating search strategy to the computer entirely, or if we explore various means of helping the searcher achieve his or her desired goal through a more symmetrical pattern of participation between the user and the computer?

The emerging cognitive engineering approach is a new paradigm for studying the man-machine interface. It attempts to describe human cognitive functioning as a recursive set of operations, including the exchange of information with the outer environment.[91-92] In contrast, certain traditional approaches, such as engineering psychology, reduced human cognitive qualities to a "black box," focusing on stimuli and responses and describing human information processes as a linear, rather than adaptive and recursive series of fixed processing stages.

By applying interdisciplinary research from cognitive engineering, psychology, expert systems, and library and information science to the design of user interfaces, I believe we can come closer to achieving man-machine interfaces that can be truly regarded as cognitive systems. While man is obviously a cognitive system, machines are not; however, the discipline of cognitive engineering provides us with well established procedures and methods, and with a set of qualitative modeling aids, that can be used to design potentially cognitive user assistance modes.

REFERENCES

1. L. C. Smith. "Artificial Intelligence Applications in Information Systems." In: M. E. Williams (ed.) *Annual Review of Information Science and Technology*, White Plains, NY: Knowledge Industry Publications, 15:67-105, 1980.

2. C. L. Borgman. "Psychological Research in Human-Computer Interaction." In: M. E. Williams (ed.) *Annual Review of Information Science and Technology*, White Plains, NY: Knowledge Industry Publications, 19:33-64, 1984a.

3. H. A. Sowizral. "Expert Systems." In: M. E. Williams (ed.) *Annual Review of Information Science and Technology*, White Plains, NY: Knowledge Industry Publications, 20:179-199, 1985.

4. W. B. Croft & R. H. Thompson. "I³R: A New Approach to the Design of Document Retrieval Systems." *Journal of the American Society for Information Science* 38(6):389-404, 1987.

5. W. R. Swartout. "XPLAIN: a System for Creating and Explaining Expert Consulting Programs." *Artificial Intelligence* 21(3):285-325, 1983.

6. J. Matthews, G. S. Lawrence & D. K. Ferguson. *Using Online Catalogs: A Nationwide Survey*. New York: Neal-Schuman, 1983.

7. C. L. Borgman. "End User Behavior in an Online Information Retrieval System: A Computer Monitoring Study." In: *Research and Development in IR.* Sixth Annual International Association for Computing Machinery (ACM) Special Interest Group in the Information Retrieval (SIGIR) Conference. New York: ACM, 17(4):162-176, 1983.

8. C. L. Borgman. "Why are Online Catalogs Hard to Use? Lessons Learned from Information-Retrieval Studies." *Journal of the American Society for Information Science* 37(6):387-400, 1986.

9. K. Markey. *Subject Searching in Library Catalogs: Before and After the Introduction of Online Catalogs.* Dublin, OH: OCLC, 1984.

10. T. E. Doszkocs. "CITE NLM: Natural Language Searching in Online Catalog." *Information Technology and Libraries* 2(4):364-380, 1983.

11. M. J. Bates. "Subject Access in Online Catalogs: A Design Model." *Journal of the American Society for Information Science* 37(6):357-376, 1986.

12. W. B. Croft & R. H. Thompson, op. cit.

13. A. S. Pollitt. *An Expert Systems Approach to Document Retrieval: A Summary of the CANSEARCH Research Project.* Report No. 8616, 2d ed. Department of Computer Science and Mathematics, Huddersfield Polytechnic, England 1986.

14. W. R. Swartout, op. cit.

15. J. P. Bennett. "The User Interface Systems." In: C. Cuadra (ed.) *Annual Review of Information Science and Technology.* Washington, D.C.: The American Society for Information Science (ASIS), 7:159-196, 1972.

16. R. N. Cuff. "On Casual Users." *International Journal of Man-Machine Studies* 12(1980):163-187.

17. T. P. Moran. "An Applied Psychology of the User." *Association for Computing Machinery (ACM) Computing Surveys* 13(1):1-12, 1981.

18. C. R. Hildreth. *Online Public Access Catalogs: The User Interface.* Dublin, OH: OCLC, 1982.

19. W. Paisley & M. Butler. *Computer Assistance in Information Work.* Palo Alto, CA: Applied Communication Research. ERIC: ED 146900, 1977.

20. M. J. Bates. "Idea Tactics." *IEEE Transactions on Professional Communication* PC-23(2):95-100, 1980.

21. M. J. Bates. "Information Search Tactics." *Journal of the American Society for Information Science* 30(4):205-214, 1979.

22. C. L. Borgman, op. cit., 1986.

23. C. H. Fenichel. "Online Searching: Measures that Discriminate Among Users with Different Types of Experience." *Journal of the American Society for Information Science* 32(1):23-32, 1981.

24. C. R. Hildreth, op. cit.

25. E. R. Siegel, K. Kameen, S. K. Sinn & F. O. Weise. "A Comparative Evaluation for the Technical Performance and User Acceptance of Two Prototype Online Catalog Systems." *Information Technology and Libraries* 3(1):35-46, 1984.

26. T. Bellardo. "An Investigation of Online Searcher Traits and Their Rela-

tionship to Search Outcome." *Journal of the American Society for Information Science* 36(4):241-250, 1985.

27. C. L. Borgman, op. cit., 1986.

28. C. H. Fenichel, op. cit.

29. R. Fidel. "Online Searching Styles: A Case-Study-Based Model of Searching Behavior." *Journal of the American Society for Information Science* 35(4): 211-221, 1984.

30. N. N. Woelfl. *Individual Differences in Online Search Behavior: The Effect of Learning Styles and Cognitive Abilities on Process and Outcomes*. PhD dissertation, Case Western University, Cleveland, OH, 1984.

31. J. Matthews and Associates, Inc. *A Study of Six Online Public Access Catalogs: A Review of Findings*. November 1982.

32. Library of Congress. *Library of Congress Online Public Access Catalog Users Survey: A Report to the Council on Library Resources*. October 1982.

33. Research Libraries Group, Inc. *Public Online Catalogs and Research Libraries*. September 1982.

34. University of California, Division of Library Automation and Library Research and Analysis Group. *Users Look at Online Catalogs. Results of a National Survey of Users and Non-Users of Online Public Access Catalogs*. November 1982.

35. J. Matthews, G. S. Lawrence & D. K. Ferguson, op. cit., Table 17, question 17.

36. P. B. Knapp. "The Subject Catalog in the College Library: An Investigation of Terminology." *The Library Quarterly* 14(3):214-228, 1944.

37. C. J. Frarey. "Studies of Use of the Subject Catalog: Summary and Evaluation." In: M. F. Tauber (ed.) *The Subject Analysis of Library Materials*. New York: School of Library Service, Columbia University, 1953, pp. 147-166.

38. M. J. Bates. "System Meets User: Problems in Matching Subject Search Terms." *Information Processing and Management* 13(6):367-375, 1977.

39. G. W. Furnas, T. K. Landauer & L. M. Gomez. "The Vocabulary Problem in Human-System Communications." *Communications of the Association for Computing Machinery (ACM)* 30(11):964-971, 1987.

40. J. Matthews, G. S. Lawrence & D. K. Ferguson, op. cit., Table 17, questions 19-20, Table 20.

41. Op. cit., Table 8.

42. C. R. Hildreth, op. cit.

43. K. Markey, op. cit.

44. Op. cit., pp. 178-9.

45. C. R. Hildreth, op. cit., p. 160.

46. J. E. Tolle & S. Hah. "Online Search Patterns: NLM CATLINE Database." *Journal of the American Society for Information Science* 36(2):82-93, 1985.

47. C. L. Borgman, *The User's Mental Model of an Information Retrieval System: Effects on Performance*. Stanford, CA: Stanford University, 1984b. (PhD dissertation)

48. W. Paisley. *The Role of Cognitive Style in the Performance of Computer-Mediated Information and Communication Tasks*. A report prepared for System Development Foundation, 1982.

49. J. Dickson. "An Analysis of User Errors in Searching an Online Catalog." *Cataloging & Classification Quarterly* 4(3):19-38, 1984.

50. C. L. Borgman, op. cit., 1983.

51. J. E. Tolle & S. Hah, op. cit.

52. J. A. Galambos, E. S. Wikler, J. B. Black & M. M. Sebrechts. "How You Tell Your Computer What You Mean: Ostension in Interactive Systems." In: A. Janda (ed.) *Human Factors in Computing Systems*. . . . New York: ACM, 1983, pp. 182-185.

53. S. Card, T. P. Moran & A. Newell. *The Psychology of Human-Computer Interaction*. Hillsdale, NJ: Lawrence Erlbaum Associates, 1983.

54. K. Efe. "A Proposed Solution to the Problem of Levels in Error-Message Generation." *Communications of the Association for Computing Machinery* 30(11):948-955, 1987.

55. A. V. Reed. "Error-Correcting Strategies and Human Interaction with Computer Systems." In: Association for Computing Machinery (ACM). *Proceedings of the Human Factors in Computer Systems Conference*. New York: ACM, 1982, pp. 236-238.

56. D. A. Norman. "Design Rules Based on Analysis of Human Error." *Communications of the Association for Computing Machinery* 26(4):254-258, 1983.

57. S. L. Smith. "Standards Versus Guidelines for Designing User Interface Software." *Behaviour and Information Technology* 5(1):47-61, 1986.

58. W. Paisley, op. cit., 1982.

59. E. Hollnagel & D. D. Woods. "Cognitive Systems Engineering: New Wine in New Bottles." *International Journal of Man-Machine Studies* 18(6):583-600, 1983.

60. J. Matthews. "Suggested Guidelines for Screen Layouts and Design of Online Catalogs." In: J. Frye-Williams (ed.) *Screen Displays in Online Catalogs: Report of a Conference Sponsored by the Council of Library Resources*. Washington, D.C.: CLR, 1986.

61. C. L. Borgman. "Online Catalog Screen Display: A Human Factors Critique." In: J. Frye-Williams (ed.) *Screen Displays in Online Catalogs*. . . . Washington, D.C.: CLR, 1986.

62. E. Hollnages & D. D. Woods, op. cit.

63. H. P. Van Cott & R. G. Kinkade. *Human Engineering Guide to Equipment Design*. Washington, D.C.: American Institute for Research, 1972.

64. T. M. Granda. *An Evaluation of Visual Search Behavior on a Cathode Ray Tube Utilizing the Window Technique*. Technical paper No. 283. Virginia: U.S. Army Research Institute for the Behavioral and Social Sciences (February). NTIS AD-A053-352, 1978.

65. M. J. Bates, op. cit., 1980.

66. S. Card, T. P. Moran & A. Newell, op. cit.

67. T. P. Norman, op. cit., 1984.
68. E. Rich. "User Modeling Via Stereotypes." *Cognitive Science* 3(4):329-354, 1979.
69. D. R. Morehead et al. "The Value of Information and Computer-Aided Information Seeking: Problem Formulation and Application of Fiction Retrieval." *Information Processing & Management* 20(5/6):583-601, 1984.
70. R. N. Oddy. "Information Retrieval Through Man-Machine Dialogue." *Journal of Documentation* 33(1):1-14, 1977.
71. W. B. Croft & R. H. Thompson, op. cit.
72. M. J. Bates, op. cit., 1980.
73. A. V. Reed, op. cit.
74. C. R. Hildreth, op. cit.
75. M. J. Bates, op. cit., 1979.
76. N. J. Belkin et al. "ASK for Information Retrieval: Part I. Background and Theory." *Journal of Documentation* 38(2):61-71, 1982.
77. E. Hollnagel & D. D. Woods, op. cit.
78. W. Paisley, op. cit., 1982.
79. W. B. Croft & R. H. Thompson, op. cit.
80. D. R. Morehead et al., op. cit.
81. R. N. Oddy, op. cit.
82. E. Rich, op. cit.
83. W. B. Croft & R. H. Thompson, op. cit.
84. A. S. Pollitt, op. cit.
85. M. J. Bates, op. cit., 1986.
86. A. B. Piternick. "Searching Vocabularies: A Developing Category of Online Search Tools." *Online Review* 8(5):441-449, 1984.
87. F. W. Lancaster. *Vocabulary Control for Information Retrieval.* 2d ed. Washington, D.C.: Information Resources Press, 1986.
88. T. E. Doszkocs, op. cit.
89. G. L. Horowitz & H. L. Bleich. "PaperChase: A Computer Program to Search the Medical Literature." *The New England Journal of Medicine* 305(16):924-930, 1981.
90. E. Hollnagel & D. D. Woods, op. cit.
91. D. A. Norman, op. cit., 1984.
92. W. Paisley, op. cit., 1982.

Knowledge-Based Systems in Information Work: A View of the Future

Irene L. Travis

ABSTRACT. Knowledge-based systems (KBS) are part of a new generation of interrelated technologies that have the potential to expand greatly both the ways in which information is conveyed and the tools available to information workers and users for finding, evaluating, analyzing, and assimilating it. These technologies can provide expanded assistance to users in such areas as reference and referral, public access catalog use, and end-user database searching. Moreover, they will allow types of knowledge to be reported and transmitted that have heretofore not been captured in permanent media using such devices as multidimensional information linkages and new forms of interactive media. These developments and KBS in particular offer exciting possibilities; however, as yet, they are only possibilities for libraries. Both further research and considerable financial resources will be required to realize the benefits of KBSs in information work.

The pace of change in electronics and the technologies it supports shows no sign of slackening. Libraries have absorbed the impacts, good and bad, of time-sharing and personal computing and are now confronting optical storage with a mixture of hope and exasperation. User and personnel requirements, library interrelationships, equipment, budgets, collection policies, and technical and public services are all in a state of flux with little prospect for consolidation or stability. Moreover, fueled by cheaper processing, cheaper

---

The author is an associate member, Senior Technical Staff, Planning Research Corporation, 1500 Planning Research Dr., McLean, VA 22102.

© 1989 by The Haworth Press, Inc. All rights reserved.

storage, and faster communications, more technology-driven change is clearly on the way.

One of the most publicized potential components of enhanced computing environments for libraries and other information service agencies is artificial intelligence (AI), especially the technologies for reasoning with knowledge-bases. Two well-known classes of such "knowledge-based" systems (KBSs) are expert systems (ESs) and natural language understanding (NLU) systems. ESs try to reproduce the performance of a person who knows how to do a particular well-bounded, but non-trivial task expertly. A commonly cited example is how to perform a differential diagnosis in some area of medicine. ESs are characterized by a capability to reason with uncertain or incomplete information, and to produce results in cases where no algorithmic solution can be specified. Typically, their knowledge bases consist of rules that specify sets of conditions that can occur in the subject domain of the system and the actions that the informant or expert takes or the conclusions he makes under those conditions. They also should incorporate a means to describe to the user how they reached a particular conclusion. This feature is called an explanation capability.

Of particular interest in information work are ESs used as tutors, which often incorporate models of users as part of the knowledge-base to be operated on in user interaction. That is, in order to help a student or other user, a tutoring system must somehow understand what the user is trying to do and how much the user already knows. This knowledge can be acquired in a number of ways, including incorporating stereotypes of users, maintaining histories of the user's previous interactions with the system, or analyzing what the user is doing in the present session. Reference librarians seek similar information as part of the reference interview.

The other KBS technology that is important to information work is NLU. It also uses knowledge-bases—lexicons and world knowledge—to process language. In fact, because the objects of information service are still usually texts, it is difficult to separate NLU capability from expert knowledge in the domain of information services. Of course, librarians are knowledgeable about such things as cataloging policies for monographic series or how to read an entry in the *Library of Congress Subject Headings*, which involve language in a minimal way. These kinds of expertise might well be expressed as rules in an ES that did not incorporate NLU, as a doctor's knowledge of a disease might be. However, much of what librarians offer users as information intermediaries is a knowledge of the indexing sublanguage of the literature of a field and of the kinds and levels of linguistic distinctions that must be made to map the user's requirements to this literature.

This prominence of NLU in information retrieval (IR) is a significant problem, since automated NLU is very difficult. Some progress has been made in providing natural language interfaces for searching structured databases, and there is some capability to process short texts to meet well-structured, pre-specified requirements. Nonetheless, NLU on the scale that may be required for use in information systems of any scope does not seem to be close at hand. However, as Croft points out,[1] we also do not really understand what these requirements are or how much an expanded natural language capability may help retrieval. Perhaps a limited NL processing may be all that is necessary to achieve a major improvement. At the time we honestly know little about how this new potential should be most effectively employed.

To this point we have spoken as though ES and NLU were separate and distinct. In fact, they have many problems in common, such as the utilization of world knowledge. Furthermore, they are increasingly co-occurring within single KBS implementations, such as those in which an NLU system serves as an interface or a knowledge-base generation system for an expert system application. Moreover, there are indications that system designers trained in AI are beginning to move to yet another level of generality—thinking in terms of the total system architecture needed to do a particular job, using both AI-based and conventional tools, rather than simply looking about for possible applications of AI technology. The appearance of this point of view in the literature reflects some maturity in AI, as it moves from being a solution in search of a problem to being simply one more technique available to systems analysts who know how to use it. This movement is being forced on the AI industry because significant applications require integration of the AI-based systems with existing databases and computing facilities. As information workers, we would be advised to adopt a similar viewpoint—to ask what problems we want to have solved and explore the ways in which KBS technologies can help rather than simply reacting to change in a completely opportunistic way.

In this article we will look at the possible impact of the emerging technology environment on information work with a focus on KBSs. We will examine it from two perspectives:

1. The introduction and use of knowledge-based tools in the provision of information services, and
2. The effect of KBS technology on library materials and the ramifications for library practice of these new kinds of information sources.

In the first area, information professionals are able to take an active role to secure better services for our clients directly and better support for our services to them. In the second, the role of the library or other information agency is indeed largely reactive. That is, we cannot control the kinds of information materials that are being produced: our problem is to accommodate them.

THE NEW TECHNOLOGIES

In the previous section, we mentioned the rapid pace of technology-driven change in computing. In this section we look more carefully at this emerging picture and how KBS technology supports and is supported by it. As shown in the middle column of Figure 1, KBSs are only one of a family of new basic applications at the disposal of the system designer. These options include sophisticated graphics, image processing and understanding, voice recognition, hypertext, and computer aided design/computer aided engineering (CAD/CAE). These broad applications are supported by fundamental advances in hardware and operating systems, which are listed in the left-hand column, such as high resolution displays. All these developments will impact the nature of library materials, on the one

NEW BASE TECHNOLOGIES
High speed integrated circuits
New computer architectures, such as parallel processors
Fast and inexpensive internal and external storage technology, such as 1 Megabyte random access memory (RAM) chips and optical disk storage systems
Rapid data communication technology, such as fiber optic local area networks (LANS);
Multi-tasking operating systems with windowing capability to allow users to run multiple programs and tasks simultaneously
Large, high resolution screens for displaying multiple windows, document facsimiles, bit-mapped graphics, and for other applications requiring that a large amount of data be displayed or that it be displayed with a high level of clarity or detail
Improved input devices, such powerful OCR, fast high resolution scanners to convert information on paper or microforms to electronic form
Improved human factors understanding
Software development environments and rapid prototyping tools for increased programmer productivity; such as expert system development environments, programmer's workbenches, and Fourth Generation Languages
New interface technologies to reduce keyboarding, such as the mouse.

NEW BASIC APPLICATIONS
Knowledge-based systems (KBS)
Graphics
Image processing and understanding
Voice recognition
Hypertext systems
Computer aided design/computer aided engineering (CAD/CAE)

NEW INFORMATION SERVICE APPLICATIONS
New Tools for Information Services
New Information Media and Genres

FIGURE 1: TECHNOLOGIES SUPPORTING NEW APPLICATIONS IN INFORMATION WORK

hand, and can be brought to bear in improving information service on the other. Image understanding, for example, may one day allow us to scan photographs for features much as we now scan text for particular combinations of words. Voice recognition will facilitate human/computer communication, and computer aided design and engineering will allow engineering specifications and documentation to be dynamic objects that are directly incorporated into a product's manufacturing and diagnostic systems.

The new technologies are a volatile and interactive mix of exciting possibilities and bewildering complexities. At a practical level, however, libraries are faced with a continual need to upgrade computer equipment and software in order to take advantage of the possibilities. Even though the equipment continues to fall in price, such rapid change is out of line with most libraries' budgets, procurement cycles, and with their ability to absorb changes in procedures and systems. The pressure is almost relentless, however. Apple Computer's hypertext package, Hypercard™, for the Macintosh™ is only one example of a very inexpensive and very seductive application package with obvious potential for information applications, such as user-friendly interfaces, that is sending us all scurrying to the computer store to make major upgrades to our internal memories and buy larger hard-disk drives in order to make full use of its possibilities. As the size of an institution's existing microcomputer base and its dependency on that base for day to day operations increases, replacement becomes increasingly expensive and disruptive. All realistic forecasts about the impact of KBS technology must keep this problem in mind.

The danger in this picture is, of course, succumbing to gadgetry for gadgetry's sake. We really know painfully little about how to employ this powerful potential for the good of library patrons, and we have little time and few resources to devote to sorting out real advances in effectiveness from things that are merely new and different. Using software such as specialized programs for building expert systems ("shells") or hypertext software, such as Hypercard, it is relatively easy to build a prototype retrieval system that looks impressive. It is much more difficult to determine (1) whether the program is actually usable by its intended consumers; (2) whether it, in fact, improves library service; and (3) whether, even if it has this potential, it can be scaled-up to meet real information system requirements within the budget of a library agency. In short, there is a major gap in time and, indeed, feasibility between the "prototype" described in the literature and a useful piece of off-the-shelf software.

KBSs AS TOOLS FOR THE PROVISION OF INFORMATION SERVICES

At this point we come to the issue of the use of KBSs to support information work, or, rather, in line with our previous discussion, we look at some persistent problems in information work and the likelihood that KBS technology can ameliorate them in, say, the next five to ten years. We will look at the following four problem areas:

1. The use of KBSs for reference and referral
2. The use of KBSs to improve public access catalogs (PACs)
3. The use of KBSs to improve end-user searching of specialized bibliographic databases with controlled vocabularies
4. The use of KBSs to improve end-user text searching.

We will consider first what these applications have in common. In all cases users must somehow refine their information need before or iteratively during an interactive search so that they can evaluate what they see against some standard for what they want to know. To be successful, they or their advisors or intermediaries must gain some sense for how the topic they are interested in appears in the literature (if it does); what terminology is used in the sublanguage(s) associated with that discussion; how the scope of the information system they are searching matches or does not match the coverage required; and how the information system indexes or otherwise identifies information on the topic(s) they seek. Finally, after seeing some results of a search, they need to have strategies for improving it if the initial results are unsatisfactory. Of course, in reality, much of this information is not known or perhaps even not knowable, which explains the many horror stories available about poor results for information seeking in all four of the problem areas listed above.

On the other hand, some of the required information is known by (1) experienced system users, (2) subject specialists, (3) the creators of the information system, and (4) librarians trained in information problem elicitation and problem solving techniques. There are undoubtedly many information intermediaries who simultaneously fill all these roles. Modeling such an expert would indeed provide very comprehensive user assistance. However, most expert system prototypes, to the degree that they are based on any close analysis of expert intermediary functions, focus on what is known by users in classes (1) and (4), that is by intermediaries when they are searching databases which they may know little about and in areas in which they do not have subject expertise.

Tests with existing end-user gateway systems, however, and, indeed most empirical research to date in searching, strongly suggests that, for simple searches, librarians with these qualifications do no better than end-users. We, therefore, can expect little enhancement in this case over that already provided by existing user-friendly interfaces that use conventional technology. The test will come in the ability of systems to identify and manage searches that are inherently difficult to carry out, which is a very challenging problem. These observations raise questions about the utility of intermediary systems that do not have detailed "domain" knowledge of the subject, the database, the indexing practices, and other things that are quite specific to a system and require large, extensive, custom-built knowledge-bases. In addition, intermediary systems require the means to understand the users' goals and needs to some degree and to provide coaching and assistance to the users in an acceptable way. Both of these problems are also very difficult. Daniels[2] provides an excellent overview of user modeling research, while Smith et al.[3] provide some insight by example into the problems in the latter area.

Reference and Referral

Turning now to the specific areas we listed above, we can note that providing guidance to reference materials is an area which has several points that distinguish it from the other applications. One is, of course, that users often come with direct, specific questions. Users, as has often been noted, do not really want to be handed a reference book, they want the answer to their question. The Answerman system at the National Agricultural Library (NAL) as described by Waters[4] gives prominence to solving this problem. Another fact in reference searching is that, contrary to the case usually seen in searching the journal literature, the user's question is much more specific than the general subject of the reference book (and, therefore, than its library cataloging). Such a system may, therefore, require a significant expansion of the general library subject heading and classification schemes if the user's natural language queries are to be processed. One might need to add, for instance, the names of particular garden pests and the accompanying taxonomic information for a gardening reference system, as was necessary to build the PLEXUS prototype developed under British Library auspices.[5,6,7] Such an expansion is non-trivial, both in terms of skill and expense.

In fact, Answerman and PLEXUS represent an interesting study in contrast of the problems of experts system development for reference and referral on a number of levels. In a sense they represent the extremes of the approaches that are found to AI in the IR. In Answerman, an off-the-shelf, inexpensive, AI shell was used by working librarians to develop a rapid, exploratory prototype in order to see how AI capability might be integrated into a library environment. The developers of PLEXUS, on the other hand, were more directly focused on IR expert system research, as such. The system results from a major research project in ES and IR that includes studying intermediary behavior in depth and building a sophisticated, state-of-the-art expert system.

Answerman, to take each system in turn, is more general in scope—agriculture—than PLEXUS, which covers only gardening. It is based on a general knowledge of library materials, rather than how librarians solve problems, and was designed basically as a front-end to a complex of retrieval capabilities. It is built, as we said, using a simple expert system shell that runs on a microcomputer.

Basically, the shell facilitates inputting IF-THEN information, in this case combinations of infotype (form), topic, and occupation/ organization (e.g., researcher, Congressman) with their associated specific reference works and a probability that the work will contain the answer to questions that can be characterized with this set of descriptors. The system then sets up its rules based on this input, provides the logic to process them, and assists in building a user-friendly, menu driven interface. As Waters himself says "The beauty of the shell approach is that it allows librarians to create their own user-friendly system to select appropriate reference tools in any specialized field easily and quickly." It does not differ much from, say, existing online database directories. One could implement this system in a relational database management system or other conventional software, but it would require more programming expertise. The expert system shell is primarily a programming tool that makes this job easier.

On the other hand, while the AI component may be minimal, the overall view and intention of the investigators certainly is not. The ES is an interface that has been experimentally linked to optical disk systems with reference book text and the Agricola database (in development), as well as with a gateway system that gives access to other commercial bibliographic and full-text databases available by dial-up. This case well illustrates our previous point about the synergism and interdependence among new technologies and the role of KBS as simply one aspect. It is also significant because it is an attempt to prototype a full online reference service, where all types of informations services—reference books, bibliographic databases, actual journal text, and other sources both inhouse and out-of-house—are available through a single comprehensive system. Here the NAL staff is not supplying an existing service in a new way; they really are attempting to change the type of service available to patrons. The system may be an unpolished prototype, but the potential is clear.

PLEXUS is, as we have said, a much more sophisticated system from an AI point of view. Unlike Answerman, it is a stand-alone system at present. In developing PLEXUS, the researchers realized that no existing shell was capable of supporting their complex application, and, thus, they wisely built the system "from scratch." They hoped, as we will see below, that part of their system might form the basis of a shell designed specifically for KB IR systems.

Plexus contains 10,000 lines of Pascal code, 1,000 rules, 1,400 stopwords, and 1,750 word stems, which makes it a fairly large expert system by current standards. It consists of a number of cooperating experts covering such areas as processing the user's natural language input; building the user model; deciding whether the input is sufficient to use to construct a search; interacting with the user to gain more information; constructing a search; evaluating a search; and modifying search strategies. Nonetheless, it has a number of limitations, most obviously in its scope (gardening). On this subject, Brian Vickery states:

> One initial hope of the project was . . . that the system could be constructed in such a way that knowledge specific to the original subject domain was separate from the general structure of the program—so that, in effect, from PLEXUS could be extracted a shell which would be available to others wishing to develop an expert retrieval system. One important feature of the attempt to extend the subject domain of PLEXUS will be to test whether this is a real possibility. At the most general level of control, the set and sequence of procedures to be carried out will remain the same whatever the subject field. But much of the fine detail of PLEXUS processing is based upon the use of semantic categories and the extent to which these can be made adaptable to different subject fields has to be explored.[8]

In other words, it is not altogether easy to divorce the processes from the subject matter in retrieval systems. The ultimate feasibility and power of a shell, which, for instance, contains only procedures and gains its semantic information solely from a thesaurus or lexicon without other specific domain-related knowledge remains to be seen.

Answerman and PLEXUS, thus, present a contrast in focus: Answerman has more scope but very limited KB capabilities, while PLEXUS has more power but very limited subject matter. Ideally, what we are seeking is the scope of one with the power of the other, but this marriage will not be easily achieved. Each research group has pointed to major barriers to scaling-up their systems for practical use. We have already discussed the reservations voiced by Vickery, while Waters makes an eloquent plea in his paper to the library community, which he feels must cooperate in the enterprise if the necessary research and investment is to be made. The necessary research in IR and AI and the cost of building the necessary knowledge bases certainly exceeds the resources of any individual library.

Public Access Catalogs

One distinguishing characteristic of PACs is that they are at present largely searched by end users, rather than intermediaries. One might think that there is no intermediary to model in this case. On the other hand, purely on the basis of personal observation, I would wager that there is no area in library service where the difference between a librarian and an end user is more marked than in completing both known item and subject searching successfully in a large traditional card catalog or its electronic replacement, providing, of course, that the librarian is thoroughly familiar with the library's collection and cataloging policies and tools. Surely the basic rules of practice of, for instance, the *Library of Congress Subject Headings*, can somehow be incorporated into an online catalog interface to help the user. On the other hand, how to present such help to the user is a non-trivial problem. If the user has found the heading "Fire prevention," should one automatically find all the headings with "Fire prevention" as a subheading, as well as all the other cross references? Or should the system probe first and only suggest headings that appear to be appropriate? Which do users prefer? Does it make a difference whether they are using their own PC in the privacy of their own home or whether there are four people waiting in line to use the terminal they are occupying? Moreover, we must face the fact that most libraries have not even managed to get their card catalog subject reference structure incorporated into their PACs, much less anything more radical. Funding is a major barrier, even to conventional technology.

End-User Searching of Specialized Bibliographic Databases

The potential of KBSs in text and database searching is an area that has received a great deal of attention, as witnessed by a recent issue of *Information Processing and Management*[9] that was devoted almost entirely to this topic. The overview articles provided by

Croft[10] and Brooks[11] in that issue are particularly recommended as providing somewhat more technical introductions to AI and retrieval than is given here. The problems represented by database retrieval applications are primarily variations on problems we have already seen. However, the possibility of a more specialized, self-selected, paying clientele for these systems makes certain types of user support more feasible. A specialized interface, such as Pollitt's experimental CANSEARCH[12] for cancer therapy, may have a volume of users, a well enough defined problem area, and a base of economic support that can make it a sensible and useful tool for medical practitioners, cancer researchers, and laymen interested in the topic. It uses a menuing approach, thus avoiding the natural language interface problem, and basically helps the user with the technicalities of formulating a MEDLINE search, given MEDLINE sub-heading usage and other complications of the National Library of Medicine's indexing, which is admittedly difficult to negotiate without training. CANSEARCH is very specifically tailored to MEDLINE and a relatively narrow subject field, so it does not contradict our previous observation that both the viability of more generalized retrieval systems and the power and feasibility of portable shells for building retrieval applications remain to be seen.

Free- and/or Full-Text Searching

The problem of natural language text retrieval, on the other hand, is one that we have not discussed thus far. The good and bad points of text searching are well known at this point, using both Boolean technologies and statistical retrieval techniques. The question is whether AI, particularly KBSs, can be any help in overcoming the limits of word-based searching. Put another way, free-text searching allows the user to escape when necessary from the constraints of the world view provided by a concept-based indexing language or to perform subject searches when no indexing is available at all. The principal problem with concept-based indexing is not that it is wrong, though it may be unnecessary in some cases, but rather that a priori indexing of any kind has its limitation in that the uses to which texts will be put and the conceptual frameworks of new classes of users are not completely predictable. It is this problem that explains why automatic statistical approaches can be competitive with retrieval based on human indexing. Building an expert system on top of statistical retrieval base is, therefore, an alternative approach to reproducing human indexing and is being pursued by Croft,[13] Fox[14] and others.

Nonetheless, certain kinds of searches are almost impossible to perform without what is now human assessment of the subject of the document. Fidel[15] reports that her studies show that searchers in the humanities, for instance, almost never use free-text searching. Moreover, in many cases, even successful free-text searches suffer from poor precision. Can natural language processing help these problems?

Some things are feasible here in the short term, and others are more difficult. Among the simpler things is screening retrieval. In several of the systems we have mentioned, such as CANSEARCH and PLEXUS, the user's query has been analyzed to identify the role of the query terms. That is, in CANSEARCH does a term fill such roles as a therapy, a site, a body system, a symptom, or characteristic of a patient? If such an analysis exists from previous processing or directly from user specification, retrieved text passages can be evaluated relatively simply to see if the terms that match the query occur in the proper roles. If not, the text can be discarded.

Another KBS enhancement with near-term feasibility is to build extended user profiles for selective dissemination of information (SDI) using AI techniques pioneered by the RUBRIC system.[16] Here, the investment can be amortized over time, providing that the user's knowledge requirements are fairly stable. Both individuals and organizations may have such requirements. In cases where the information need continues, but the users change because of personnel turnover, the knowledge captured in the profiles is particularly valuable. Similar efforts may be warranted, even for single searches, if a very large number of records must be scanned. If, for instance, an historian must go through millions of military messages in an archive looking for certain types of events, it may well be worth a week's effort on the part of the information specialist and the user to put together a sophisticated query statement. Such profiles are labor-intensive to construct, but within the state of the art. Other uses include selecting texts to be analyzed to update knowledge or databases automatically through further natural language processing and automatic indexing or re-indexing.

The examples above have presumed that the text being searched was only selectively processed with the major analytical work being reflected in the query formulation. Moreover, the primary object of the operations was to match passages of text against information specifications. More ambitious NL processing includes applications that involve the system in understanding the meaning of the text and being able to reason with it or otherwise operate on the basis of understanding its content. Systems in this class include those that can perform direct question-answering, generate database entries, write summaries or abstracts, and build knowledge bases from text. Such systems exist, and some are being considered for practical applications.[17,18,19] Major problems, as above, include how to expand the scope of such systems, given their requirements for lexical information and, in many cases, for a great deal of world knowledge.

Other problems include understanding the meaning of long texts and of texts that are not event-oriented, in contrast to most of the newspaper stories and military messages that comprise the bulk of the information processed by current NLU systems. Understanding metaphor and representing common sense or common world knowledge to the system are also difficult. To take only one trivial example, suppose we consider the following sentences:

> The Librarian forgot her appointment with the new head of the cataloging department. She was embarrassed.

Our assumption that "she" is the Librarian, not the head of the cataloging department, is based on our knowledge of the common courtesies one owes one's colleagues and the reaction one should have to omitting them accidentally — as opposed, of course, to omitting them deliberately. If the first sentence had been "The Librarian ignored her appointment with the new head of the cataloging department," the "she" that was embarrassed might have been the cataloger. In any event, the second sentence would certainly be much more ambiguous. When one leaves the realm of processing straightforward factual narrative for very specific and well defined purposes, the water gets deep very quickly.

KBSs AND OTHER ELECTRONIC PRODUCTS AS INFORMATION MATERIALS

In addition to the possibilities detailed above, the dramatic and fundamental technological changes have occurred that will have an impact on information work in other positive and exciting ways. For instance, we are witnessing and will continue to see the evolution of entirely new information genres, such as those based on hypertext. It is fascinating to contemplate what such presentation tools can provide to imaginative authors trying to convey highly complex scholarly material. Whole classes of knowledge that could not easily be captured in permanent media up to this point may now be recorded in a useful form. In fact, one can see KBSs in that light — as a means of preserving and transmitting knowledge that is difficult to convey in conventional writing, or even as a new genre. Some ESs can easily be viewed as a species of space-age "how-to" manual.

The impact, however, will be much more extensive. These new vehicles have in common the ability to liberate us from linear presentation of material. At the same time, meaningful communication must still have a structure, and the structures will potentially be more complex. We, in turn, will certainly need automated tools and will almost certainly need intelligent automated tools to manage both the authoring and the use of these new forms. Bootstrapping might very well accelerate both the pace and the complexity of these new materials, that is, for instance, in the use of KBS to build KBS and other multidimensional forms.

Not only will the structures become more complex and the type of information conveyed be changed, but, of course, the potential for mixing media in a presentation and for user interaction with the material will also be factors of great importance that add new types of complexity to the electronic document. We are already seeing some initial examples in the electronic encyclopedias. A little reflection on this situation will reinforce my previous observation that it will be relatively easy to create interesting and superficially entertaining systems in this environment, but it may be several years before we have much grasp on how to use it for maximum effectiveness and before authors know how and when to exploit the numerous devices available. We are seeing an explosion of possibilities with very little notion about how to use them.

Information agencies will, nevertheless, be encountering new instances of a problem that will be no less difficult because it is familiar: namely, how to deal with a flood of new types of library materials. As with the microforms, film, phonograph records, videotapes, and computer software that libraries now incorporate in their collections, librarians must solve the problems of how to evaluate, catalog, store, and give patron access to KBSs and other new formats. Let us take an ES as a case in point. In the near future there are likely to be quite a number of ESs that are the equivalent of today's lay persons guides to legal and financial problems, such as how to make a will or how to do estate planning. Such programs written for commonly available personal computers are likely to be very popular and would seem to be a reasonable acquisition for some libraries. The problems then represent a combination of those present with other software and with media, such as film, where it is almost impossible to assess the content or presentation without expending considerable time and effort. Questions a librarian will have to consider include the following:

1. Where can I find a review of this kind of material? What are reviewer's qualifications to evaluate the content, the technical quality of the system, or both?
2. How are reviewers that librarians rely on going to assess the product? Testing and verification of ESs is at best a black art at present. In fact, it is a problem that is only beginning to be addressed in AI research. How will the reviewers independently be able to compare the coverage, accuracy, quality, or timeliness of an ES? Who is the author of the expert system insofar as its content is concerned? Whose knowledge is represented in the system? If the source is a well-known expert, how can one be sure the system represents his knowledge accurately? We have the same problem with evaluating texts, to be sure, but it is easier for the expert/author to verify what he has written than what has been incorporated into an expert system.
3. As with film and other media requiring equipment, is the li-

brary going to supply equipment so that the material is available to all users or is it only going to supply the software? If only software, is the library going to supply the proper version of the operating system as well as the application?
4. What are the plans and costs for updating the expert system, both in terms of software and content? What is the useful life of the product if it is not updated?
5. How do you catalog an expert system? If there is a single expert, is the expert the author? What are the significant things to describe about it apart from those characteristics it shares with any software? Are the number of rules of size of the knowledge base differentiating features?

Similar questions can be asked about hypertexts or any other complex medium.

Finally, we must mention that changes in format and content are not the only problem. Sheer quantity will continue to plague us. The problem with being inundated with information, much of it not useful, has been raised for hundreds of years, but electronic documents, communications, and publishing will change the complexion of the problem yet again. Hard disk drives, for instance, that can store 3,000 pages of text are scarcely worthy of notice anymore, and compact optical disks can literally store the contents of a small library.

Current search problems have fostered a class of professional on-line searchers to handle occasional major information seeking events for us. In the future, problems of that magnitude may plague us daily as we try both to find the small percentage of information in our personal collections that is of interest to us and to cope with the unmanageable volume of material which that small percentage may now represent. Libraries and other information agencies may be faced with the need to develop entirely new classes of tools to handle the increase.

CONCLUSION

Overall, our prognosis for the impact of KBS systems on information work in the next five to ten years has been mixed. It is fair to say that the first five years of intensive interest in expert systems on the part of some information researchers has recently begun to yield a number of prototype applications. In addition to the systems themselves, the experience of the researchers has yielded a number of very thoughtful discussions of the topic with much more meat than the early speculations. The efforts by Brooks, Croft, Daniels and others have been mentioned. Waters also comments trenchantly on the practical problems of mustering the limited resources of libraries to exploit new technology cooperatively. For systems of any size, a large funding base will be necessary, whether through cooperatives, from government subsidy, or from venture capital invested by the information industry, as has been true for most other library automation.

A recent article in AI Magazine by an industry analyst[20] stresses that KBSs for many other applications, systems which libraries might collect, are about to appear in quantity. Here, too, the amount of attention such systems have received seems greatly out of proportion to the utility gained from them to date, but that situation could change very rapidly. If a large number of good applications are suddenly unveiled, the use of the technology could escalate rapidly. The number of KBS applications will certainly have to grow greatly if any real impact is to be felt in our day to day experience as information professionals in the next few years. However, the groundwork is being laid for such growth, and it will come to fruition when we have gathered the necessary resources and experience to utilize the KBS potential.

REFERENCES

1. Croft, W. Bruce, "Approaches to intelligent information retrieval," *Information processing and management*, v. 23 no. 4, 1987, p. 222.
2. Daniels, P.J., "Progress in documentation: cognitive models in information retrieval—an evaluative review," *Journal of documentation*, v. 42 no.4, 1986, pp. 272-304.
3. Smith, P. et al. *The role of the human factors engineer in designing the interface to a knowledge-based system.* (Technical Report ISSE-174) Columbus, OH: Department of Industrial and Systems Engineering, Ohio State University, 1987.
4. Waters, Samuel T., "Answerman, the expert information specialists: an

expert system for retrieval of information from library reference books," *Information technology and libraries*, v. 5 no. 3, 1986, pp. 204-212.

5. Vickery, Brian, "A reference and referral system using expert system techniques," *Journal of documentation*, v. 43 no. 1, 1987, pp. 1-23.

6. Vickery, A. and Brooks, H.M., "PLEXUS—The expert system for referral," *Information processing and management*, v. 23 no. 2, 1987, pp. 99-117.

7. Vickery, Alina and Brooks, Helen, "Expert systems and their applications in LIS," *Online review*, v. 11 no. 3, 1987, pp. 149-165.

8. Vickery, Brian, op. cit, p. 21.

9. *Information processing and management*, v. 23 no. 4, 1987. Pergamon Journals Limited.

10. Croft, W. Bruce, op. cit.

11. Brooks, H.M., "Expert systems and intelligent information retrieval," *Information processing and management*, v. 23 no. 4, 1987, pp. 367-382.

12. Pollitt, Steven, "CANSEARCH: An expert systems approach to document retrieval," *Information processing and management*, v. 23 no. 2, 1987, pp. 119-138.

13. Croft, W. Bruce and Thompson, R.H., "I³R: A new approach to the design of document retrieval systems," *Journal of the American Society for Information Science*, v. 38 no. 6, 1987, pp. 389-404.

14. Fox, Edward A., "Development of the CODER system: a testbed for artificial intelligence methods in information retrieval," *Information processing and management*, v. 23 no. 4, 1987, 341-366.

15. Fidel, Raya. Private communication.

16. Tong, Richard M. et al., "Conceptual information retrieval using RUBRIC," in *Proceedings of the Tenth Annual International ACMSIGIR Conference on Research and Development in Information Retrieval*, New Orleans, Louisiana, June 3-5, 1987, edited by C. T. Yu and C. J. Van Rijsbergen, New York: ACM Press, 1987, pp. 247-253.

17. Sager, Naomi et al. *Medical language processing*. New York: Addison Wesley, 1987.

18. Loatman, R. Bruce, "A hybrid architecture for natural language understanding," in *Proceedings of the SPIE: Applications of artificial intelligence V*, v. 786, 1987, pp. 416-423.

19. Dyer, M. G. *In-depth understanding*. Cambridge, MA: MIT Press, 1983.

20. Stone, Jeffrey, "Commercial AI trends seen at AAAI-87," *AI magazine*, v. 8 no. 4, 1987, 93-95.

REFERENCE APPLICATIONS

An Expert System at the Reference Desk: Impressions from Users

Nancy J. Butkovich
Kathryn L. Taylor
Sharon H. Dent
Ann S. Moore

SUMMARY. A prototype expert system is being tested by technical writing classes at Texas A&M University. In this course students learn to conduct library research by completing a two-part assignment, the first of which is to locate basic reference materials in their fields of study. The expert system assists in this search. Loaded into the database are records for standard reference sources in selected disciplines. When a student types a natural language request, such as "I need bibliographies on geology," the system analyzes the request and provides a list of titles, call numbers, locations, types of sources, and broad subject headings. The students can then use this list in the second part, a research project. Students were given two questionnaires. The first evaluated their familiarity with reference sources and prior library research experience; the second surveyed

---

Nancy J. Butkovich is Science and Technology Reference Librarian, Kathryn L. Taylor is Library Assistant II, and Ann S. Moore is Assistant Head of Reference Division, Sterling C. Evans Library, Texas A&M University, College Station, TX 77843. Sharon H. Dent is Instructor, English Department, Texas A&M University, College Station, TX 77843.

© 1989 by The Haworth Press, Inc. All rights reserved.

their opinion of the expert system. Patron reactions, problems encountered, and future changes will be discussed.

INTRODUCTION

The utilization of an expert system to enhance reference services is one way for reference librarians to contribute to the automation process in the libraries of today. This should be done with the library user in mind. When an assignment is repeated each semester, reference librarians should consider how an expert system might assist the librarian as well as the patron. In this article we will discuss our experiences in planning, developing, and implementing an expert system.

COURSE AND STUDENT DESCRIPTION

Technical Writing is a 300-level course, with a prerequisite of 6 credit hours of Freshman English composition classes and at least 60 credit hours overall. It is recommended that students enrolling in Technical Writing have completed at least half the courses in their major, although this is not required. Typically, the students have senior classification (90+ credit hours), and about one-third are enrolled in their last semester.

Most of the students have had some experience writing research papers, usually for Freshman English classes. Few have done research for upper level courses. This generally means that they are familiar with the *Reader's Guide*, the card catalog, and perhaps newspapers and broad-based encyclopedias to gather information. Their experience with other reference materials is limited or non-existent.

Among other requirements, Technical Writing students must learn to prepare professional quality reports on topics selected from their major field of study and approved by the instructor. The report must be fully researched from current, reputable sources and the information must be correlated to produce original conclusions or solutions to a specific, tightly focused application or problem. The report may not be a review of the literature or an "everything you ever wanted to know about _____" paper.

There are four separate major steps in completing the research project after a topic has been selected. The first is a two-part library assignment for which the students must familiarize themselves with major periodicals, indexes, reference works, and government documents that pertain to their major. They are also asked to locate specific research materials for the topic they have chosen. It is this part with which we are most concerned.

The next step required is a proposal for their project which includes a written review of the literature as well as a preliminary bibliography. Students are encouraged to expand the preliminary bibliography as they work through the project. A progress report is submitted next, and finally the complete project report. The process from the selection of a topic to completion of the report takes about three months.

LITERATURE REVIEW

Expert systems are computer systems which employ human knowledge to solve problems that ordinarily require human intelligence. Expert systems can be taught to answer the rote, repetitive and less complex questions a patron might ask.[1] *Library Literature, ERIC, Information Science Abstracts, Library and Information Science Abstracts* and *Education Index* were searched for articles concerning the use of expert systems in the reference setting. Because of the "newness" of expert system technology, particularly in regard to reference work, little research has been published to date.

Vickery, Brooks, Robinson and Vickery[2] discussed the problems associated with designing an expert system, PLEXUS, to be used in a public library. PLEXUS, a PASCAL-based prototype software package, is designed to analyze patron inquiries, ask any necessary questions and suggest possible sources of information which may contain the answer. This article discusses the processes used by PLEXUS in analyzing and responding to questions. A second article by Vickery and Brooks[3] also discusses the way in which the system analyzes and responds to questions. Numerous examples of prompts and query screens are presented.

Micco and Smith[4] discussed "building an expert system that would serve as an assistant to the reference librarian by helping end users to refine their search strategies before going on line." This system would provide access to a wide array of in-house as well as online databases; however, they did not have sufficient funding to finish the project and presently do not have an operating system.

An expert system currently in use at the National Agricultural Library is described by Waters.[5] Their system, which they named Answerman, is based on a shell called 1st CLASS. This system can be used to tap into external information sources as well as a local database and provides textual as well as bibliographic information.

Smith developed an expert system to ease a severe staffing problem in the government documents department of an academic library. She stresses the potential of an expert system "to provide a consistent, if minimal, level of service at the reference desk freeing the librarian to work on problems requiring more creativity."[6]

HARDWARE AND SOFTWARE

The software selected for this project was Q&A, produced by Symantec Corporation of Cupertino, California, which was chosen because of its low cost and natural language ability. We were specifically concerned with Q&A's database management capabilities and its natural language expert system, the Intelligent Assistant, which we have renamed Technical Writing Assistant. We found that this combination of features would be best suited for our project.

Because this was a prototype, we did not have any hardware permanently assigned to the project; instead we used what was available at the time in the Wiley Laser Disk Service portion of the Automated Information Retrieval Services center. This equipment was an IBM PC-AT computer with 640K memory and a 30mb hard disk, an IBM monochrome monitor, and a Hewlett-Packard ThinkJet printer. Since this computer also served as a CD-ROM search station, Wiley area staff members assisted patrons in switching from the CD-ROM to the Technical Writing Assistant, which was installed on the hard disk, and back again.

Hardware and software costs vary depending on the time ordered, the vendor, and any appropriate state contracts or bids. Table 1 provides the hardware and software costs for the equipment used based on our purchase prices. This does not include transportation

TABLE 1

Hardware

IBM PC-AT (includes CPU, keyboard, monochrome monitor).....$4,383.00
Hewlett-Packard Think-Jet printer..........................$ 272.00
Parallel cable...$ 30.00
128K Memory Expansion......................................$ 245.00
Total hardware.............$4,930.00

Software

Q&A (version 2.0)..$ 250.00
Total software.............$ 250.00

Total costs................$5,180.00

costs, and dollar amounts are rounded to the nearest dollar. If an IBM PC-XT or AT or XT clone is used, costs could be significantly reduced; however, the software requires a memory capacity of at least 512K, which should be considered when allotting equipment for a similar purpose. In fact, Heid reported that "performance is greatly enhanced if you have 640K and a hard disk."[7]

THE DATABASE

The database was constructed with two basic factors in mind. The first factor was the target patron group, students enrolled in Technical Writing classes. Class rolls from several sections were analyzed to determine majors most frequently represented. Since this course is required for students in the Colleges of Business, Agriculture, and Engineering, a special effort was made to cover these areas in the database. Disciplines covered included business, engineering, agriculture, the sciences and geosciences.

The other factor which influenced the database was the nature of the assignment. Students were required to choose a topic for a research paper and then locate various reference tools which would be useful for the topic. The types of sources were: bibliographies, encyclopedias, dictionaries, handbooks, indexes and abstracting services. Therefore, titles in each of these categories covering the predetermined disciplines were identified for inclusion in the database.

Various methods were used to collect titles. Standard reference tools such as Sheehy's *Guide to Reference Books*, Walford's *Guide to Reference Material* and Malinowsky's *Science and Engineering Literature* were used. Other sources consulted were *Business Information Sources* by Lorna M. Daniells and the sixth edition of the *Encyclopedia of Business Information Sources*, edited by James Woy. The subject section of the card catalog was checked and reference shelves were browsed. For each title in the database, the following information was given: title, call number, location, type of source and broad subject area (see Figure 1). The prototype database contains 428 records but will be expanded to cover more titles and subject areas.

The expert system was located in the Wiley Laser Disk Service area alongside several bibliographic databases on CD-ROM, i.e. *InfoTrac*, *PsycLIT*, *Agricola* and *Datext*. This location seemed ap-

Figure 1

TITLE	CALL NUMBER	LOCATION	TYPE OF SOURCE	BROAD SUBJECT AREA
Computer and Information Systems Abstracts Journal	QA/76/I4.6	Reference Table 10	Index	Computer Science; Mathematics; Electronics
Key Abstracts: Electrical Measurements & Instrumentation	TA/165/K4	Reference Stacks	Index	Electronics; Engineering
Solid State Abstracts Journal	TK/7800/S6.2	Reference Stacks	Index	Electronics; Electrical Engineering; Engineering
Electronics and Communications Abstracts Journal	TK/7800/E4.386	Reference Stacks	Index	Electrical Engineering; Electronics; Engineering; Communications
Electrical and Electronics Abstracts	TK/1/E2.3	Reference Stacks	Index	Electrical Engineering; Engineering; Electronics
Science Citation Index	Z/7401/S365	Reference Counter H	Index	Engineering; Geology; Biology; Chemistry; Mathematics; Physics; Medicine; Aquatic Science; Geochemistry; Geophysics; Biochemistry; Aeronautics; Agriculture; Astronomy; Botany; Zoology; Computer Science; Food Science; Electronics; Environmental Science; Forestry; Fisheries; Horticulture; Meteorology; Soil Science; Oceanography

Printout of results for the query, "I need indexes on electronics."

propriate, since users of the expert system would also be potential users of the laser disk services. The Wiley area is staffed during the same hours as the reference desk to assist users with the various search services. A brief manual was produced outlining the use of the expert system. The manual contained several examples of actual screens, a typical search and step-by-step directions for printing. Each Wiley staff member attended a training session which provided instruction and hands-on experience. They then provided instruction in the use of the system to each patron as needed. When a patron typed in a request such as "I need indexes on electronics," the expert system, with its natural language processing capability, analyzed the request. Searching its database for records which met the two criteria "indexes" and "electronics," the expert system produced a list of sources (see Figure 1).

USER RESPONSE

To elicit reactions to the system, each user was required to complete a questionnaire (see Figure 2), which asked for basic information such as the student's major and the topic of his paper. In order to evaluate the system, we asked questions such as "Did you find what you were looking for?" and "After using the system did you still need to ask a librarian for assistance with the same question?" Also included were general questions such as "What features did you like?" and "What features did you dislike?"

Every student who responded to the questionnaire (see Figure 3) stated that the instructions were clear and the system was easy to use, yet one-third of the students did not find what they were looking for. Given the limited scope of the database, this was predictable. About half of the respondents still needed to ask a librarian for assistance with the same question. This response confirms our assumption that an expert system can provide assistance in some cases but cannot totally replace the services of a reference librarian. To our great delight, the students overwhelmingly responded that they would use this system again. Staff response was, in general, also favorable. Despite problems with software, hardware and the database, which will be discussed later, the staff felt that the expert system was a useful endeavor which could help to stem the enormous tide of repetitive questions resulting from this assignment.

Figure 2

TECHNICAL WRITING ASSISTANT QUESTIONNAIRE

Your professor's name: _____

Your major: _____

Your topic (subject area): _____

Have you ever used a menu-driven database? ____Yes ____No

For what kind of materials were you looking? (Check all that apply.)

____Dictionaries   ____Index/Abstracting Services

____Handbooks   ____Encyclopedias

____Directories   ____Biographies

____Bibliographies

____Other (please list): _____

Were the instructions clear? ____Yes ____No

Did you find this easy to use? ____Yes ____No

Did you find what you were looking for? ____Yes ____No

If not what was missing? _____

_____

After using the system did you still need to ask a librarian for assistance with the same question? ____Yes ____No

Would you use this system again? ____Yes ____No

What features did you like? _____

_____

What features did you dislike? _____

_____

If you have any additional comments, please feel free to write them on the back of this form. Thank you for your cooperation.

Sterling C. Evans Library
Reference Division 09/87

Figure 3

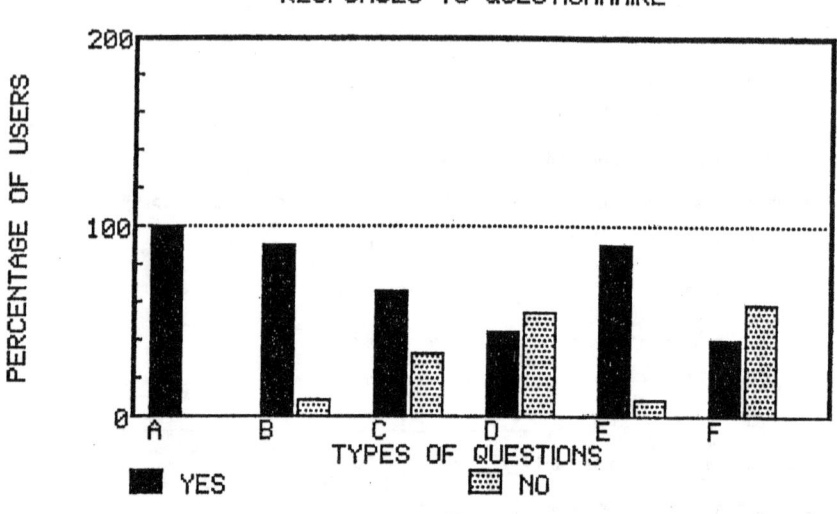

A= Were the instructions clear?	%100 yes	% 0 no
B= Did you find this easy to use?	% 91 yes	% 9 no
C= Did you find what you were looking for?	% 67 yes	% 33 no
D= After using the system did you still need to ask a librarian?	% 45 yes	% 55 no
E= Would you use this system again?	% 91 yes	% 9 no
F= Have you ever used a menu-driven database?	% 41 yes	% 59

Number of respondents to questionnaires= 12

PROBLEMS

A number of problems were encountered involving hardware, software, and the database. Each of these problems and their solutions will be identified and discussed below.

Software limitations presented the stickiest problems, since this was the area over which we had the least control. The difficulties encountered with Q&A were related to the help screens, database integrity, and output. Help screens are designed to provide instructions concerning aspects of the software which might not be readily apparent. When the first user sits down at Q&A, there is a clearly defined inquiry block with instructions and examples concerning the proper way to ask a question. However, this screen changes after the first inquiry, and subsequent users are given a blank block with no instructions, resulting in confusion. We would have preferred this screen to reappear each time an inquiry is made. We also would have liked the ability to modify the examples, making them more suitable for our purposes; unfortunately we were unable to do either. This necessitated explanations for most patrons using the system.

A powerful feature used by the Intelligent Assistant is the ability of the system to recognize words it does not know, query the operator about them and allow the operator to teach the words to the system. Unfortunately for public service applications, the operator is a patron who does not know the system or the proper way to teach the system. This results in erroneous answers. For example, the patron types "I need a business handbook." Technical Writing Assistant does not recognize the word "business" because we did not use it as a subject heading, so it asks the patron if he or she would like to add the word to its vocabulary. The patron does and proceeds to enter "business" as an alternate name for the field "broad subject heading."

From the patron's point of view, he or she has now created a new subject heading called "business." However, Technical Writing Assistant interprets this as meaning the patron wants "business" to be synonymous with the phrase "broad subject area." For example, when a patron asks for dictionaries about business, the Assistant will obligingly provide a list of all dictionaries in the database, on all subjects. This occurred at least once, and we suspect more often than that. The possible results could be spectacular, depending on the size of the database and the particular format requested. We finally instituted periodic checks of the teaching instructions to eliminate extraneous vocabulary.

Output proved to be a problem as well. Answers appeared as spreadsheets which required three screens to read from left to right;

the image did not compress to one screen width. The authors found this to be an irritation, although the students did not seem to object.

More significant was the fact that the print process was too long. Q&A defaults to the screen, not to the printer. When patrons wanted a print-out of the answer, they had to follow a lengthy eight-step process in order to obtain the hard copy. This involved filling in printer specifications each time a print was desired; the system would not "remember" the instructions from one search to another. In retrospect we should have tried to create a macro which would reduce the number of keystrokes and the possibilities for confusion, but we did not.

Hardware also proved to be a bigger problem than we had anticipated. We were unable to utilize Q&A's color capabilities with our monochrome monitor. This was actually an aesthetic problem, since the patrons probably never missed the color screens. Unfortunately, we had seen Q&A on a color monitor, and we missed the vivid displays.

Lack of color was a minor irritation which can be easily corrected; the problems with the printer were not as minor. Although the Think-Jet did everything we required of it, it most assuredly was not the best printer for the job. Several problems arose. First, it was slow; some questions produced as much as three pages of answers, and these seemed to take forever to print. Second, the compression type on a Think-Jet is difficult to read. We were printing at 15 characters per inch, which was the least we could use and still get the results of the search on an 8-1/2 inch wide piece of paper. This is the only paper size the Think-Jet can accommodate. If the ink cartridge was getting low, the letters of the type formed only partially, and the text was illegible. Third, the ink often smeared, which further reduced legibility. These problems, combined with the lengthy printing instructions already described, resulted in students frequently choosing to write the answer themselves rather than trying to obtain a print-out.

The two biggest problems with the database involved subject headings and limited scope. Several students complained that we did not have anything in the database on their topic. We anticipated this problem, since the database was not intended to be exhaustive. As was discussed in a previous section of this paper, the test database included only selected sources from business, engineering, agriculture, and the sciences.

A related problem with subject access concerned the actual terms used to index individual records. An example of this concerned the business and engineering titles. "Business" was not used as a subject heading; all records were indexed under the specific subject, e.g., finance, marketing, management, etc. Engineering titles were indexed differently. Each record concerning engineering received "engineering" as a subject heading, and only some of the major branches of engineering, such as civil engineering, nuclear engineering, etc., were included. We found that students in the business related disciplines wanted to be able to search "business," while the engineering students preferred the more specific headings. Both the general and specific headings probably should be available.

SUMMARY AND CONCLUSIONS

The benefit of an expert system for use with a defined audience to handle routine, less complex questions has been proven to our satisfaction. However, the software selected did not perform as well in a public setting as we had hoped. This was primarily due to inadequacies with help screens, vulnerability to tampering, and problems with the printing process. In a setting where the operators are trained staff members, such as at a reference desk, we believe that Q&A would be a powerful resource. The expert system was also well-received by those who responded to the evaluative questionnaire, but assistance with the system and a user's manual are recommended for first-time users. Patrons found Q&A to be very user-friendly, and they were generally very tolerant of the shortcomings of the database.

Our future plans include significantly expanding the database to cover other disciplines and rectifying problems with the subject headings. Authority control for keyword subject headings may be necessary. Also, we plan to utilize a software package which is more resistant to tampering and better fits our needs. Finally, we will publicize the expert system to all class sections of this course rather than limiting it to just a few sections. We believe that expert systems have a definite place in public service and that their utilization can result in improved service to the patron.

REFERENCES

1. F. Hayes-Roth, "Expert Systems," in *Encyclopedia of Artificial Intelligence* ed. by Stuart C. Shapiro (New York: John Wiley & Sons, 1987), p. 287.
2. Alina Vickery, Helen Brooks, Bruce Robinson and Brian Vickery, "A Reference and Referral System Using Expert System Techniques," *Journal of Documentation* 43 (March 1987): 1-23.
3. Alina Vickery and H. M. Brooks, "PLEXUS—The Expert System for Referral," *Information Processing and Management* 23 (1987): 99-117.
4. H. Mary Micco and Irma Smith, "Designing an Expert System for the Reference Function Subject Access to Information," ASIS '86: *Proceedings of the 49th ASIS Annual Meeting* 23 (1986): 204-210.
5. Samuel T. Waters, "Answerman, the Expert Information Specialist: An Expert System for Retrieval of Information from Library Reference Books," *Information Technology and Libraries* 5 (September 1986): 204-213.
6. Karen F. Smith, "Robot at the Reference Desk?" *College and Research Libraries* 47 (September 1986): 486-489.
7. Jim Heid, "Q&A: Smarter Searching," *PC World* 4 (April 1986): 221.

The Information Machine: A Microcomputer-Based Reference Service

Jeff Fadell
Judy E. Myers

SUMMARY. This article describes the development and use of a microcomputer reference assistance program at the University of Houston Library. We discuss the development environment, including the interests and concerns of the staff and the limitations on available resources. We describe the development process, which began with a concept, continued with the formulation of objectives and the preparation of initial drafts of both the computer program and the content of the presentation, and has been carried through to completion and public implementation. We describe the major modules of our computer presentation of over 350 screens of information, which has been available for public use on four IBM XTs since January 1987. We then address the integration of the ongoing management of the changes of content and the statistics produced by the program into the clerical support functions of our department. Finally, we present what we have learned from users of the public presentation, discuss how the system has worked to date, and touch on some future directions we are contemplating.

The Information Machine is a microcomputer presentation that we developed at the University of Houston Library to provide reference assistance.

The authors are Reference Librarians, University of Houston Library, 4800 Calhoun, Houston, TX 77204-2091.

© 1989 by The Haworth Press, Inc. All rights reserved.

THE DEVELOPMENT ENVIRONMENT AND PROCESS

Background

It is important to note that our project was quite different from the type of automation project that is typically described in library school automation courses or in computer texts for managers. We could not have begun by listing the sort of detailed system specifications that should be produced for an online catalog, for example, because we didn't know in the beginning exactly what would work. We treated the initial stages of development as a creative process, and we began with objectives and expectations that were general and incomplete. First, we realized that our computerized presentation would not emulate the process that occurs at the reference desk, but would vary in several ways. Second, we expected that it might appeal to a different group of library users. We had already noted that our printed library guides reached a different audience than our reference desk service. With this project we hoped to reach the video generation. Third, the computer presentation would be much more limited than the information available at the reference desk. Fourth, the computer presentation would be much more structured than a reference interview and also much more consistent.

This was also a group process, and from the beginning we believed that it was important to develop a common group understanding of the general effect of the product in operation and either to work within those bounds or to redefine them as a group. The process of developing and maintaining a constant focus in a creative group has been well described in two books, *Disney animation: the illusion of life*,[1] which has become a cult classic in computer programming groups, and *Chariots for Apollo*.[2]

Why Did We Want to Do It?

Our reference staff had a number of reasons for wanting to produce a computerized presentation. We knew that we were not serving all users: the library was open more hours than the reference desk. And we suspected, despite our active reference and library instruction program, that we were not reaching some people who could use help even when the desk was open. We had seen computerized presentations from two other libraries, and so we knew that the concept could work.

The Starting Point

The germ of the idea that became the Information Machine had been in Myers' mind for several years. She had envisioned a menu-driven computer presentation that could provide basic information about the Library and could also refer users to appropriate reference books or periodical indexes. She had done some initial development on her Apple II, in the days before the Library had microcomputers. She gave up this effort because it appeared that the Library was unlikely to provide Apple IIs for the public, and the floppy disc capacity of the Apple II was inadequate for the scale of presentation that she envisioned. She had mentally designed a program to manage such a presentation in Applesoft Basic but had not created a program.

In 1985, the University of Houston Library began a public service automation project in order to focus attention on needs in this area and to begin to develop a comprehensive set of computer-based services for library users. Eighteen concepts were considered for development in this initial project. Six of the eighteen were implemented over the next two years, including one proposed by Myers as a "menu-driven ready-reference program." The initial description consisted of nothing but the title. The idea was intentionally left vague at this point, because we believed that group discussion and cooperative development would produce a sounder concept and a better product than any one person was likely to create alone.

There were a number of significant resources available for this project. One of the most important was that the library director supported the concept and offered to purchase equipment to deliver the presentation to the public, if we would create one. The equipment was to consist of several IBM PCs or XTs with hard disks and color monitors. The staff had most of the resources needed to develop both a presentation and a program to present it, including an IBM PC for office use, the IBM Basica interpreter, the WordPerfect word processor, and the present authors, who were interested in working on the project.

We also faced a few limitations. Our IBM PC was a fairly new acquisition, and although the staff was beginning to be comfortable with WordPerfect, no one in the department had ever programmed an IBM PC or even done any serious programming at all outside of introductory college courses. The project could not utilize expensive software or programming assistance. And our time was limited.

Also on the negative side, it was immediately obvious that there was a considerable amount of anxiety about the project on the part of some members of the staff. There seemed to be three sources of anxiety. First, staff members could not visualize the end product. This was certainly understandable, because one of the tasks of the project would be to create that product.

Second, there was a feeling that such a computerized presentation was inappropriate. This concern was expressed in various ways, such as that the computerized presentation would lead users to conclusions that were incorrect or that were not responsive to their needs, or that this proposal was part of a longterm plan to reduce staff and eventually close the reference desk. Some staff members recommended that the content of The Information Machine be limited to directional information.

Third, staff members doubted that the project could be accomplished without enormous computing resources. They felt that the development and maintenance of the project would require technical skills beyond the ability of anyone on the staff. This concern was typically expressed as a reservation about spending time on the content until there was a working version of the computer program that would deliver the result to the public.

Process

It seemed to the two of us that two types of actions could be taken to allay the anxieties. First, the concerns were taken seriously and discussed openly, informally, and *individually* with the people who were concerned. Second, the two of us began to develop a partial working version, so that the staff would have something specific to respond to.

A few provisional decisions had to be made in order to develop presentations and a program to show to the group. We wanted to be able to create our screens with WordPerfect, because there would be a great deal of text, and we wanted to use a full-featured word processor with which we were familiar. We planned to then capture the screen images and manipulate them with a computer program in Basic. We decided that the presentations we developed would be mostly text, enhanced with fairly simple graphics that could be produced with WordPerfect. We had neither the time nor the expertise to create elaborate graphics screens.

Fadell began to draft presentations on two topics, "Finding Journals" and "Locating Call Numbers." These two topics were chosen because the staff felt that these were two of the most common questions. Myers found several public-domain programs designed to capture screens as binary files and wrote an initial version of the computer program. Both of us discussed our work with interested staff and asked for comments. Once the word processor texts and a working computer program were available, some of the anxiety was dissipated.

A committee was then established, chaired by Fadell, which was to serve as both the working group and the steering committee for the project. The committee included supporters of the project as well as members with strong reservations.

Several months elapsed between the appointment of the committee and the official start of the project, because several other projects were under way at this time. Much of the work that determined the look and feel of the final presentation was done in the time between the appointment of the committee and the first meeting. For example, during this time we continued to work on the program and the content and developed provisional opening menus, drafts of the closing screens, and a working title, "The Library Oracle." We also continued to discuss ideas and the decisions that would be required with interested staff, both those on the committee and others. The programs from other libraries were also made available for staff review: the Pointer program from SUNY Buffalo[3] and a program from the Purdue University Undergraduate Library.[4] There was agreement on the general objectives: that the presentation was to serve those who did not ask—because the desk was busy, or because they didn't feel confident enough—and, if the presentation could not help, to encourage them to come to the desk. We also wanted the program to collect statistics on use and helpfulness.

One of the major discussion topics during this time was the design of the opening menus. The opening menus were a critical component of the presentation, because they would determine not only the user interface but also the structure of the ensuing presentation. What should we ask? How might we focus on a user's question in a menu-driven presentation? This was a time for creative thinking and for keeping part of our minds on the project while working at the reference desk, to try to think of a structure that would accommodate as many of the queries as possible.

Several drafts of provisional opening menus were created. We wanted a user to be able to tell whether the information being sought was in the computer presentation by at least the second screen of the presentation. We tried several approaches. Finally, one seemed right (Figures 1-5). The closing screens were also drafted; these would encourage those who had not been helped by the presentation to come to the reference desk for assistance.

Also during the time before the first meeting of the committee, we developed discussion documents on specific project objectives, the content of the presentation, and enhancements needed for the program. Some conflicts were resolved in the process of creating the drafts. Some differences of opinion could not be resolved at this stage, and in those cases we sought to express the issue clearly and in a way that would facilitate discussion at the first meeting of the committee. Committee members were asked to review Fadell's two presentations, the three discussion documents, and the drafts of the opening and closing screens, and to be prepared to comment on them at the meeting.

The First Meeting

We asked the Assistant Director for Public Services to attend the first meeting, because we were still not sure that the committee supported the project enough to take it forward. She opened the meeting by expressing her strong belief in the value of the project and her confidence in the committee's ability to explore the potential for a presentation of this type, instead of limiting our efforts in

FIGURE 1

```
UH-UP M. D. Anderson Library      * The Information Machine *         MU1

                            THE INFORMATION MACHINE

    This service is designed to provide assistance when the Reference/Information
    Desk is busy or is closed. For information that is not provided here, please
    go to or call the Reference/Information Desk. This is not the Library Online
    Catalog. The Online Catalog is next to the tall display cases.

    To start, select one of the following:

    1. How do I begin research, identify books and articles on my topic, find
       microfiche, interpret and locate call numbers, locate journals, etc.?

    2. Where can I find a photocopier, change, a study area, a pencil sharpener,
       material my professor has put on Reserve, Library Guides, etc.?

    3. When is the Library open, the next Library tour, etc.?

    4. Who may borrow books, have a study carrel, have a computer search
       done, etc.?

    5. What are the Reference/Information Desk hours and phone numbers?

    Type the number of your selection.
                           [Or, press 'Q' to quit]
```

This is the opening menu of The Information Machine. The text is in white on a blue background. Material printed in **bold** above is displayed as bright white. Material in **bold underline** above is printed in yellow.

FIGURE 2

```
UH-UP M. D. Anderson Library      * The Information Machine *    MU2

   How do I:

   1. Find books, by author, title, or subject?

   2. Find articles on my topic? I have a subject in mind.

   3. Find journals? I have a list of the articles I want.

   4. Find other kinds of materials, such as book and
      film reviews, conference proceedings, textbooks and
      curriculum guides, microforms and videocassettes?

   5. Interpret call numbers and location codes?

   Type the number of your selection.

          ****  MORE TOPICS COMING SOON TO THIS MENU  ****

   How do I: Begin research in my subject; Find library materials in
   other special formats, such as, newspapers, maps, etc.; Find other
   kinds of information, such as Government publications or statistics.

[OTHER OPTIONS: PRESS 'P' for previous screen, 'Q' to quit, 'Z' to start over]
```

Figures 2 through 5 are the second-level menus. One of our design objectives was that users should recognize, by the second screen of the presentation, whether the presentation is likely to answer their question. The stars underlined above are displayed in light red.

FIGURE 3

```
UH-UP M. D. Anderson Library      * The Information Machine *    MU3

Where can I find:

1. A place to study?

2. The Serials List, the Library of Congress Subject Headings,
   Library Guides, a dictionary, a suggestion box?

3. A pencil sharpener, copier, typewriter, change machine,
   scissors, paper cutter, paper punch, stapler, tape, etc.?

4. A water fountain, restroom, telephone, snack bar?

5. The material my professor has put on reserve?

6. A particular room or wing of the Library building such as the
   Vista Room, Current Journals Room, Brown Wing, Honors Lounge?

7. Other libraries: a UH branch library, on this campus or
   another UH campus, or other libraries in the Houston area?

Type the number of your selection.

[OTHER OPTIONS: PRESS 'P' for previous screen, 'Q' to quit, 'Z' to start over]
```

FIGURE 4

```
UH-UP M. D. Anderson Library      * The Information Machine *      MU4

When is/are:

1. The hours for this library (the M. D. Anderson Library) and
   each of its services?

2. The hours for the University of Houston-University Park
   Branch and Law Libraries?

3. The general Library Tours this semester?

4. The next Library Book Sale?

5. The hours for other University of Houston System Libraries
   and other Houston area research libraries?

Type the number of your selection.

6. To return to the Opening Menu, type 6.


[OTHER OPTIONS: PRESS 'P' for previous screen, 'Q' to quit, 'Z' to start over]
```

FIGURE 5

```
UH-UP M. D. Anderson Library     *·The Information Machine *          WM1

Who may:

 1.  Use this library?

 2.  Borrow books?

 3.  Borrow Reserve materials?

 4.  Borrow journals?

 5.  Have a book put on hold or recalled?

 6.  Have the use of a study carrel?

 7.  Obtain a group study room?

 8.  Have a computer search done?

Type the number of your selection, or type 9 to return to the
opening menu.
```

[OTHER OPTIONS: PRESS 'P' for previous screen, 'Q' to quit, 'Z' to start over] predetermined ways. This statement succeeded in setting the tone for the meeting and for the succeeding work. From this point on, the committee worked as a team, with team members having diverse roles as creators, editors, and critics, but with a common understanding that we would do our best to take the project as far as we could with the available resources.

During the first meeting of the committee, the objectives for the scope of the presentation were approved as follows:

1. Provide limited information and basic reference service, especially when the reference desk is closed or is very busy.
2. Provide interactive tutorials on basic library information-seeking processes.
3. Provide a structured decision-making environment for users to deal with their information needs.
4. Enable users to find any service area, major in-building location, and the locations of libraries and library materials on campus and within the University of Houston System.
5. Describe locations of frequently needed supplies, equipment, and other amenities.
6. Provide basic information on library policies that affect users.
7. Provide the hours buildings are open, hours of services, and dates of special events.
8. Do the above in a manner that is flexible and easily modified or supplemented.

The next item of discussion at the first meeting was the opening menu screens, which also included suggested topics for the presentation (Figures 2-5). Only minor revisions were suggested; this approach still seemed right. Discussion continued and decisions were made on which topics should be developed before the presentation was made available to the public, and topics were assigned to members for development. A procedure was established for committee review of presentations as they were developed.

The working title of the presentation was changed from The Library Oracle to The Information Machine — Oracle had too many distracting meanings, and the new title emphasized that it was only a machine.

During the first meeting the committee also discussed the requirements for the computer program (which Myers had named ScreenRunner) that would display the content of the presentation. We knew at the time that Dan Bricklin's Demo Program was under development. (This program received a great deal of advance publicity, because Dan Bricklin had been one of the originators of VisiCalc, had subsequently been ousted from the company he co-founded, and was thus a favorite of computer columnists.) Demo Program (and the spate of presentation managers that followed it) would have some of the features we needed, but it would not keep statistics, and it would not facilitate the development and maintenance of large presentations with many branches.

The committee requested the capability to return to the opening menu from any screen, to back up 10 screens, to start over if there had been no user input for some time (we would try different lengths of time and see what worked), and to keep daily statistics on the number of viewers of each topic. The committee also wanted the program to collect data on whether users found the presentation to be helpful, and the total number of screens viewed. We considered whether to collect statistics each time a user changed to a new topic (as the Purdue program does), but we decided not to, because we found the constant interruptions to be an annoying feature of that presentation.

We decided that it was very important for each screen to have a header that described what computer presentation this was and which screen the user was on. The header would probably not be very important now—we could, after all, put a sign on the machine that said what it was. But in the future, we expect users to have access to several electronic environments from a single terminal, and it will be important to tell users where they are. We designed a header with a form similar to the header on the screens of our Geac online catalog.

There was considerable discussion on whether to include an electronic message system, so that users could comment on the presentation, could point out errors, and could tell us their additional information needs. We decided that users would instead be more likely to enter reference questions for which they wanted answers, and we were not ready to provide this service. We therefore decided to provide a paper questionnaire adjacent to the machines for the first month or so, to encourage users to comment.

Myers was particularly adamant that none of the data for the presentations should be contained in the program itself, as was the case with the two examples we had seen. Content is much harder to edit when it is part of the program, because a knowledge of programming is required in order to make revisions. We wanted to be able to create and revise the entire presentation with WordPerfect.

Several programming suggestions that were offered were not seen by the committee to be necessary: "help" screens, hourly statistics, and statistics on the number of users who finished the presentation on a topic.

By the end of the first meeting most of the concern was gone. It was clear that there would be open discussion, consensus, and full review. This group could agree that it was appropriate to use a computer to present the type of information that we had discussed. Now all that remained was to do the work.

Doing the Work

We made many decisions during this time about color conventions, screen content, and variety and pacing of presentations. We distilled the available literature on screen design into a set of guidelines for our presentations (Figure 6).

FIGURE 6
**GENERAL GUIDELINES FOR DEVELOPING
SCREEN PRESENTATIONS**

1. Reduce density.
   A computerized presentation is not just print in another guise. It is considered a virtue to express many concepts compactly in print, but this just does not work when the information is being presented on a screen. Ideally, there should be **one concept per screen**.

2. Provide multiple choices.
   Give users options to review a unit, to take a quiz, or to decide what they want to see next. The strength of this medium is the opportunity to make choices in order to tailor an individual presentation.

3. Use layout and color for emphasis.
   We recommend that you not conform to print conventions, such as using

bold or underline for a title just because it is a title. Bold it only if the title is being emphasized.

4. Present information graphically.
   Use the line drawing ASCII characters to create illustrations, borders, pointers, maps, large letters, etc.

5. Vary the density and the look of the presentation.
   It is especially dull to have screen after screen of wall-to-wall 80-column text, each screen ending with "[To continue, press the **Spacebar**]." Alternate fuller screens with briefer ones. Use margins set at 1 and 80 for some screens, and 10 and 74 (or even 15 and 70) for others. Provide title screens at major conceptual breaks.

6. When you reach the limits of what you can present in this form, encourage users to seek assistance.
   You can help users by telling them in your presentation that they have reached a limit. Tell them what to ask and where to ask it. Many library users do not ask for assistance because the are afraid that we will think they are stupid. Assuring them that they have a valid question can help to overcome this obstacle.

7. Describe the limitations as well as the strengths of your resources and services.
   We all want to give a good impression of our library, but don't make the presentation a commercial. Level with your users.

8. Present the underlying structure of the library's organization of knowledge.
   It is very hard for people to understand where they are in a computerized presentation because there is no physical context. It is therefore necessary to emphasize the intellectual context. When you present a sequence of steps, try to explain what each step is for and where each step fits into a whole process. Be especially clear about what the whole process is and what it is for.
   A computerized presentation may be the very worst imaginable form in which to give people a list of 10 steps or items. They probably can't see it all on one screen, and they can't take it with them. When you need to give your users this sort of information, do it in print.

9. Get advice.
   A presentation can be as clear as glass to its creator and still be much less than effective for its intended audience. We found it helpful to have not one, but at least two levels of review. If you can work with someone else or a small group to create and review word processor drafts of text, you will catch many problems.
   We also found it useful to withhold the early drafts from some of our best reviewers, so that they could see the (hopefully) nearly finished versions without having seen the earlier ones. The early reviewers will have all of the

versions in mind, and it will be hard for them to remember whether an essential fact or relationship is present in the current version, or if they are remembering something from an earlier draft.

As we experimented with possible WordPerfect screens using various layouts, formats, highlights, etc., we found that this software provided great flexibility along with much more graphics capability than we had expected. Because WordPerfect allowed easy access to the full range of ASCII characters, we could easily and quickly create graphics more elaborate than we had anticipated. To highlight text, we made arrows, boxes, etc. We used block graphic characters to draw large letters for use on title screens (Figure 7). The Line-Draw feature also made it easy to draw maps of various floors of the building. We had to draw the outline only once, and with the Typeover mode we could add text to the map without disturbing the boundary lines.

Besides the foreground and background colors (we chose white on blue), WordPerfect would let us use three other colors from the 13 remaining. We generally used yellow to highlight choices of keys to press and high-intensity white to bold words and phrases we wanted to emphasize.

The three wings of the University of Houston library building are labeled by color. We decided to draw the building maps in black on a white background and then highlight areas of the Red Wing in red, the Blue Wing in blue, and the Brown Wing in brown (Figure 8).

The development of the content of the presentation was not evenly distributed among committee members. Fadell developed about two thirds of the content and served as our general editor, Myers developed about a quarter of the content, and other committee members less. It had been understood from the beginning that committee members had various roles to play, and in fact most of the members were expected to serve primarily as reviewers and critics.

We learned more than we expected to have to learn about some pretty basic library operations. It took weeks of discussion, for example, to find a useful way to describe the process for finding the valid form of a personal name used as a subject in the library catalog.

FIGURE 7

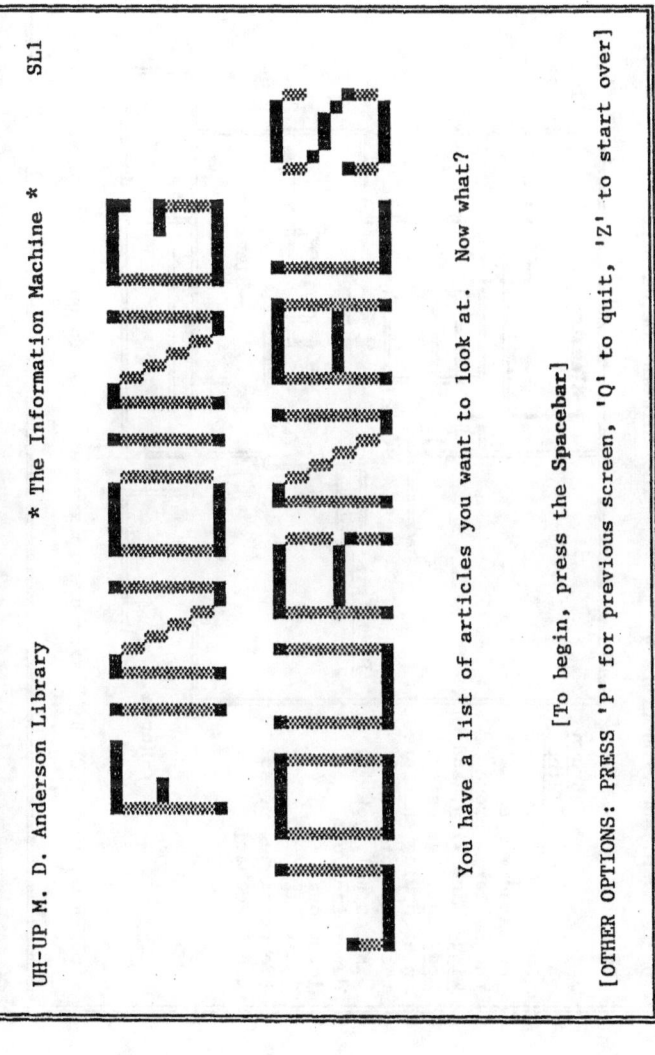

A section header, created with WordPerfect, using the IBM graphics characters.

FIGURE 8

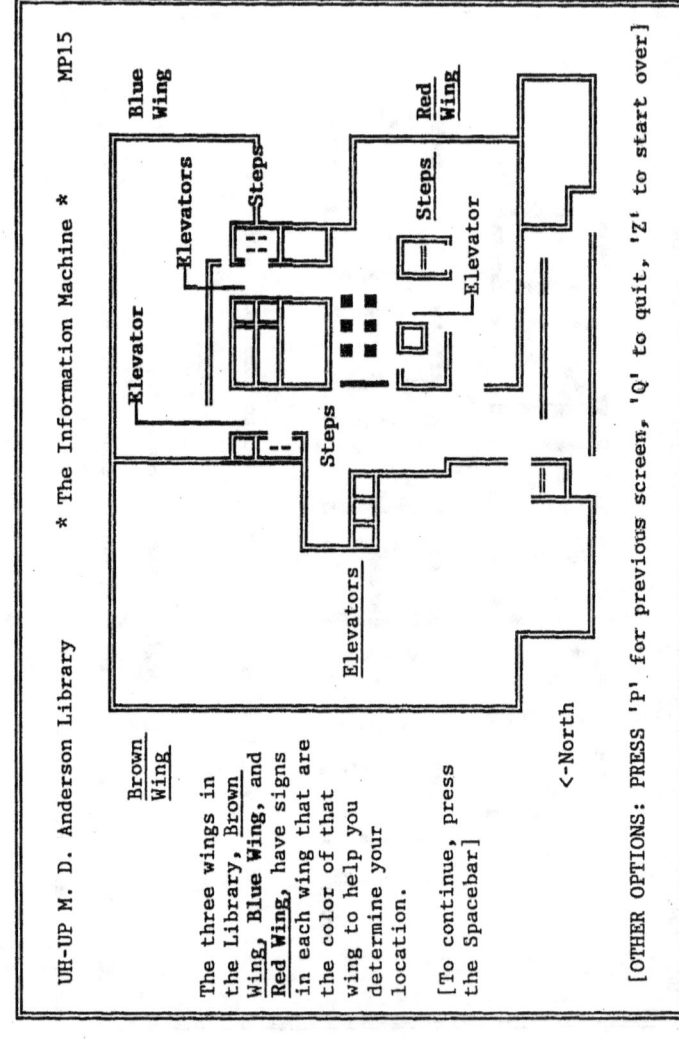

The building maps were created with the line draw feature of WordPerfect. The maps have black text on a white background. Bold text appears on the screen in blue, underlined text in brown, and bold/underlined text in red.

Prototypes

A powerful feature of WordPerfect is its macro capability. Using this, along with the Hard Page feature, we were able to simulate the presentation on the word processor. The committee could thus see early on how the program would actually work in practice even before the software to run it was ready. For example, we could simulate branching by making macros for one PgDn, two PgDns, or three PgDns. We could then present the user with a question on the screen and instruct him to type the macro, for example Alt-Y if his answer was Yes, Alt-N if his answer was No, or Alt-M if his answer was Maybe. The appropriate screen (from one, two, or three pages down) would then appear. The tutorials on using the Serials List and locating call numbers were prototyped in this way.

Program Development

By the time the first few presentations were completed, the version of the computer program that could accommodate presentations on several topics was ready to test. Myers had switched from Basica to Microsoft Quick Basic so that the program would run faster and would not require the presence of the Basica interpreter.

The ScreenRunner presentation manager at that point met all of the criteria established at the first meeting. It would allow the user to see the previous screen, start over, or quit at any time, and it displayed these choices as a footer on each screen. It disabled all keystrokes except the ones designated as choices on a given screen. The program could not be stopped by the normal break or reboot keystrokes. If, in the middle of a presentation, there was no keystroke after a certain length of time, it beeped and asked if the user was still there; if there was no response, it restarted the presentation. It kept daily statistics on which scripts were used by how many users, how many "Yes," "No," or "Partly" answers there were when people were asked, when they quit, whether they found the information they were looking for, and how many users walked away without answering or without quitting the program. It also counted the total number of screens viewed. This provided large numbers for those who like them and also let us calculate an average number of screens per viewer. Two books were particularly helpful references during program development.[5,6]

Fadell added one final enhancement to the program. We had particularly liked the opening screen of the Purdue program, an attention-getting mandala pattern. We could see that something with motion and many colors would be a better grabber than our opening menu. By the time we were writing our program, mandalas were out, and fractals were in. (Mandalas and fractals are evolving patterns produced as mathematical equations are recalculated. Mandalas are composed of square tiles. Fractals may emulate natural rocky landscapes or dragon-shaped curves.) We could find public-domain fractal programs, but programming a text window surrounded by a fractal pattern was beyond us. It also occurred to us that fractals might soon be out of fashion as well. Fadell came up with the idea of a marquee, with a band of lights running around the border. Substituting question marks for lights, he had the concept he wanted. He then took Lon Poole's book[7] home one weekend and figured out how to program an opening marquee (Figure 9) with question marks in random colors running around the border, some upside-down as a nod to our Spanish-speaking users.

THE PRODUCT

Putting the Pieces Together

To create the final presentation, each page of the WordPerfect text was first captured as a separate binary file by a modified public domain program, which saved these files with numeric filenames corresponding to the exact time they were created.

Groups of files were then run through a small Basic program that eliminated the WordPerfect status line from the bottom of each screen and renamed the screen with the name we wanted to use. The files were then saved on a diskette and copied into The Information Machine's directory on the hard disk, where they were ready for manipulation by the program and the appropriate script.

The next step was to use WordPerfect to write scripts that control the branchings from each screen to other screens. From some screens the user can go only to the next screen in the presentation,

FIGURE 9

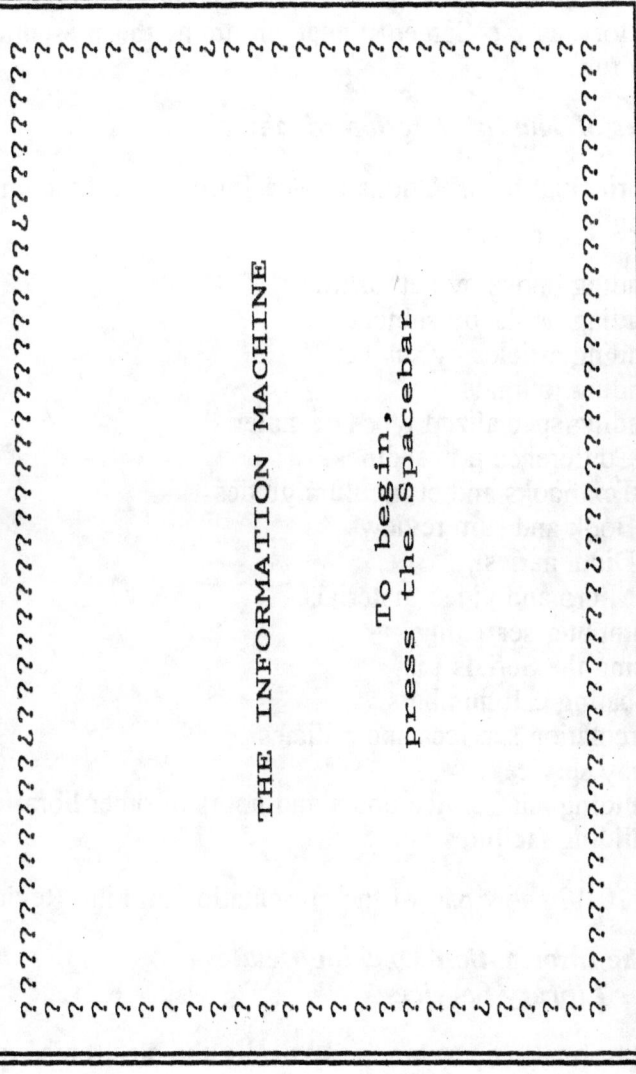

This is the opening marquee of The Information Machine.

but other screens have as many as nine choices of what to see next. Choices can be screens in the same script or in any other script.

One other small file was then created, consisting of a list of the scripts contained in the presentation.

When all of these files had been created and copied into the same subdirectory as the ScreenRunner program, the presentation was ready to run.

Contents of The Information Machine

The principal presentations in The Information Machine are the following:

    Finding books by author/title
    Finding books by subject
    Finding articles by subject
    Finding journals
    Finding specialized types of material
        Conference proceedings
        Textbooks and curriculum guides
        Book and film reviews
        Dictionaries
        Micro and video materials
    Computer searching
    Using the Serials List
    Locating call numbers
    Circulation services and policies
    Copy service
    Building and service hours and hours of other libraries
    Building facilities

Figures 10-17 show part of the presentation on Film Reviews.

How The Information Machine Relates to Other Library Services

The Information Machine is basically the electronic equivalent, with pizazz and pretty colors, of the types of printed material libraries have been making available for years, with these differences:

— Each user can construct his own tailor-made library guide, i.e., choose exactly what information he wants presented and go directly to it instead of having to scan in a linear manner through irrelevant material in search of the particular points he wants addressed.
— Presentations can include multiple-choice tests with immediate feedback and reinforcement.
— Presentations are broken down into easily digestible units of no more than 21 lines each.
— Information can be added or updated quickly without additional expense.
— Use statistics are generated daily.

The Information Machine is not intended to replace printed materials. We have a strong user-education publishing program that puts out what we think are some of the best library instruction publications in the business. Their availability reduces the need for a printer on The Information Machine. A screen printout cannot do the job of a handsome and well organized sheet, bookmark, or pamphlet designed as a print medium from the first.

Nor is The Information Machine intended to replace the reference staff. It is intended to be one more way of reaching people, especially those who are intimidated by a four-page printed guide or by a person at the reference desk to whom they are unwilling to reveal their ignorance.

The First Year

The Information Machine was made available to the public on four IBM PCs, upgraded with larger power supplies and hard disks, complete with security devices. (Two of these machines are used for end-user online searching during evenings and weekends.) The complete presentation of 350 or so screens, along with the computer program, scripts, etc., takes about two megabytes of space on the disk. We placed the machines so that users would have to pass both the reference desk and the online catalog to get to them. We could have placed the machines near the door and gotten many more users, but we did not want the machines to seem to be the primary source of assistance. This is still a limited, alternative resource.

FIGURE 10

```
UH-UP M. D. Anderson Library      * The Information Machine *          FR1

There are a variety of different indexes that will provide you with citations
to film reviews, including the information you need (publication titles,
volume numbers, page numbers, dates, etc.) to look for the reviews in the
Library.

Since film reviews are evaluations of a film that were written at the time the
film was released or shortly afterwards, you will ordinarily have to know the
year your film was released in order to find reviews of it.

If you don't already know the release date of your film, you will probably be
able to find the date by looking in one or more of the film reference books
shelved in the Reference Room with call numbers in the PN 1990's.  (For a list
of these titles, as well as help in finding further information on films,
consult the printed Library Guide FILM.)

1. To see the location of the film reference books, type 1.
2. To see the location of FILM guide, type 2.
3. To continue this presentation, type 3.
4. To return to the Opening Menu, type 4.

[OTHER OPTIONS: PRESS 'P' for previous screen, 'Q' to quit, 'Z' to start over]
```

Figures 10 through 17 illustrate part of the presentation on Film Reviews.
If the user selects choice 1 from this screen, Figure 11 is displayed.

FIGURE 11

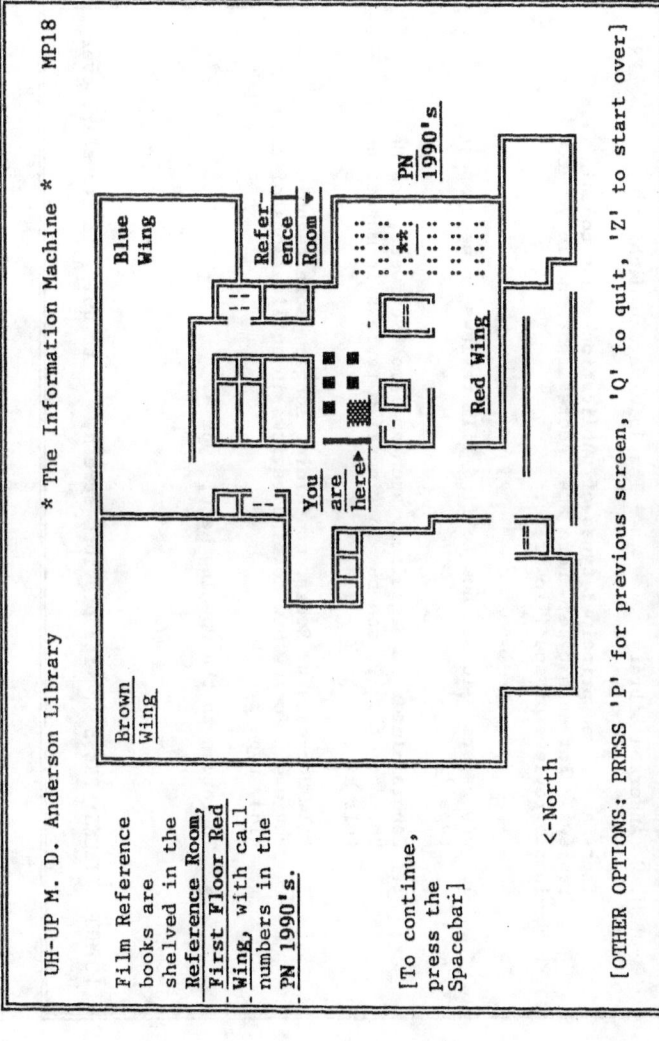

A user may press the spacebar to continue the presentation on film reviews, or may select any of the options from the bottom line of the screen. Figure 12 is displayed if the spacebar is pressed.

FIGURE 12

```
UH-UP M. D. Anderson Library     * The Information Machine *      FR2

    There are three principal types of publications that contain film
    reviews. For each type, there are indexes that enable you to
    locate reviews of specific films:

    1. Newspapers. To see how to find film reviews in newspapers,
       type 1.

    2. General-Interest Magazines, such as Time, Newsweek, the New
       Yorker, etc. To see how to find film reviews in magazines of
       this kind, type 2.

    3. Film Journals or Books, containing longer, more technical
       reviews. To see how to find reviews in publications of this
       kind, type 3.

    4. To return to the Opening Menu, type 4.


    [OTHER OPTIONS: PRESS 'P' for previous screen, 'Q' to quit, 'Z' to start over]
```

Notice that users are often given a numbered option to go to the opening menu, in addition to being able to restart the presentation by typing "Z". Figure 13 will be displayed when a user selects choice 1.

FIGURE 13

```
┌─────────────────────────────────────────────────────────────┐
│                                                             │
│ UH-UP M. D. Anderson Library    * The Information Machine *         FR3 │
│                                                             │
│    Most major newspapers carry film reviews, but (as is the case    │
│    with any newspaper article) to find a review of a particular film│
│    you must either know the exact date the review appeared or use an│
│    index.                                                   │
│                                                             │
│    Indexes exist for only a small number of newspapers. The New     │
│    York Times, the Times of London, the Christian Science Monitor,  │
│    and the Wall Street Journal have indexes that go back many years.│
│    Most other newspaper indexes, including the index to the Houston │
│    Post, began in 1976. There is no printed index to the Houston    │
│    Chronicle.                                               │
│                                                             │
│                                                             │
│                         [To continue, press the **Spacebar**]       │
│                                                             │
│                                                             │
│ [OTHER OPTIONS: PRESS 'P' for previous screen, 'Q' to quit, 'Z' to start over] │
└─────────────────────────────────────────────────────────────┘
```

FIGURE 14

```
UH-UP M. D. Anderson Library      * The Information Machine *           FR4

   Recent volumes of the Wall Street Journal Index are located on
   Index Table 4; older volumes are located in the Index Backfiles
   area of the Reference Room with the call number HG 1 W26. Film
   reviews are listed beginning with the 1968 volume. For the years
   1968 to 1977, look in the "General" section of the Index under
   the heading Movie Industry. In the 1978 and subsequent volumes,
   look under the heading Movie Reviews.

   The rest of our newspaper indexes are located on Index Table 15
   and in the Index Backfiles area. In all but two of them, you
   will find reviews under the heading Motion Picture Reviews. The
   exceptions are the index to the Times (London), where you will
   need to look under the heading Film, and the 1960-1978 volumes of
   the Christian Science Monitor, where you will need to look under
   the heading Movies.

   1. To see the location of Index Tables 4 and 15 and the Index
      Backfiles area, type 1.

   2. To continue this presentation, type 2.

[OTHER OPTIONS: PRESS 'P' for previous screen, 'Q' to quit, 'Z' to start over]
```

FIGURE 15

```
UH-UP M. D. Anderson Library     * The Information Machine *         FR5


In the case of film reviews in the **New York Times**, there is a
handy shortcut you can take if your film was released **before 1983**:

On **Index Table 14** there is a thirteen-volume set entitled **New
York Times Film Reviews**, which contains the complete text of film
reviews that appeared in the New York Times between 1913 and
1982.

<u>1.</u>  To see the location of **Index Table 14**, type <u>1</u>.

<u>2.</u>  To return to the Film Reviews menu, type <u>2</u>.





[OTHER OPTIONS: PRESS 'P' for previous screen, 'Q' to quit, 'Z' to start over]
```

FIGURE 16

```
UH-UP M. D. Anderson Library     * The Information Machine *              FR6

The following indexes list film reviews published in general-
interest magazines:

The **Readers' Guide to Periodical Literature**, located on **Index
Table 1**, has been published since 1900 and is a good source for
older as well as current film reviews. Look up the heading
**Moving Pictures** in volumes **before 1977** and the heading **Motion
Picture Reviews** in volumes **from 1977 on**.

The **Magazine Index**, located at the end of **Index Table 15**, is
published in microform. Listings for the latest four to **five
years**, in a single alphabet, are on a motor-driven film reader
and are updated monthly. Microfiche containing older years (back
to 1977) are in the fiche cabinet near the Reference/Information
Desk. Reviews are not found under a separate heading, so look up
the **title** of your film directly.

**1**.  To see the location of **Index Tables** 1 and 15, type **1**.

**2**.  To return to the Film Reviews menu, type **2**.

[OTHER OPTIONS: PRESS 'P' for previous screen, 'Q' to quit, 'Z' to start over]
```

This screen is choice 2 from the film reviews menu (Figure 10).

FIGURE 17

```
┌─────────────────────────────────────────────────────────────────┐
│ UH-UP M. D. Anderson Library    * The Information Machine *  FR7│
│                                                                 │
│ There are several indexes on Index Table 14 that will lead you  │
│ to longer, more technical reviews published in film journals or │
│ books. In most of them you can look up the title of the film    │
│ directly:                                                       │
│                                                                 │
│    Film Literature Index                                        │
│    Retrospective Index to Film Periodicals                      │
│    International Index to Film Periodicals                      │
│    Guide to Critical Reviews: Part IV: The Screenplay           │
│    Cumulated Dramatic Index, 1909-1949                          │
│    Macmillan Film Bibliography                                  │
│    Art Index                                                    │
│                                                                 │
│      (In the Art Index, look up the heading Moving Pictures--   │
│      Criticisms, Plots, etc. or Moving Picture Reviews in       │
│      volumes before 1977 and the heading Motion Picture         │
│      Reviews in volumes from 1977 on.)                          │
│                                                                 │
│ 1. To see the location of Index Table 14, type 1.               │
│                                                                 │
│ 2. To return to the film reviews menu, type 2.                  │
│                                                                 │
│ [OTHER OPTIONS: PRESS 'P' for previous screen, 'Q' to quit,     │
│                 'Z' to start over]                              │
└─────────────────────────────────────────────────────────────────┘
```

This screen is chioce 3 from the film reviews menu.

The Information Machine has now been publicly available at the University of Houston since January, 1987. The presentation has been viewed by over 30,000 people and has been helpful to the majority of them. Our users are serious people—the most popular topics are Finding Books by Author/Title and by Subject and Finding Journals. People do mistake The Information Machine for the adjacent Online Catalog, despite our disclaimer on the first screen (Figure 1).

During the first month of use, and again near the end of 1987, we offered users a questionnaire. The intent of the questionnaire was to see if there was anything seriously wrong and to ask for recommendations on topics to develop in the future. The majority of the eighty responses were very positive. Most respondents understand what the presentation is intended to accomplish—only a couple of people complained that it did not include the Gettysburg Address or the names of the members of the Russian Politburo. Two respondents failed to find something they were seeking that was actually included in the presentation. A few people complained that computers should not be used for such trivial purposes. We asked respondents to rank three topics we were considering for future development, but, since respondents wanted all three with equal fervor, we received no help with our decision.

One of the hypotheses we followed during the design of the presentation appears to be incorrect. The Information Machine includes frequent encouragement for users to come to the reference desk if the computer presentation does not provide the information they need. We had expected that people would come to the desk if they were assured by the presentation that they had a valid question and were given a suggestion of how to present it. However, we have observed that very few people leave The Information Machine and come to the reference desk, even when they leave the presentation from a screen that strongly encourages them to do so.

The statistics indicate that none of the presentation modules are seriously defective—they all are reported to be much more often helpful than not. The least successful module is the one on finding articles on a topic. In The Information Machine we strongly encourage users to come to the reference desk for assistance in selecting an appropriate index, and, if they choose not to do so, we suggest that they look for a printed library guide on their topic or look at the labels on the index tables (which identify the general subject coverage of the indexes on each table). This is not what they want to hear. We could have developed a module that handled this topic more extensively. However, we decided that The Information Machine was not a good vehicle for this topic, because we would have had to write a number of menus of choices that would lead to many combinations of recommended indexes. We would have to change several screens every time we added, deleted, or moved an index. We are developing an expert system that is to help users identify and select reference materials, including indexes. The expert system is being designed so that the knowledge base is easy to create and maintain.

Hardware Problems

We have had two hard disks go out, one during the warranty period and one after. We lost one month's worth of statistics the second time — the first disk failed at the first of the month, after we had copied the prior month's statistics to a floppy disk.

During the first year we used a version of the program that had a single opening marquee, with the text "The Information Machine," in bright white, in the same place on the screen all year. This began to burn in the monitor, but not to the extent that it makes the screen hard to read. We have revised the program to cycle monthly through four marquees that do not use the same screen locations and that use regular white instead of bright. Based on our experience with the first version of the marquee, we calculate that the new version will take at least eight years to burn in the monitors.

The program is breakproof, but we have had the program stop running a couple of times due to severe electrical power fluctuations. Twice users have erased the hard disk during those times when our Information Machines had turned into silicon pumpkins. Our copy of the Norton Utilities arrived just in time to allow us to recover the statistics.

There have been no other hardware problems.

Turning a Project into Standard Operating Procedure

The Information Machine began as a project and, because of its apparent success, is now a fixture. The next step has been to integrate Information Machine maintenance into the routine clerical workflow of the Department. This involves regular updates, such as the holiday, final examination, and intersession hours that need to be changed every semester, and the monthly gathering and reporting of user statistics.

To facilitate this, we have identified all the screens that need to be substituted or edited on a regular basis and have saved them in a separate WordPerfect file. Editing, converting, and copying procedures have been fully documented, practically keystroke by keystroke.

Each month the statistics from each machine are copied on to a diskette and imported into a Lotus 1-2-3 spreadsheet. A report is printed showing the monthly totals for each machine and the monthly and year-to-date totals for the four machines combined (Figure 18).

We have fully documented the procedures for collecting the monthly statistics from each machine, entering them into the spreadsheet (we created Lotus macros to make the process almost automatic), and printing the report.

Fully documented as well is the process of loading The Information Machine from the backup diskettes on to a hard-disk PC.

REFLECTIONS

How Do We Know We Got It Right?

We don't know. At this stage, the product is as good as the common sense of its creators. We improved our odds by involving a number of intelligent, creative, committed people. Anyone who has reviewed a number of the current CD-ROM resources knows that such a process does not inevitably result in the development of an excellent product. It is our belief that no one knows yet how to produce the best product of this type, and that what the world needs is for several people or groups to give it their best, so that the results can be compared, contrasted, and tested.

Future Directions

We are negotiating with a vendor to make The Information Machine available for sale. The product includes the ScreenRunner presentation manager, the conversion program, a number of utility programs, and our complete presentation for use as a guide. We found that developing the conversion program and the documentation for use by others was at least as much work as the development of our initial release of a working version for our own public. One advantage to us of developing a version for broader use is that we now have programs and documentation that are much easier for our own staff to use.

We have lots of ideas for electronic reference services. Some of them may be implemented as direct extensions of The Information Machine, and others may require other development vehicles, such as the expert system that we have begun to work on. We do not consider The Information Machine to be an expert system. There is plenty of expertise in the presentation, but none in the computer program. It is nevertheless an important building block of our electronic services, which we expect eventually to coexist on integrated terminals.

Here are some of the components of our long-term plan for The Information Machine:

- Dial-up access for those who can already dial into the Library's Public Online Catalog.
- Inclusion of new presentations on topics such as beginning research, finding newspapers, maps, and statistics, and accessing government documents.
- Versions for the University of Houston branch libraries.
- Link to an expert system to facilitate access to reference materials.
- Eventual integration with the Geac Online Catalog, OCLC, CD-ROM and online databases, etc., into single workstations.

The materials housed in reference collections are increasingly

FIGURE 18

INFORMATION MACHINE STATISTICS

June, 1987

IM1	QY	QN	QP	QW	WA	TOT
MU	136	92	47	35	168	478
SL	7	5	2	2	5	21
SM	2	0	0	0	0	2
CN	12	5	5	2	3	27
AR	16	16	8	4	24	68
JN	5	2	4	0	6	17
MP	29	16	11	2	20	78
MQ	6	3	1	0	1	11
BK	30	30	10	5	22	97
CP	1	0	0	1	0	2
CY	6	1	0	0	3	10
WM	27	11	15	7	12	72
SB	23	23	6	3	13	68
HR	13	4	5	0	7	29
ID	7	6	3	3	8	27
DC	4	1	0	1	0	6
BR	2	1	0	0	1	4
LG	0	0	0	0	1	1
TL	0	0	0	0	0	0
SP	3	2	0	0	0	5
FR	0	0	0	0	0	0
Scr	4105		Total Users			478

IM2	QY	QN	QP	QW	WA	TOT
MU	156	98	56	27	197	534
SL	9	4	0	3	7	23
SM	3	0	0	1	0	4
CN	7	3	3	1	4	18
AR	20	12	8	4	25	69
JN	7	2	2	3	8	22
MP	43	21	7	5	18	94
MQ	15	4	5	0	7	31
BK	24	20	12	3	28	87
CP	2	0	0	0	0	2
CY	15	3	0	0	1	19
WM	31	11	9	0	12	63
SB	17	16	7	1	16	57
HR	23	7	6	1	12	49
ID	7	8	4	0	16	35
DC	7	2	3	0	3	15
BR	1	1	2	0	0	4
LG	2	1	0	0	0	3
TL	1	0	0	0	0	1
SP	2	1	0	1	0	4
FR	0	0	0	0	1	1
Scr	4374		Total Users			534

IM3	QY	QN	QP	QW	WA	TOT
MU	32	24	22	4	43	125
SL	1	0	1	0	2	4
SM	0	0	0	0	0	0
CN	3	3	1	1	2	10
AR	4	1	3	0	4	12
JN	3	1	0	0	3	7
MP	7	2	6	0	4	19
MQ	2	0	3	1	0	6
BK	6	7	8	1	10	32
CP	1	0	2	0	0	3
CY	5	1	1	1	0	8
WM	6	2	3	0	5	16
SB	3	4	6	1	7	21
HR	2	1	4	1	2	10
ID	2	1	1	0	0	4
DC	2	0	1	1	2	6
BR	0	0	0	0	0	0
LG	0	0	0	0	0	0
TL	0	0	0	0	0	0
SP	0	1	0	0	0	1
FR	0	0	0	0	0	0
Scr	1168		Total Users			125

IM4	QY	QN	QP	QW	WA	TOT
MU	55	51	23	18	83	230
SL	3	5	2	0	1	11
SM	0	0	0	1	0	1
CN	2	1	2	1	3	9
AR	4	19	6	1	9	39
JN	6	3	2	0	2	13
MP	13	5	7	1	14	40
MQ	3	0	0	1	0	4
BK	9	7	7	3	13	39
CP	0	0	1	0	0	4
CY	5	0	0	0	1	6
WM	13	2	4	1	8	28
SB	4	6	6	3	5	24
HR	11	3	2	0	5	20
ID	3	6	3	0	2	14
DC	2	1	0	0	1	5
BR	0	0	0	1	0	2
LG	0	0	0	0	0	0
TL	0	0	0	0	0	0
SP	1	0	0	0	0	1
FR	0	1	0	0	1	2
Scr	1814		Total Users			230

FIGURE 18 (continued)

TOTAL MONTH-TO-DATE

IM	QY	QN	QP	QW	WA	TOT
MU	379	265	148	84	491	1367
SL	20	14	5	5	15	59
SM	5	0	0	1	1	7
CN	24	12	11	5	12	64
AR	44	48	25	9	62	188
JN	21	8	8	3	19	59
MP	92	44	31	8	56	231
MQ	26	7	10	1	8	52
BK	69	64	37	12	73	255
CP	4	2	3	1	1	11
CY	31	5	1	1	5	43
WM	77	26	31	8	37	179
SB	47	49	25	8	41	170
HR	49	14	17	1	27	108
ID	19	21	11	3	26	80
DC	15	4	4	2	7	32
BR	3	2	3	0	2	10
LG	2	1	0	0	1	4
TL	1	0	0	0	0	1
SP	6	4	1	0	0	11
FR	0	2	0	0	2	4
Scr	11461		Total Users			1367

TOTAL YEAR-TO-DATE

Information Machine	Typed "Yes"	Typed "No"	Typed "Partly"	Walked Away	Walked Away from a Program	TOTAL
Menus	3355	2558	1484	700	4358	12455
Serials List 1	211	148	96	19	187	661
Serials List 2	15	5	2	1	2	25
Call Numbers	177	137	90	24	137	565
Articles on a Topic	470	403	334	84	559	1850
Finding Journals	177	139	90	31	190	627
Building Maps 1	966	524	397	92	617	2596
Building Maps 2	216	126	109	15	87	553
Books (A/T)	564	545	327	101	689	2226
Conference Proceedings	21	12	13	6	21	73
Copiers	190	39	36	17	65	347
Who May	657	268	260	61	350	1596
Books (Subject)	396	377	236	67	458	1534
Hours	389	215	156	29	213	1002
Ref/Info Desk	214	188	139	35	219	795
Dictionaries, etc.	116	80	70	13	63	342
Book Reviews	26	12	14	5	22	79
Library Guides	10	12	9	0	8	39
TILII	8	11	3	0	9	31
Supplies	58	35	39	5	23	160
Film Reviews	31	13	21	2	15	82
Total Screens	110078		Total Users			12455

available in machine-readable form, and many of them are already available on user terminals at home and in offices. Where will the reference librarian be when the user is on a terminal at home? How will we assist users to navigate in the universe of electronic information? We believe that, if the reference librarian is to continue to have a role in improving access to information, it is time for us to organize our knowledge and to deliver it in new ways. The Information Machine is our first step in this larger process.

REFERENCES

1. Thomas, Frank, and Ollie Johnston, *Disney animation: the illusion of life*, New York: Abbeville Press, 1984.
2. Pellegrino, Charles R. and Joshua Stoff, *Chariots for Apollo: the making of the lunar module*, New York: Athenaeum, 1985.
3. *Pointer*, computer program [IBM PC Basica], available from Karen Smith, Lockwood Memorial Library, SUNY at Buffalo; copyright 1986 by the State University of New York. Described in Karen F. Smith, "Robot at the reference desk?," *Energies for transition, proceedings of the Fourth National Conference of the Association of College and Research Libraries*, Chicago: ACRL, 1986, p. 198-201.
4. Unnamed computer program (Applesoft Basic), available from Dana Smith, Purdue University Undergraduate Library, circa 1983. Described in Smith, Dana E., and Steve M. Hutton, "Back at 8:00 am: microcomputer reference support programs," *Collegiate Microcomputer*, vol 11 no. 4, November 1984, p. 289-294.
5. Jourdain, Robert, *Programmer's problem solver for the IBM PC and XT*, New York: Brady, 1986.
6. Davies, Russ, *Compute!'s mapping the IBM PC and XT*, Greensboro, NC: Compute! Publications, 1985.
7. Poole, Lon, *Using your IBM personal computer*, Indianapolis: Howard W. Sams, 1983.

The Information Machine will be made available for sale by the

Amigos Bibliographic Council
11300 North Central Expressway
Suite 321
Dallas, Texas 75243
(800)843-8482

AquaRef:
An Expert Advisory System for Reference Support

Deborah Hanfman

SUMMARY. The National Agricultural Library's Aquaculture Information Center has developed an expert-system based Advisor for supporting reference-related inquiries. The system was created to help improve access to basic resource tools and information in aquaculture, one of the rapidly expanding disciplines within agriculture. System developmental stages are described, including the selection of software and determination of types of information to incorporate into the system. Data distribution is discussed in terms of user groups and feedback mechanisms. The basic expert advisory system was enhanced and linked to external programs, including bibliographic databases through remote access and CD-ROMs. Future projections include external linkage to full-text files and images on laser videodiscs and CD-ROMs. Cooperative updating is encouraged as a means to facilitate the universal role of libraries and information services to disseminate information.

The National Agricultural Library (NAL) has been exploring the concept of "expert systems" to assist reference librarians and subject specialists in their role of disseminating agricultural information. The Aquaculture Information Center, which is one of several specialized Information Centers at NAL, initiated a project using expert system "shell" software that would provide basic reference tools on aquaculture.

Deborah Hanfman is Coordinator for the Aquaculture Information Center, National Agricultural Library, Beltsville, MD. This article was written by Mrs. Hanfman as part of her official duties as a Federal employee. No copyright is claimed on this article.

The need for an Expert Advisory System was based on the Agriculture Information Center's past history. In 1985, the Aquaculture Information Center (AIC) was established by Congressional mandate to serve as a repository for national aquaculture information. Since that time it has also supported a formal agreement with the National Oceanic and Atmospheric Administration to provide access to internal aquaculture literature. Based on these two responsibilities, the volume of national and international requests has sharply risen over the years. With professional staff and time at a premium, the AIC recognized that additional resources were needed. Staff of the Center designed and created an "expert advisory system" on aquaculture called AquaRef to handle the large number of reference requests received daily by both the AIC and the Reference Branch of NAL.

Some libraries and information services have looked into the area of expert systems to support them in their work. POINTER, a microcomputer reference program for Federal documents, was developed by Karen F. Smith and others at the State University of New York at Buffalo, under a Council of Library Resources grant. The program was originally created using Lisp (an artificial intelligence programming language), and then later modified to BASIC. POINTER could be used by both the reference staff and patrons, guiding them through a series of menu selections to appropriate government documents. This early work was one of the first approaches to relieve the reference librarian from commonly confronted problems such as overwork, limited staff, frustration, and burnout.

In early 1986, a demonstration program called ANSWERMAN was developed at the National Agricultural Library by the Associate Director, Samuel T. Waters using expert system "shell" software. Shells are expert system tools that facilitate the creation of expert systems, without requiring previous experience with programming languages. ANSWERMAN was designed as a small microcomputer-based expert system to point users to a wide variety of agricultural-related reference books and corresponding page numbers for easy access to answers. This exploration of expert systems for reference support set the stage for developing slightly more expanded systems at the library using an "expert system shell." AquaRef soon followed as a pilot project to determine the usefulness of expert advisory systems in specialized fields.

Private companies such as Du Pont have also investigated expert system shells to create programs that can assist them in their everyday operations. Corporation experts predict that by 1991, 2,000 expert systems will be in use which could yield a 10% increase in net profits.*

The terminology "Expert Advisory System" is used at NAL to identify a microcomputer-based system that mimics the advisory work done by human experts, in this case, reference librarians. An expert system "shell" is utilized for the system creation. Users of the system are directed to bibliographic citations on a subject in agriculture. They are also provided with names of appropriate associations and experts, legal references, textual information, and other reference-oriented materials. These resources aid end-users in locating information to conduct their own research. They also provide the information professionals with an affordable vehicle to disseminate information to their patrons. No single librarian or information specialist can be expected to consistently remember the best sources for locating answers on a particular subject; expert advisory systems offer compensation for this and free professionals for more complex inquiries requiring indepth effort.

AquaRef focuses on the specialized field of aquaculture, with intent that evaluation of its usefulness could set the tone for other areas in the library to follow.

AquaRef is the first "expert advisory system" developed at NAL for distribution to the public. This paper describes the developmental stages involved in the creation of AquaRef, the data distribution phase, and projections for a networking of specialized collections and expertise in aquaculture and other growing disciplines within agriculture.

---

*Mickey Williamson, "At Du Pont, Expert Systems Are Key to AI Implementation." *PC Week*. January 13, 1987, p. 35.

SOFTWARE SELECTION CRITERIA

A prerequisite to the development of an expert advisory system was the identification of software that would run on an IBM PC or compatible. This microcomputer capability enables a broader audience to utilize the program, avoiding the need for individuals to obtain access to minicomputers or mainframes.

Since librarians and subject specialists would be serving the roles of both "domain experts" (field experts) and "knowledge engineers" (information gatherers, assimilators, and developers of expert system structure), an expert system "shell" was required. Shells are expert system tools that facilitate the creation of expert systems. System developers could create relatively sophisticated advisory systems without prior knowledge in artificial intelligence programming languages such as Lisp or Prolog.

Additional criteria considered during software selection included: cost, data updating capability, friendly user interface, Run-Time program, and advanced capabilities such as linking to external files or databases.

Following careful analysis of various demonstration disks, documentation for a number of shells, and review of available literature on expert system software, 1stCLASS was selected as the expert system "shell" of choice. It was produced by Programs in Motion, Inc., 10 Sycamore Road, Wayland, MA 01778. A preliminary evaluation of 1stCLASS was initiated at NAL in 1985 to test its usefulness for providing bibliographic access to literature.

NAL called this test demonstration product ANSWERMAN. The ease with which this system was created convinced the library to acquire 1stCLASS Shell Software to develop expert advisory systems in specialized subject areas of agriculture. They would aid reference librarians and subject specialists in handling ready-reference inquiries.

1stCLASS met all of the above specified selection criteria. The software package was affordable; NAL purchased the package for $495.00, which included a Run-Time (ADVISOR) Program, allowing the purchaser to make copies of the Run-Time Program and distribute or sell such copies. The software runs on IBM PC or compatible computers.

Data entered into the system can be easily revised or updated at any time, allowing the specialist to compensate for rapidly changing information.

Users of the system follow a series of menu-driven input screens. The input screens are modified by the system developer during the creation phase, which permits the end-user to quickly and easily retrieve the desired response.

Advanced capabilities of the software enabled NAL to utilize videodiscs and CD-ROM systems currently existing at the library as enhancement features to the expert advisory system. The additional ability to dial-up remotely to databases for bibliographic access permitted users to expand the number of retrievable records and conduct more complex searches.

1stCLASS also offered a wide variety of other options including interfacing with Lotus 1-2-3 for exchanging numeric and logical data, and a "chaining feature" which allows system developers to freely build up to thousands of modular knowledge bases (specific rules and their associated facts and text) into complex collections (a useful option for cooperative updating).

DATA ANALYSIS PHASE

The first approach to developing any expert system is deciding the types of information to include in that system and determining how the information will be arranged. Staff of the Aquaculture Information Center reviewed patrons' correspondence collected over the past two years and selected the topics most frequently asked. Seven species of animals and two species of plants were chosen for inclusion, as well as a general aquaculture information category.

Steps taken to locate answers were analyzed. It is noteworthy that repeated questions received by staff at various times provided answers that were new and unique. These varied responses to the same questions can be easily incorporated into the shell, and represent a "gathering of the minds" in the final package.

SYSTEM CREATION

Once the types of aquaculture information were determined and organized into a tree-like structure, knowledge bases could be created.

Development Screens

1stCLASS shell software provides six basic screens for system creation. Using these screens, the system developer can quickly define the elements of the knowledge base, enter examples, select a rule building method, and run the resulting knowledge-base module. With 1stCLASS, knowledge bases are created directly from a rule. The resulting knowledge-base module(s) represent the "Advisor" program, which is the program visible to end-users of the system.

The Files Screen identifies the knowledge-based files that have been built by the system developer and can be accessed within the program. (Figure 1 illustrates the Files Screen for AquaRef.)

The Definitions Screen is where the system developer defines his knowledge base. Results or recommendations of the program, factors that influence what those results might be, and possible values (categories) for each factor that can influence the outcome are entered in this screen. (Figure 2 illustrates a Definitions Screen for AquaRef.)

This screen is also used to select the "editing text" feature of the 1stCLASS program. This is where the system developer can enhance text that he wants visible to the end-user.

Figures 3a-c show samples of Text Editor Screens in AquaRef.

The Examples Screen permits the developer to create combinations of the previously defined values that lead to various outcomes or recommendations; these can be thought of as "if . . . then" rules expressed as individual examples. For instance, the system developer could create an example such as: "If I am interested in prawns and want post-larvae suppliers, then I can consult these resources." The Examples Screen is laid out in an easy spreadsheet format.

The Methods Screen allows the system developer to create the rule for the series of "if . . . then" statements created in the Exam-

```
Get,  Save,  New,  Print/export,  Dos,  Quit    [Memory left = 100.%]
          Files  Definitions  Examples  Methods    Rule Advisor
[F1=Help]        File = --new file--                [F9=Quit] [F10=Definitions]

File       Type  Date      Time      Directory: A:\

ALGAE      KBM   12/17/86   5:07 PM
ANIMAL     KBM    1/01/87   0:20 AM
CATFISH    KBM    4/13/87   4:20 PM
CRAYFISH   KBM   12/17/87   6:42 PM
GENERAL    KBM   12/22/86   2:40 PM
INTEREST   KBM    1/06/87   3:33 PM       ëëëëëëëëëëëëëëëëëëëëëëëf
OPTION1    KBM    4/29/87   2:42 PM       ¤To Get a file from disk, ¤
OPTIONS    KBM    1/29/87  10:49 AM       ¤Press G and select it.   ¤
OYSTERS    KBM   12/23/86   7:48 AM       ¤                         ¤
PLANT      KBM    1/01/87   0:21 AM       ¤To start building a New  ¤
PRAWNS     KBM   12/22/86   4:47 PM       ¤knowledge base, press N. ¤
SALMON     KBM   12/23/86   8:22 AM       ¤                         ¤
SEAWEED    KBM   12/18/86   5:32 PM       ¤F9 and F10 change screens.¤
SPECIFIC   KBM    1/01/87   0:39 AM       ¤                         ¤
TILAPIA    KBM   12/18/86   5:42 PM       ¤For more help, press F1. ¤
TROUT      KBM   12/23/86   8:33 AM       äëëëëëëëëëëëëëëëëëëëëëëë¥
---- end of files ----
```

FIGURE 1. A Sample Files Screen for AquaRef

```
new_Factor, new_Value, edit_Text, Change, Activate, Move, Delete
        Files  Definitions   Examples    Methods    Rule  Advisor
[F1=Help]   1 Factors in CATFISH              [F9=Files] [F10=Examples]

    subject      result                  êêêêêêêêêêêêêêêêêêêêêêêêêêêêêêêf
    culture      #option1                ¤Complete the definitions, then  ¤
    technical    techcit                 ¤press F10 to give some examples.¤
    marketing    marketcit               ¤                                 ¤
    legislation  legiscit                ¤For more help, press F1.        ¤
    association  assnscit                âêêêêêêêêêêêêêêêêêêêêêêêêêêêêêêê¥

What kind of information would you like about catfish?

              FIGURE 2. A Sample Definitions Screen for AquaRef
```

[F5=Clear] [F6=Del_Eol] [F8=Read file] [Esc=Discard edit] [F10=Keep edit]
[F1=Help]   Enter/edit text for factor "species", value "trout"
trout (Salmo gairdneri, S. trutta; Salvelinus fontinalis, S. namaycush)

Enter only 1 line for values

FIGURE 3a. A Sample of Edited Text for the Value "Trout"

121

```
[F5=Clear]   [F6=Del_Eol]   [F8=Read file]   [Esc=Discard edit]   [F10=Keep edit]
[F1=Help]      Enter/edit text for factor "result", value "assnscit"

Louisiana Crawfish Farmers Assn.    South Carolina Crawfish Growers Assn.
P. O. Box 91544                     Rt. 3, Box 188
Lafayette, LA 70509                 Edgefield, SC 29824
(318) 235-7072

International Association of Astacology
(for information, US contact is:
Dr. James F. Payne
Dept. of Biology
Memphis State University
Memphis, TN 38152)
```

FIGURE 3b. A Sample of Edited Text for the Value "assnscit" (crawfish associations)

```
[F1=Help]           1st-CLASS Advisor for OPTION1              [F9=Rule] [Esc=Stop]

Perhaps these citations will be adequate for your needs:
1. Catfish farming. USDA Farmer's Bulletin No. 2260. 1981. 19 pp.
   (NAL call no.: 1AG84F no. 1160)
2. Channel catfish culture. Tucker, S. S. 1985. 658 pp. (NAL call
   no.: SH1.D43 v. 15)
3. Catfish farming: 1970-1985. Decker, L. National Agricultural Library,
   Quick Bibliography 86-33, February, 1986. (Free copy upon request)

If you are an experienced DIALOG searcher, you may want to have a more
detailed bibliography from the Aquatic Sciences and Fisheries Abstracts
database (DIALOG 44); if so, select "ASFA" below.

Will you take a few minutes to give us feed-back on your use of our
system? Please select "evaluation" below.
₴╀╀╀╀╀╀╀╀╀╀╀╀╀╀╀╀╀╀╀╀╀╀╀╀╀╀╀╀╀╀╀╀╀╀╀╀╀╀╀╀╀╀╀╀╀╀╀╀╀╀╀╀╀╀╀╀╀╀╀╀╀╀;
:ASFA                                                              ‥ ‥ ‥
:evaluation
:I prefer to end the search now
μ╀╀╀╀╀╀╀╀╀╀╀╀╀╀╀╀╀╀╀╀╀╀╀╀╀╀╀╀╀╀╀╀╀╀╀╀╀╀╀╀╀╀╀╀╀╀╀╀╀╀╀╀╀╀╀╀╀╀╀╀╀╀╀‡
                                                          PgDn, or End
```

FIGURE 3c. A Sample of Edited Text for Factor Called "OPTION1" ples Screen. There are four methods to create a rule. An example of the Methods Screen is shown in Figure 4.

The rule determines which questions to ask and in what sequence, and which results (advice) to display. In AquaRef, we chose to "Optimize" the rule.

The fifth type of screen is the Rule Screen. It permits the developer to see the created rule.

The Advisor represents a "series of screens" that are automatically generated for access by the library patron or other end-user. The screens are based on the rule sequence selected and use any text entered earlier by the developer. An example of three Advisor screens in AquaRef are illustrated in Figure 5.

The Advisor is the portion of the program that can be sold or distributed by the software purchaser.

The above overview of 1stCLASS Screens represents only the "basics" for system creation. Once the developer is familiar with the basic framework of the software, he can utilize a range of advanced capabilities.

Chaining

The chaining feature allows the system developer to freely build (chain) thousands of knowledge bases together into complex collections of knowledge bases. Staff of the Aquaculture Information Center realized this feature would be an asset in the development of AquaRef and other expert advisory systems at NAL. It would permit the independent creation of knowledge bases (KBs). These KBs could be linked together and automatically provide the user with a very large number of results that could assist them in their work. Chaining permits cooperative updating and independent development of knowledge bases to occur. Remote libraries could develop a knowledge base representing their own specialized collection and have that knowledge base chained to NAL's program.

Louisiana State University has already initiated this concept for AquaRef. Based on their expertise and specialized collection of aquaculture in the State, staff have developed a knowledge base on crawfish and submitted the data to NAL for chaining to the existing crawfish knowledge base in AquaRef. The resulting module is more

```
Optimize, Left-right, Customize, Match, ICO, ?, Test, Save, Advisor
     Files   Definitions   Examples  Methods      Rule Advisor
[F1=Help]       File = shell                           [F9=Examples] [F10=Rule]
```

Select a method to build the rule:

O = Optimize the rule

L = Use the factors in order, Left-to-right

M = Match the advisor responses against the examples

C = Customize the rule with the rule editor

FIGURE 4. Methods Screen

FIGURE 5. Three Advisor Screens in AquaRef

```
[F1=Help]          1st-CLASS Advisor for INTEREST          [F9=Rule] [Esc=Stop]

                                    AquaRef

     AquaRef is a small-scale aquaculture advisory system which was
created by the staff of the Aquaculture Information Center at the
National Agricultural Library. The system provides references to
appropriate sources of information and gives the call number or location
in the Library; some answers and advice are also given in response
to commonly asked questions. The information contained is for educational
purposes only; no discrimination is intended and no endorsement by the
National Agricultural is implied.


Are you interested in general or specific information on aquaculture?

Use the UP- and DOWN-ARROW keys to highlight your answer; press <cr>
►††††††††††††††††††††††††††††††††††††††††††††††††††††††††††††††††††††††††;
 :general                                                                ··
 :specific                                                               ··
 µ†††††††††††††††††††††††††††††††††††††††††††††††††††††††††††††††††††††††‡
                                                             , PgDn, or End
```

```
[F1=Help]          1st-CLASS Advisor for GENERAL           [F9=Rule]  [Esc=Stop]

Please select a category under general aquaculture:
ß†††††††††††††††††††††††††††††††††††††††††††††††††††††††††††††††††††††††;
:current and pending Federal legislation                                 ..
:citations to general aquaculture literature                             ..
:citations to National Agricultural Library bibliographies               ..
:list of NAL Information Alerts related to aquaculture                   ..
:titles of general aquaculture magazines and journals                    ..
:sources of aquaculture supplies                                         ..
:associations to contact                                                 ..
:sources of names of experts to contact                                  ..
:services of the Aquaculture Information Center                          ..
µ†††††††††††††††††††††††††††††††††††††††††††††††††††††††††††††††††††††††‡

                                                          , PgDn, or End
```

127

FIGURE 5 (continued)

[F1=Help]　　　　1st-CLASS Advisor for PRAWNS　　　　[F9=Rule] [Esc=Stop]

```
What kind of information would you like about freshwater prawns?
ß†††††††††††††††††††††††††††††††††††††††††††††††††††††††††††††††††;
:culture techniques                                                :
:technical information such as nutrition, diseases, pond water quality, etc. :
:marketing information                                             :
:existing Federal legislation and pending Federal legislation      :
:associations to contact                                           :
:suppliers of Macrobrachium postlarvae                             :
µ†††††††††††††††††††††††††††††††††††††††††††††††††††††††††††††††††‡
```

, PgDn, or End

comprehensive and depicts an excellent representation of materials on the subject.

Chaining also gets the developer around the designing limitations of the software. 1stCLASS allows one to define up to 31 factors and 32 results (answers) per knowledge base. If more factors or results are desired, the system developer can chain the data to another knowledge base. AquaRef exceeded the "results" limitations, and utilized the chaining feature for its primary design. A new upgraded software package called FUSION, produced by Programs in Motion, Inc., is commercially available and allows the developer to define a much larger number of factors and results.

Enhancement Features

By utilizing an expert system shell, staff of the AIC could easily explore the feasibility of linking AquaRef to external files. NAL has been actively participating in projects that mount full-text publications onto high storage 12" discs, called laser videodiscs. Linkage of AquaRef to videodiscs considerably expands user options and the availability of full-text information.

CD-ROMs (Compact-Disks, Read-Only Memory) are commercially available for searching databases that are primarily bibliographic in nature. Each disk holds a large volume of data stored in digital form. Some of the databases commercially available in the field of aquaculture include: AGRICOLA (AGRICultural Online Access), which represents NAL's computerized agricultural database; and ASFA (Aquatic Sciences and Fisheries Abstracts database), produced by Cambridge Scientific Abstracts, Rockville, MD). Both of these CD-ROM databases are available to users through subscription and can provide them with additional resources in aquaculture in a user-friendly menu-driven environment. The AIC has successfully linked AquaRef to the ASFA database on CD-ROM as an enhancement feature to the basic advisory program.

External linkage to "remote" aquaculture databases has also been successfully completed as a way for users to access the ASFA, AGRICOLA, and other aquaculture-related databases through DIALOG Information Service in Palo Alto, California. The same remote linkage could be done through BRS (Bibliographic Retrieval

Service, Latham, NY) in other subject areas; aquaculture-specific databases are not currently available through BRS.

Staff used a Crosstalk script file to enable the telecommunications link to DIALOG. Once the user entered DIALOG, he could conduct independent searching using DIALOG searching protocol.

Evaluation of AquaRef was necessary to determine if the advisory product was indeed useful to patrons. To encourage feedback from users, a small program written in BASIC was incorporated into the Advisor program. Users accessing AquaRef were asked at the end of the program to take a minute and provide comments regarding usefulness of AquaRef to their specific needs. Users desiring a followup by a professional from the Center could key their name, address, and phone number in the appropriate space on the evaluation program. The subject specialist and/or librarian would then be able to contact them for personal consultation.

Feedback to the evaluation was stored on the hard-disk and periodically reviewed by AIC Center staff. An individual that completed the evaluation from a remote area had several options for providing feedback. He/she could send the AIC a diskette containing his/her responses, a computer printout of the answers, a completed "printed evaluation form" identical to the automated evaluation program, or informal responses by phone or letter.

AquaRef DISTRIBUTION

Once the basic Advisor package was completed, the AIC staff requested a review and testing of the AquaRef program. User documentation was written by AIC staff and reviewed by staff of the Information Systems Division at NAL. Following this phase, modifications were made to the program and user documentation. The availability of the AquaRef Advisor in floppy disk form was then announced to the public. Since the AquaRef project was a pilot study to determine the usefulness of AquaRef for reference support, NAL chose to distribute the data free for a limited time period. Approximately six hundred floppy disks containing the AquaRef data were distributed between January and September of 1987 in the U.S. and overseas.

Requestors of the AquaRef diskettes were from a wide variety of backgrounds. Librarians, State Extension Specialists, County Agents, students, and potential and practicing aquaculturists were the most concentrated user groups. Feedback indicated that these groups received the most benefit from the system. Many private companies, systems experts, and groups unaffiliated with the field of aquaculture requested the disk for use as a prototype to develop their own systems in other subject areas.

Requestors of the AquaRef Advisor provided the AIC with a double-sided, double-density floppy disk. In response, staff of the Center copied the data onto the requestor's diskette and returned it to them with accompanying user documentation.

Individuals receiving the AquaRef Advisor were encouraged in the written user documentation to provide the AIC with feedback regarding the usefulness of system. They were also encouraged to make recommendations for ways to improve the system.

CURRENT PERSPECTIVES AND FUTURE OUTLOOK

Although AquaRef is currently limited in its coverage of commercially important aquaculture species, it provides a basic foundation for expanded development of the system in the future. The large number of both national and international requests received for AquaRef indicates that there is a real need for improved information transfer in this field. AquaRef represents one of the ways in which librarians can help meet the information needs of patrons and yet save time for themselves for more detailed inquiries.

Although feedback has been very positive and encouraging, it has also been sporadic. Approximately one-fifth of the total requestors for the AquaRef Advisor provided the AIC with feedback. Feedback was received in the form of printed copies of the online evaluation, diskettes, computer printouts, and informal correspondence. Future prospects for updated versions of AquaRef indicate a need for a more formalized mechanism of end-user feedback. Predetermined test sites and controlled monitoring of the evaluation study would provide staff of the AIC with more definitive data.

Cooperative updating is an important way to improve on topics and expertise involved in creating expert systems. LSU has set the precedent for this concept by creating a knowledge base to chain to

AquaRef. With the availability of large, specialized collections and expertise throughout the world, there is hope that librarians and other subject specialists can codify this knowledge into a useful program for dissemination.

Soon underway in early 1988, the National Agricultural Library will digitize and mount aquaculture publications onto a CD-ROM for full-text and page-image access as Phase I of a cooperative "National Agricultural Text Digitizing Project." With AquaRef as a front-end to the aquaculture disk, it should open the doors for patrons to a wealth of literature.

Future prospects also include linking AquaRef to NAL's upcoming integrated library system for cataloging, indexing, and circulation information on the topic.

Other specialized Information Centers at NAL are creating systems based on the AquaRef prototype. They include Food and Nutrition, Critical Agricultural Materials, and Herbs. It is not inconceivable that upon completion, these agricultural-related programs could be successfully integrated into a full-scale "agricultural expert advisory system."

In the meantime, NAL staff regularly provide basic training classes on the development of expert advisory systems using 1st-CLASS software. It is hoped that this will spark interest in the area of expert systems for future explorations.

The challenge of the reference librarian to meet the needs of the library patron is here! Librarians now have the opportunity to explore inexpensive expert system software packages for creating programs that can handle ready-reference requests. We need to be able to provide patrons with the best service possible, yet manage our time efficiently under periods of heavy workload and limited staff. Expert systems can help us more easily accept this challenge.

AquaRef represents a small-scale production of an advisory system in aquaculture, yet has provided mutual benefit for both the librarian and patron. Similar systems of this kind can contribute greatly to the information needs of patrons in other subject areas. With cooperative updating, what begins as a small-scale system can develop into a much larger system representing specialized collections and a wealth of subject expertise. The final product is an asset to the user community and helps the library serve its role in information transfer.

REFERENCES

Cavanagh, J.M.A. The Automated Readers' Advisor: Expert Systems Technology for a Reference Function. *1987 Proceedings of the National Online Meeting* (New York; May 5-7, 1987), 57-65.

Harmon, Paul; King, David. Expert Systems: Artificial Intelligence in Business. 1985. John Wiley & Sons, Inc. 283 p.

Hawkins, Donald T. Artificial Intelligence (AI) and Expert Systems for Information Professionals—Basic AI Terminology. *Online*. September 1987, 11 (5), 91-98.

Hawkins, William J. Expert Systems Promise Supersmart PCs. *Popular Science*. March 1986, 83-85, 116.

Parrott, James R. Expert Systems for Reference Work. *Microcomputers for Information Management*. September 1986, 3 (3), 155-171.

Pollitt, Steven. CANSEARCH: An Expert Systems Approach to Document Retrieval. *Information Processing & Management*. 1987, 23 (2), 119-138.

Smith, Karen F. POINTER: The Microcomputer Reference Program for Federal Documents (Buffalo, NY 1986).

Smith, Karen F.; Shapiro, Stuart C. Final Report on the Development of a Computer Assisted Government Documents Reference Capability: First Phase (Buffalo, NY: St. Univ. of New York at Buffalo, 1984).

Tyson, Reuben K.; Herrod, Richard. Capturing 32 Years on Computer. *Food Engineering*. December 1985, 69-71.

Van Horn, Mike. *Understanding Expert Systems*. 1986. Bantam Books. 233 p.

Waters, Samuel T. Answerman, the Expert Information Specialist: An Expert System for Retrieval of Information from Library Reference Books. *Information Technology & Libraries*. September 1986, 5 (3), 204-212.

Williamson, Mickey. At Du Pont, Expert Systems Are Key to AI Implementation. *PC Week*. January 13, 1987, 35.

Designing a Workstation for Information Seekers

Mary Micco
Irma Smith

SUMMARY. The goal of our research project is to explore the use of new technologies in providing more sophisticated delivery systems for information services in situations where the services of skilled reference librarians are not available. We are working on developing an advanced function workstation equipped with a CD-ROM jukebox of reference books and vocabulary control tools on laser disks with keyword access. The user interface will include an expert system to guide users in selecting the types of material best suited to their needs. It will also provide guidance in developing the best search strategy by mapping the terms selected by the users to the more controlled vocabularies of the data bases. Searches that are too broad and yield too much material will be narrowed. Conversely, searches that are too specific will be broadened. The system will also be designed to connect to a full service integrated library network also enabling the user to access the on-line card catalog, check circulation and do interlibrary loans.

In developing this system we will be taking advantage of many new technologies including the advanced function workstations, expert systems components, hypertext and optical disk storage.

I. PROBLEM STATEMENT

Not only is it increasingly difficult for even experienced reference librarians to keep up with the information explosion, but also these "experts" are in short supply. In many situations, hapless end

---

Mary Micco, Associate Professor, Computer Science Dept., Indiana University of Pennsylvania, Indiana, PA 15705.
Irma Smith, Head Reference Librarian, Chatham College Library, Woodland Rd., Pittsburgh, PA 15632.

© 1989 by The Haworth Press, Inc. All rights reserved.

users are left to their own devices as they struggle to find the information they need, packaged and presented in a form they can deal with.

In attempting to build an expert system to emulate the reference librarian, we have found that two major difficulties must be overcome, both of which require the application of new technologies.

The first challenge is to find an adequate knowledge representation scheme that will enable us to organize and retrieve the recorded wisdom of mankind in a dynamic online environment. We have considered both Dewey and the LC classification schemes, but both suffer from the fact that they are static, allow for only one main entry per item, and were designed to organize books in a collection. In the last two years, we have experimented with a number of frame-based expert systems that would enable us to organize knowledge in frames and then use these to provide context for the user's query.

"Brute force" searching, such as is currently used in most bibliographic data bases, is less than satisfactory, offering little assistance in the selection of terms other than alphabetic lists. A number of studies (Sinkankas, 1974; Micco, 1980; Cochrane, 1978) have shown that the syndetic structures of existing vocabulary control tools are poor, leading the reader quickly away from the subject.

There exist wide variations in specificity and cross-references among the different independent data bases. Automating such systems will not necessarily result in an improvement in service.

The second problem is the lack of consistency in the approach to indexing. The bibliographic record used in on-line public access catalogs (OPACs) today is not designed to provide many searchable keywords. Apart from the title, and very rarely a contents note, few useful terms exist other than the subject headings selected by the cataloger. Subject headings have traditionally been limited to describing the "aboutness" of the book. Standard library cataloging practice currently results in an average of slightly under 1.5 LC subject headings (O'Neill & Aluri, 1981) per title. Only about half of the terms used by readers in their first try correspond to a reference (Haftner, 1979). Mandel (Mandel & Herschman, 1983) maintains that this is *prima facie* evidence that the entry vocabulary of library catalogs is inadequate. It seems clear that the natural language of the readers is not being mapped to the controlled language of the LC subject headings. Another explanation for the frequent failures to match a term is the lack of specificity of LCSH. This is in part due to the fact that readers' requests often may be too specific to be covered by a whole monograph. Another related problem in analyzing search failure is that users often select terms that are either too broad or too narrow (Kaske, 1986).

Access to reference books is even worse. Yet we find we need 30-40 keywords for a brief periodical article.

Our goal is to design a system that will relate both broad and narrow user terms to subject terms describing both the "aboutness" of the book and also its contents in one bibliographic data base. Once this is accomplished the next step will be to add in the much more specific terms to be found in the indexes of a basic collection of reference books (both encyclopedias and subject specific dictionaries and thesauri).

II. CONVERGING TECHNOLOGIES

Cost-effective new technologies are now available that can have a major impact on the level of support that can be provided for end users searching for information in the world's recorded literature. The problem that we will address is managing this vast array of resources in such a way that users can be reasonably sure they are in fact finding the relevant literature and overlooking little of importance. We are proposing a more comprehensive approach to the problem of bibliographic control and subject access. The technologies we will be exploring include:

1. *Advanced function workstations:* These are much more powerful than the current crop of microcomputers and will provide the necessary capacity to handle the level of sophistication required in a fully integrated system. Our main goal is to enhance the MARC records with subject terms taken from the table of contents and where needed the index, as has already been done by Cochrane (*Books are for use*, 1978). These terms will be described as "chapter level" terms and will each become an entry in a lookup table with a pointer to the main heading or "anchor" term for the whole book. We hope to develop a series of interconnected maps of chap-

ter level terms that will provide a context to the term originally selected and will also offer alternatives drawn from actual usage by authors in the discipline.

2. *Expert system shells:* These programs enable us to build more complex logic in the user-system interface. We have written a number of small prototypes in Prolog to test our methodology. We also plan to experiment with KEE, an expert system shell with considerably more flexibility that will allow us to build a frame-based knowledge representation scheme.

   a. *Vocabulary control tools:* We are proposing to build a system that will provide online access to the vocabulary control tools used by skilled reference librarians, through the use of a CD-ROM jukebox with keyword access. All the tools will be organized by class number and linked in this way to the online databases as well.
   b. *Strategies to narrow the search space:* We hope to be able to duplicate many of the search strategies and patterns of skilled searchers. No reference librarian would think of undertaking a "brute force" search of an entire collection. Instead, they narrow the search space to manageable proportions. Whoever heard of a librarian who confused "blind Venetians" and "venetian blinds"? Expert systems have given us a new tool that can handle the more complex logic required to make such distinctions.

3. *Hypertext or hypercard:* This relatively new software will enable us to build an interconnected, classified knowledge representation scheme that will support the expert system logic described above. The system of subject area maps generated from the books themselves (see VI., Methodology, below) will involve a frame of textual information for each anchor term (main heading) selected. Hypercard will enable us to manage these for effective display.

4. *Optical disk storage:* Hypermedia technology is making possible much greater local storage that can be used for on-line versions of a whole range of subject access tools as well as a much wider range of materials. We are proposing in the last phase of this research project to experiment with an online jukebox (a Sony prod-

uct), that will enable us to perform keyword searching in subject access tools such as dictionaries, thesauri and classification schedules. We will experiment with erasable laser disks to find a convenient medium on which to build our system of maps.

III. BACKGROUND

The project we are currently working on is Phase III of a larger project to explore the use of expert systems and other emerging technologies in information retrieval. Initially we felt it would be easier to obtain funding if the project were broken down into independent but related phases. Two of the phases are now completed and have been reported in the literature.

A. Phase I: The Chatham Experiment: Systems Analysis and Design

Funding for this research was provided by Alcoa, the Benjamin Franklin Foundation and Westinghouse.
Researchers: Dr. Mary Micco and Dr. Irma Smith.

Two years ago, at Chatham College, we designed and built a small prototype of a system that will run on an advanced function workstation, can be networked with the whole range of library databases, and includes several different expert system modules, each performing a specialized task in the information retrieval process. We were designing these workstations for use by the general public, and therefore took advantage of windowing and mouse technologies to build a helpful, flexible and friendly user interface. This prototype was intended to explore and delineate the methodology for a larger system. We determined that it would be necessary to have a number of specialized modules each with a unique function. Such a modular system is much easier to write and test since each module can be tested separately. It also has the advantage of making the system much more flexible. The user can backtrack or skip modules without difficulty. Unfortunately at this stage in the design process we did not have access to the hardware to actually implement a full-sized system but each of the components was tested individually.

1. *Traffic control:* Just as in the non-automated library, many

users of automated library systems are simply looking for an author or a title. The first task of the system then, is to screen incoming requests and direct simple searches to the appropriate data bases in the network. Searches for a known author or title require little more than access to the MARC records and a name authority list or a permuted keyword listing of titles to help the users who cannot readily locate the one they are searching for. Note that the Chatham network was designed to be a full service system with access to all library files/data bases including circulation, acquisitions and interlibrary loan (see Figures 1 and 2).

2. *Developing the end user profile:* The next task, accomplished almost intuitively by our expert reference librarian, is to develop the user profile. This involves assessing the reading skill of the user, the type of project being undertaken, the user's knowledge of the topic being researched, and last, but not least, the user's stage in the research process. All of these factors influence the choice of databases and the type of literature recommended by the system. The information has to be collected from the user by a screen questionnaire so that it can be supplied to the expert system. As we developed the rules for our prototype system, written in Prolog, it became clear that many enhancements need to be added to the bibliographic record as we know it. For some reason, publishers do not pass on valuable information that could be used to match the book to the reader profile. The intended audience, reading level, and type of information package are all important factors that could easily be added through the use of additional tags.

3. *Selecting the broad subject area:* In order to limit the amount of material the system has to search, the next step in the process is to determine the broad subject area of interest. Existing "brute force" key word searching tools currently make no effort to use classification to limit the search area with the exception of the MEDLARS system which uses the explode feature to enable one to search all the narrower class numbers in one broad group such as cancer. Clearly if a user were looking for "peplums," the librarian would quickly determine that an art project was involved. Subsequent questioning might reveal that the user was interested in the shadowing on the drapes of the peplums of the Caryatids on the Erychthion. By establishing the broad class number involved, the

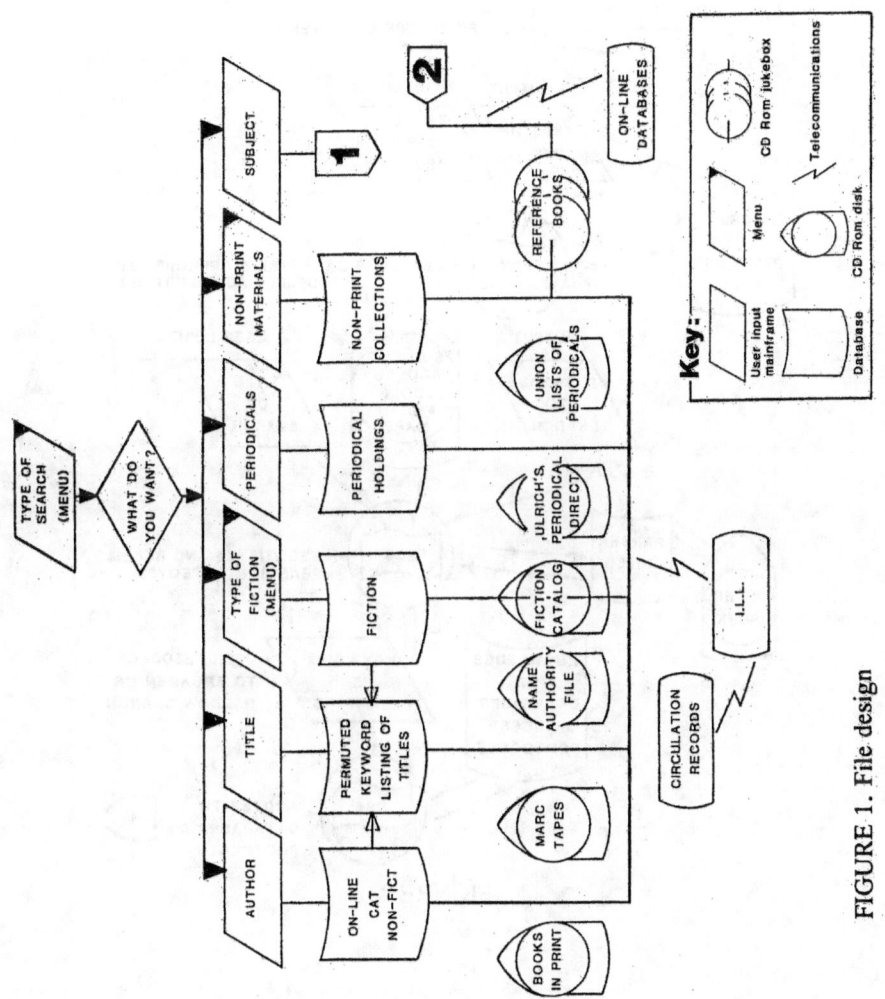

FIGURE 1. File design

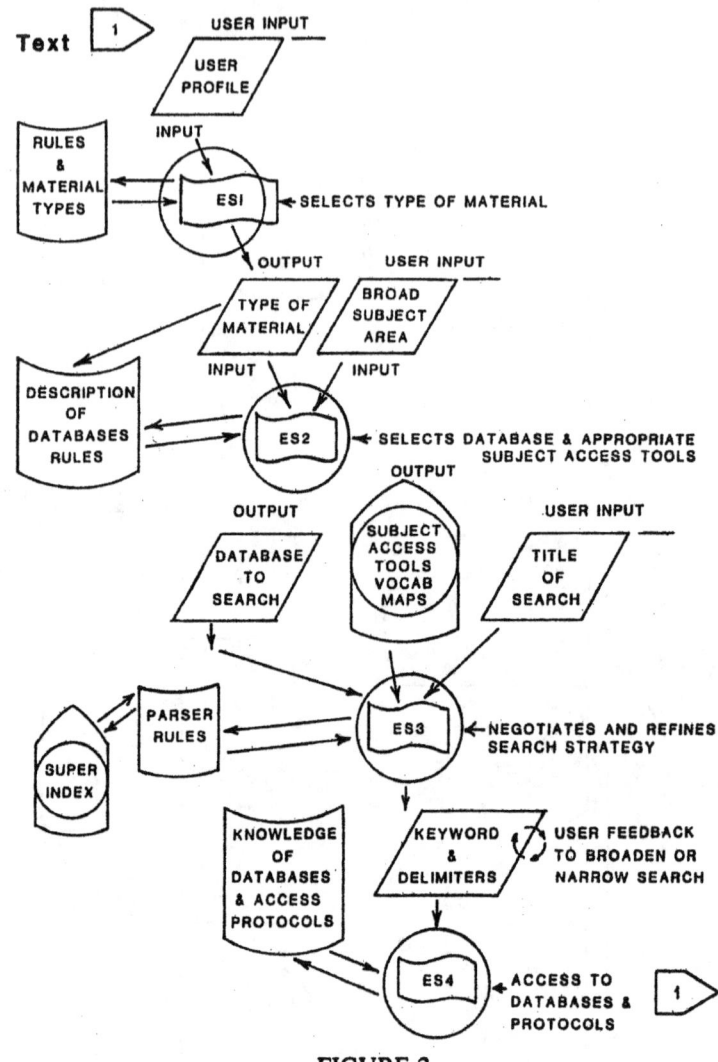

FIGURE 2.

system can readily reduce the search space to manageable proportions. This reduction also eliminates the problem of false drops of the type generated by the confusion between, for example,

— blind Venetians (blindness, Venice)
— Venetian blinds (window covering).

4. *A fully integrated three-tier system:* During the Chatham experiment, it became apparent from our observations of skilled reference librarians that they move readily from one type of information package to another as the need dictates. Over half of the searches done online in the periodical literature by unskilled searchers were in fact better satisfied by reference books or books selected by skilled searchers.

We could only conclude that a fully integrated three-tier system was needed, providing first some tools such as dictionaries and thesauri to help in determining the vocabulary to use. On the second level we proposed placing the data bases that involved access to books and the reference collection. As we all know, the subject access provided to reference books is virtually nonexistent at this time, except for a few data bases, such as the SuperIndex from Pergamon. As a solution to this problem, we suggested that optical disk storage of the jukebox variety (available from Sony), could be used to provide a basic reference collection. To make these accessible, and to permit our expert system to search the vocabularies of these books efficiently, we are proposing a comprehensive index to this collection that contains at least the table of contents and the indices of all commonly used reference works with a Boolean searching capability.

Finally, on the third level, we are proposing a gateway to the online periodical data bases that will assist the user in the key word selection process by providing online access to the thesauri relevant to the user's request. This means that all data bases and thesauri are assigned classification numbers and coded to be accessible from any level when the system determines that in fact the information being sought is most likely to be found in current periodicals.

Once the user has selected the general subject area he wants and checked the terminology, the system will pass the search in to the periodical literature on the third level in the data bases appropriate for that general subject area.

5. *Subject searching—Search strategy negotiation:* This expert system module proved to be very complex and was not completed in the Chatham experiment. It became the focal point of Phase II, and we are now ready to develop and test a proposed solution, a series of subject area maps derived from table of contents terms.

B. Phase II: The ADFA Experiment: Feasibility Study

This research was completed with funding and a great deal of support from the Australian Defence Force Academy Library in Canberra, Australia. The principal investigator, Dr. Micco, was awarded a teaching fellowship there in 1987, and worked closely with Mr. Alex Byrne, the Deputy Librarian, and his staff. The research results have been accepted for publication in a 1988 issue of *College & Research Libraries*.

In this experiment, 6,000 MARC records were enhanced with table of contents terms and then added to the Academy's OPAC, a URICA system. The procedures used were standardized, based on the manual developed by Pauline Cochrane and Barbara Settel (Settel, 1977). The terms were entered as local subject headings in the 653 field with 4 levels of subdivision at the suggestion of the Australian National Bibliography. Because the project was called the Enhanced Subject Project, the chapter level headings drawn from the table of contents were referred to as ESP terms.

The impact of subject access enhancement on the library cataloging workload, on library resources, and most importantly, on user search retrieval were studied. Our goal was to increase the number of access points to books, for which an average of less than 2 subject headings are provided. Clearly, this limited provision of subject headings is woefully inadequate when compared with the 50 or so reference points that we see as necessary for much less substantial periodical articles. Reference books have even fewer access points, consisting generally of only one broad subject heading. After careful study, we determined that not only were the number of access points different for each type of information package, but also the specificity of the vocabulary.

In the ADFA library, an undergraduate campus library of 160,000 monographs, the number of distinct keywords found in the MARC 650 field for the entire library collection was a little over 30,000. This would appear to support our hypothesis that only broader terms appear in the LCSH headings for books. Our most significant finding was that the addition of chapter level terms increased document retrieval by a dramatic 400%, with a not unacceptable increase in false drops. Nor was the system slowed down appreciably by the addition of the terms. However, it was clear that the OPAC end user interface was not designed to handle the increased number of books being retrieved. Users who were surveyed reported frustration at having to scroll through 50 to 100 screens of records.

The ADFA project enabled us to test the feasibility of the research being proposed here, and also helped us to refine our methodology.

IV. UPGRADING EXISTING SUBJECT ACCESS TOOLS (PROPOSED)

Given the background, we are currently seeking funding to enable us to continue our research by building and testing an improved keyword and subject access system for books.

We hope to develop a prototype that can successfully be integrated as a module in any existing OPAC. The prototype will be designed to build the subject headings and table of contents maps from bibliographic records actually being entered as new holdings in the OPAC. Therefore the maps will be dynamically updated as new material is added and should accurately reflect changing terminology.

Theoretical base: Vocabulary control tools that assist the user in obtaining the correct level of specificity are still relatively primitive, consisting mainly of alphabetical lists of keywords or at best a very limited display of narrower and broader terms. Micco, in her dissertation, analyzed the syndetic structure of LCSH, PRECIS and MeSH and found all of them lacking (Micco, 1980). Additional ammunition in explaining the failure of keyword access derives from the research on memory and cognition — the verbal context in which a word is learned can be very important in recall. If a word is learned while embedded in a particular semantic context (e.g., between two other words), free recall of that word will be much higher if the surrounding words are presented during the recall efforts (Baker & Santa, 1977).

Psychologists agree that our ability to recall is not nearly as great as our ability to recognize members of a set (Rubin & Kontis, 1983). We have obtained ample proof of this in our research on searching behavior. Human subjects typically have great difficulty and strenuously resist being asked to come up with a number of synonyms for their chosen topic. However, when presented with lists of options, they have no hesitation in selecting numerous subordinate concepts for their topic. Librarians accomplish this by browsing through the table of contents of relevant books. Our goal is to build a system that can provide this level of support to the end user of any OPAC.

V. METHODOLOGY: BUILDING THE SYSTEM OF SUBJECT ACCESS MAPS

The user interface we are proposing consists of a series of interconnected subject area maps that will graphically display the syndetic structure of the vocabulary in the system. It will be dynamically updated every time a book is added to the collection. There are three major components of the project:

1. The procedures for building and maintaining the subject area maps from the enhanced MARC records.
2. The procedures for managing the end user interface and particularly determining which maps to display and under what conditions.
3. In the case where the term or terms being sought are not found in the MARC records, we plan to refer the user to a comprehensive index to a set of basic reference books mounted on a CD-ROM disk and keyword searchable. Given a CD-ROM jukebox, it is entirely feasible that the user could then have full text access to the given reference work.

A. Building the Maps

First the MARC record for a new book is processed, and the enhanced subject access terms (ESP terms) drawn from the table of contents added according to the procedures developed in Phase II. Then each book will go through additional processing as follows:

1. *Extraction of terms:* The software will extract from the record the following tagged fields: title, subject headings, ESP terms and classification number.

2. *Selection of the anchor term:* For each book, the system will use a set of heuristics to determine the one compound term that best describes its contents. For example:

   a. When the term appears in both the title and the subject heading, then of course it is preferred.
   b. For conferences, workshops, etc., the title term is favored.
   c. If there is only one subject heading, of course it is selected.
   d. If several subject headings exist, favor the one which most closely fits with the classification number.

The expert system that will be making this determination will be also evaluating the class number, and its English equivalent, as well as title and subject headings. The goal here is to find the one best term to describe the "aboutness" of the book.

The anchor term selected in this manner will become the focal point of a frame which will be displayed as a subject area map of related relevant terms. The user will be able to browse through the chapter level terms when they request the map for the topic of their choice.

3. *Posting the dictionary entry for the anchor term:* Central to the whole system will be a dictionary table of all terms in the system, both chapter level headings and anchor terms. This dictionary will contain both single and compound terms since in many cases the anchor terms will be compound, e.g., artificial intelligence. The chief function of this table will be to provide a detailed entry for every term in the system showing the class numbers associated with the term, the anchor map number for each class number in which it has been selected as an anchor term, and also the map numbers in which the term appears as a chapter heading.

If the anchor term already has a map, the book counter for that map will be incremented by 1. Each map can then show how many books are associated with that term and that class number. The system is dynamic and interlinked, enabling the user to display the interconnections between terms. Chapter terms will be considered as narrower, anchor terms will be broader. Each anchor term can use its class number to move upwards to broader terms in the same general class or to related class numbers. Some terms will appear as anchor terms for a book, and elsewhere as chapters.

The central dictionary will reflect this. Any chapter term in one map that is also an anchor term elsewhere, will be marked to indicate this connection, e.g., a book on natural language has a chapter on parsing. We note in the central dictionary that there are also complete books on parsing. Therefore, the chapter term will be coded to show that complete books exist on this topic.

4. *Posting the dictionary entries for the chapter level headings:* A dictionary entry will be made for every chapter level term. The only additional burden on the cataloger will be that he will be asked to indicate bound terms such as "natural language" with special codes.

Every chapter-level heading for the book will then be added to the map frame for the anchor term chosen. These will then be available for display on the map. When a user selects a term that is not an anchor term, the table will indicate in what maps (books) that term has appeared as a chapter heading.

The system derived in this manner will consist of a series of frames or maps, one for each anchor term in the system. The dictionary table will provide the user with entry to the system. The design is simple and self-maintaining. The syndetic structure developed in this manner will reflect current usage in the literature. We will use Hypercard to manage the frames of text.

B. Building the End User Interface

We anticipate using the technology offered by hypercard systems to effectively manage and display the map frames generated in the manner described in the preceding paragraph.

To provide added structure to the system, the maps will also be linked by their classification numbers so that hierarchical displays can be generated at several levels of abstraction. This will make it possible for a data base user to narrow or broaden a search, by displaying either the anchor terms at different levels in the hierarchy or whole maps as desired.

The more difficult problem will be developing the expert system that will assist in determining which maps to display in response to the user query. We have identified two problems that will occur here.

1. If the term being searched is not found in the data dictionary generated from the table of contents terms then we must have the ability to switch to different sets of tools, just as the reference librarian does. For this step we are proposing a fully integrated set of vocabulary tools stored on CD-ROM, with a comprehensive index and Boolean searching capabilities. For example, if an art student were looking for material on the shadows of the drapes of the peplums on the Caryatids of the Erichthion, the search mechanism should be able to determine quickly that such material exists in an article in an art encyclopedia.
2. Given the phrase or search request submitted by the user, determining the weighting of the terms and deciding what to search and in what order can prove to be quite challenging. We have worked on developing a weighting system, but it will need a lot more field testing and experimentation.

VI. EVALUATION

We have already built a very small prototype. This was not difficult to do. The acid test will come when the size of the data base increases.

Stage 1: We will test it with several carefully selected sets of records clustered in a particular subject area, independently of the OPAC. The system will be deemed successful if it can extract the required information from the MARC record, post the entries in the dictionary, update the maps and then display them effectively. The user should be able to move freely about the system of maps to locate books on the topic selected and also obtaining information about chapters in each of the books.

Stage 2: We plan to build a test data base of 6,000 general acquisitions with enhanced subject terms. In this testing stage we will process all 6,000 records through the regular library catalog system and then make the system available for online searching by end users using the enhanced OPAC software. We will have to add menu options so that users can view the maps. We anticipate that the size of the system may create management problems and various modifications in the design may be necessary. It is very difficult to anticipate these difficulties without actually working with the data.

Stage 3: (Projected for the following year [if Stage 2 is a success]): We would like to attempt loading the entire library data base and evaluate the impact on the system. We do not yet have any idea of the total number of maps that will be generated, although we expect to use the test data of 6,000 to make reasonable predictions. This will obviously require a substantial investment in hardware and staff to become a reality.

Stage 4: Once we have the subject area maps moved into the OPAC, the next stage is to integrate it with the acquisitions systems so that the maps are dynamically updated every time a new book is added. For the front end, the expert system will select the type of material that is appropriate, and the terms for searching. If a term is not found in the central dictionary, we are proposing a 2-tier support system.

> *Step 1.* The expert system will search the general index to the basic collection of reference books maintained in the proposed CD-ROM jukebox and hopefully will then retrieve the full text of the material located in this way.
>
> *Step 2.* Failing success in the reference collection, the system will switch over to the thesauri for the periodical data bases and attempt to find it there.

VII. CONCLUSION

Until we have the hardware and software to develop a full scale test system, many of the interesting research questions that could be explored will have to remain unanswered. We have gone as far as is possible with the limited hardware available to us. The methodology for developing the subject area maps is interesting and valuable in and of itself. Its power will be greatly enhanced if we can also add the expert system components proposed.

Over ten years of research and testing have been devoted to developing the background and roots for this project. The potential contribution of this work to increase access to the content of the nation's libraries is unquestioned. At present librarians are resigned to the realization that 20% of their collections provide 80% of the users' satisfaction. With enhanced subject access and its promise of increasing retrieval 400% we may see more of the collection being used. There is also a very real concern that much of the world's recorded knowledge is being lost into a black hole due to the very inadequate retrieval provided by "brute force" keyword searching particularly when this is restricted to the keywords found in titles and subject headings.

The dividends to be reaped through the design of system generated aboutness and contents maps are potentially immense for both users and librarians.

REFERENCES

Baker, L. and Santa, J. L. "Semantic Integration and Context," *Memory and Cognition* 5: 151-43, 1977.

Books Are For Use. Final Report to the Council on Library Resources. Syracuse University, School of Information Studies. Subject Access Project. Pauline Atherton (Cochrane), Director. Syracuse, NY, 1978. ED156131. Pp. 177.

Haftner, Ruth. "The Performance of Card Catalogs: A Review of the Research," *Library Research* 1: 199-220, 1970.

Hudson, Judith and Walker, Geraldene. "The Year's Work in Technical Services Research, 1986," *Library Resources & Technical Services* 31 (December 1987): 275-86.

Kaske, Neal K. and Sanders, Nancy P. "On-line Subject Access: the Human Side of the Problem," *RQ* 20 (Fall 1980): 52-58.

Mandel, Carol A. and Herschman, Judith. "Online Subject Access—Enhancing the Library Catalog," *Journal of Academic Librarianship* 9 (3): 148-55, 1983.

Micco, Mary H. *An Exploratory Study of Three Subject Access Systems in Medicine: LCSH, MeSH, PRECIS.* Thesis. University of Pittsburgh, 1980.

O'Neill, Edward T. and Aluri, Rao. "Library of Congress Subject Heading Patterns in OCLC Monographic Records," *Library Resources and Technical Services* 25 (January/March 1981): 63-80.

Rubin, David C. and Kontis, Theda C. "A Schema for Common Cents," *Memory and Cognition* 11 (4): 333-41, July 1983.

Settel, Barbara, ed. *Subject Description of Books: A Manual of Procedures for*

Augmenting Subject Descriptions in Library Catalogs. Syracuse, NY: Syracuse University, School of Information Studies, 1977. Research study no. 3.

Sinkankas, George Martin. *An Investigation and Comparison of Three Associative Systems in a General Subject Heading List*. PhD dissertation, University of Pittsburgh, 1974.

Watstein, Sarah and Kesselman, Martin. "Artificial Intelligence: A High-Tech Bibliography," *Library Hi Tech Bibliography* no. 1 (1987): 1-9.

Simulation of the Reference Process, Part II: REFSIM, an Implementation with Expert System and ICAI Modes

James R. Parrott

SUMMARY. This paper is a continuation of a previous one in *The Reference Librarian*, exploring the advantages of a simulation (rather than expert system) approach to designing a system to relieve reference desk overload. Another paper examined the correlation between four expert systems and various reference models; it made several recommendations for future research. The ideas presented in those two earlier papers have now been implemented in a prototype system named REFSIM, which can be used by either client or librarian. REFSIM can simulate a reference librarian, a teacher of reference librarians and a client, singly or in combination. It has an expert-system consultation mode and several Intelligent Computer-Assisted Instruction (ICAI) modes.

The components and architecture of REFSIM are described in this paper. Details, including a sample transaction, are given for the expert system mode, which is to be used for consultation by library clients. An overview is supplied for two ICAI modes, which can be used to instruct clients or train reference librarians.

SIMULATION OF THE CONSULTATION PROCESS IN REFERENCE

In the last few years, the contemporary crisis in reference service has received a thorough and much deserved airing.[1,2] On the one hand, time and staffing are often inadequate to handle the large number of reference questions (many of them simple and repetitive). On the other hand, a significant number of transactions are

---

The author is Reference Librarian, The Library, University of Waterloo, Waterloo, Ontario, Canada N2L 3G1.

characterized by unsatisfactory answers, abrasive behaviour and few referrals by staff. To a large extent, current interest in reference expert systems can be seen as a response to this crisis.

A previous paper in *Reference Librarian*[3] explored the advantages of adopting a simulation perspective rather than an expert system perspective in creating a system to relieve reference desk overload. It was shown that this shift in perspective necessitates the simulation not only of the problem-solving skills of a reference librarian, but of the information-seeking behaviour of a client as well. It was argued further that such a system could assist not only at the reference desk, but also in case-oriented training for reference librarianship. In another paper,[4] four expert systems for reference work were described and compared with various theories of the reference process. (These systems, incidentally, have concentrated on consultational rather than instructional aspects of the reference process.) Interesting theoretical features that had not been implemented well or at all by any of the systems were identified. Based on this, recommendations were made for future areas of research in constructing reference expert systems. The present paper describes a prototype system with the objective of implementing those recommendations from a simulation perspective. The system has been named REFSIM to reflect the fact that it attempts to simulate not just the librarian, but the entire reference process. An interesting feature of REFSIM is its implementation of the recommendation to use the system's expertise knowledge base to drive Intelligent Computer-Assisted Instruction (ICAI) modes as well as the expert system consultation mode.

SIMULATION OF THE INSTRUCTIONAL PROCESS IN REFERENCE

Before going further, it may be useful to review why one might want to extend a reference-consultation expert system to handle instructional tasks. The principal reason is that reference librarians generally act not only as consultants but also as instructors at the reference desk. The relative importance of these two modes of service is, of course, a function of the specific reference environment and philosophy. For example, in a particular special library, librarians may put much less emphasis on instruction than in a particular academic library. Instruction in the reference process is, however, important to all reference librarians during at least one stage in their careers—when they themselves are being instructed at library school. An additional reason for including instructional tasks, therefore, is that it allows the creation of a system that may be of direct use in the training of reference librarians.

Computer-assisted instruction (CAI) systems have already achieved some success in helping library clients.[5] CAI modules have also been integrated with one reference expert system, ORA.[6] In addition, CAI has been used in teaching reference skills in the library science curriculum. Probably the most innovative systems of this type were constructed by Thomas P. Slavens[7,8] to address certain problems in teaching reference. Among the problems identified were the lack of individual instruction, varying levels of student sophistication, and limited opportunities for practice in reference service before graduation. Karen Y. Stabler[9] has recently reported a similar problem, namely, limited opportunities for practice in answering sample questions during in-service training. Slavens included two modes of instruction. The *drill-and-practice* mode presented and tested the library school student on information about reference service. Here the system simulated a tutor with the skills of an experienced reference librarian. The *inquiry* mode, on the other hand, allowed the library school student to practice reference skills by interacting with a library client simulated by the system.

All the CAI systems referred to above suffer from problems characteristic of traditional CAI systems. An extension of CAI known as Intelligent CAI (ICAI) has been developed to overcome these problems. In an article on intelligent tutoring systems (another term for ICAI), Darwyn R. Peachy and Gordon I. McCalla[10] point out that traditional CAI systems have trouble teaching effectively. This is because they require the student to follow a pathway along an inflexible tree structure in the lesson. In a recent review of research on ICAI, Christopher Dede[11] indicates that ICAI systems are able, by contrast, to "tailor content and method to the needs of an individual learner without being limited to a repertoire of prescribed responses." Dede divides ICAI systems into *tutors* and *coaches*. He also notes that using both these instructional approaches can create a very powerful learning environment. ICAI tutors are intended to give the student a foundation of descriptive knowledge covering the problem-solving skills being taught. ICAI tutors may be either presentation-oriented (presenting and testing knowledge) or Socratic (revealing and resolving paradoxes in the student's belief structure). ICAI coaches, on the other hand, provide the student with an opportunity to learn problem-solving skills by practicing in a realistic context, usually a simulated situation. It should be recognized that the pioneering research of Slavens was unique in that it did provide both tutor and coach modes, albeit using traditional CAI. The Slavens drill-and-practice mode was a presentation-oriented tutor in Dede's terminology, and the Slavens inquiry mode was a simulation-based coach.

A COMMON KNOWLEDGE BASE FOR CONSULTATION AND INSTRUCTION

As is pointed out in a paper by Harmon,[12] one of the components of an ICAI system is a domain knowledge system, which includes a knowledge base on the subject domain to be taught. Harmon indicates that this domain knowledge system could also function as an expert system or intelligent job aid. Hence, a knowledge base on the reference process could be used for both an ICAI system for reference instruction and an expert system for reference consultation. This twofold use of a knowledge base seemed both a natural and an efficient approach to system design for REFSIM. In fact, it has already been employed in systems for other disciplines. Probably the best example is the use of the MYCIN knowledge base on infectious diseases to drive GUIDON, an ICAI system for training experts in that area.

It should be noted, however, that experience with GUIDON has indicated that simply using the expertise knowledge base of an existing expert system to create an ICAI mode can cause problems.[13] A major problem is that an expert system can function reasonably well by applying a set of specific rules that do not concern themselves with overall strategy. In such a case, the system is using fairly superficial knowledge, rather than a deeper knowledge of the processes being addressed. People, unlike machines, find it easier to remember and apply a rule when it is presented as a logical consequence of a strategy. Clancey and Letsinger[14] therefore developed NEOMYCIN, a new version of MYCIN that includes not only specific rules, but also "meta-rules" for overall strategy and justification. From the NEOMYCIN knowledge base, they are developing GUIDON2, which should perform better, since it will give the students explanations citing not only specific rules, but also the strategies on which the rules are based. Because of these problems, the expertise knowledge base of REFSIM has been designed to include meta-rules. Consequently, when REFSIM is used in ICAI mode, reference processes can be presented through rules not only for specific tactics but also for overall strategy. This permits an effective use of the expertise knowledge base for both consultation and ICAI modes.

As mentioned above, the goal of REFSIM is to implement various aspects of reference theory by simulating the entire reference process. Varying the roles played by the system and by the person using it, and varying pedagogical strategy allow the system to operate in several modes. REFSIM has an expert system consultation mode that gives advice in answering reference questions. It also has three ICAI modes that give instruction in the reference process. The ICAI modes include: a presentation-oriented tutor, a Socratic tutor, and a simulation-based coach that behaves one way for library clients and another for librarians. The system uses frames, semantic nets, IF-THEN production rules and databases. A prototype of REFSIM running on an IBM PC-XT has been developed in Arity PROLOG by the author. A full version of the REFSIM knowledge base is being developed in collaboration with Linda C. Smith (Graduate School of Library and Information Science, University of Illinois) for eventual testing by library clients and library school students. In the discussion that follows, the components and architecture of the REFSIM knowledge base will be described. Next, details of the consultation mode of REFSIM will be given. Then the ICAI simulation-based coach mode and the ICAI Socratic tutor mode will be examined briefly.

REPRESENTING KNOWLEDGE ABOUT THE REFERENCE PROCESS

A knowledge base on the reference process must represent the kinds of knowledge that reference librarians have about the reference process. For the reference interview, that includes knowing typical language used by clients, typical kinds of information (subject area, geographical area, etc.) that have to be clarified by the librarian for different types of reference questions, and typical client attitudes and behaviour. For search strategy prescription, the kinds of knowledge include knowing that certain classes of reference tools can be prescribed for certain types of reference questions, and knowing characteristics of specific reference tools.

There are several techniques for representing knowledge in a computer, each suited to certain kinds of knowledge. Knowledge about language can be represented by a device called a *parser*, which takes English sentences and makes "sense" out of them. Such a device could therefore represent typical language used by clients in the reference process.

Knowledge about stable situations can be represented by *databases*, which consist of records of information, with each record organized into fields. Because the characteristics of specific reference tools are relatively stable, knowledge about them could therefore be represented by a database.

Knowledge about situations involving change can be represented by *frames*, which are organized into slots (like the fields in database records), the information in which can vary over time. Because the state of clarification (in the librarian's mind) of the information associated with a reference question can vary during the reference interview, that state of clarification could be represented by frames. Similarly, the state of the librarian's conception of a client's attitude and behaviour can change during the reference interview, and could therefore also be represented by frames.

Finally, knowledge about the taking of action can be represented by *rules*, which indicate that, if certain circumstances are true, then certain actions are appropriate. Because the prescription of certain classes of reference tools under certain circumstances implies recommending the taking of action, such prescriptions could therefore be represented by rules.

CONNECTIONS BETWEEN KNOWLEDGE BASE CONSTITUENTS

In REFSIM, first the parser determines the basic question type by scanning the client's question for characteristic words. Once this has been done, a frame corresponding to that question type is invoked. This frame handles the reference interview by asking the client questions to determine the value of each empty slot. The frame's changing state represents the system's evolving understanding of the nature of the client's request. (Further details about REFSIM frames for particular question types are given in a later section.) The reference interview ends when all the questions have been asked and the frame slots are therefore as full as possible.

The system then finds all the action-prescribing rules that satisfy both the question type and the values gathered by the associated frame. As will be seen, the REFSIM rules are in an IF-THEN format. The rules range from trivial (for directional transactions) to complex. Many of the REFSIM rules are really *meta-rules* (in the NEOMYCIN terminology). That is, they specify strategy or fairly general tactics. For example, "IF the client's motivation is writing a term paper, THEN consult appropriate periodical indexes."

By linking these meta-rules to *databases*, it becomes possible to make prescriptions appropriate to the specific situation. For example, by linking the above-mentioned meta-rule to a database of reference tools, and sending over information from the frame (e.g., about the subject area), it is possible to suggest the use of specific periodical indexes. It is clear that these meta-rules could also be linked to external databases, such as online catalogues, CD-ROM reference tools, and commercial online bibliographic databases. The system would then act as an intelligent front-end to these external databases.

NATURAL-LANGUAGE PARSER

Some natural-language parsers are syntactically oriented: that is, among other things they categorize the words in the sentence as nouns, verbs, adjectives, and so on. The natural-language parser in REFSIM is not syntactically oriented. Instead, it is a "fuzzy semantically-driven" parser like that used by Burton for an intelligent tutoring system known as SOPHIE.[15] It is fuzzy because unknown words can be skipped if the parser recognizes enough of the important words. It is semantically-driven since the parser looks for semantic entities like the concepts of "address" and "patent" rather than syntactic entities like nouns.

Parsing proceeds in REFSIM as follows:

1. The parser first searches for the occurrence of certain keywords (like "address" and "patent") that are characteristic of ready-reference questions.
2. The parser then attempts to determine the ready-reference question type in the following manner.
   a. If it finds a keyword, then it assumes this is the ready-reference question type. Next it examines the structure of the sentence to see if the basic keyword is modified in some way.
   b. If so, it identifies each modifier as such, and uses the prepositions and a database of some common modifiers to determine the type of modifier (e.g., subject or geographical).
   c. If it has trouble determining the type, it asks the user for semantic assistance.
   d. It then finds the ready-reference frame (see the next section) where the main slot matches the basic keyword already found.
   e. Next, it puts the appropriate modifiers from the sentence into the empty slots of the frame chosen.
   f. Finally, the frame asks questions to try to elicit information for slots still empty.
3. If the parser doesn't find a match on the ready-reference keywords, then it treats the question as potentially a substantive or holdings question in the following manner.

a. It looks for sentence constructions that are characteristic of substantive subject questions or of holdings questions (e.g., "I'm looking for some information on a medical topic," and "I'm having trouble finding a particular item in the catalogue.")
b. If it finds any of the proper sentence constructions, it checks for modifiers as in part (2.) above.
c. It then goes to the appropriate frame for the question type (e.g., subject substantive or holdings) and fills in empty slots with information from the modifiers in the original sentence.
d. As in (f.) of (2.) above, the system attempts to determine missing information.

REFERENCE INTERVIEW FRAMES

Below are given some details of the slot structures of frames for different types of reference questions. The distinction between the name of a slot (e.g., *subject area*) and its value or content (e.g., "biology") should be noted.

Slots for *directional* transaction frames include:

MAIN SLOT NAME	MAIN SLOT VALUES
directional info type	"info on typing rooms," "info on loans," etc.
SECONDARY SLOT NAME	SECONDARY SLOT VALUES
which library	"Arts," "Science," etc.
material type	"book," "periodical," etc.

Slots for *ready-reference* transaction frames include:

MAIN SLOT NAME	MAIN SLOT VALUES
rr question type	"address," "definition," "patent," etc.

SECONDARY SLOT NAME	SECONDARY SLOT VALUES
subject area	"biology," "philosophy," etc.
geographical area	"France," "U.S.A.," etc.

The set of secondary slots required for any ready-reference frame depends upon the value of the main slot.

Slots for *substantive* transaction frames include:

MAIN SLOT NAME	MAIN SLOT VALUES
subst question type	"complex subject search," "bibliographic verification"

SECONDARY SLOT NAME	SECONDARY SLOT VALUES
subject area	"economics," "physics," etc.
motivation	"writing a short report," "writing a term paper," etc.
acceptable answers	"data," "periodical articles," "critical reviews," etc.
prior action	"none," "tried catalogue," "online search," etc.

The substantive frames simulate the Taylor filters[16] and elements in the Lynch category scheme for the substantive-transaction reference interview.[17]

Slots for *holdings* transaction frames include:

MAIN SLOT NAME	MAIN SLOT VALUES
bibliographic form	"book," "book chapter," "conference paper," etc.

SECONDARY SLOT NAME	SECONDARY SLOT VALUES
user characteristics	"familiar with names of bibl. components," "not familiar..."
bibliographic details	[see below]

source of information	"abstract/index," "reference in book/paper," "a person," etc.
function	"this item is essential," "something else on subject would be OK," etc.
prior action	"asked reference librarian," "looked in another library," etc.
item previously used	"yes," "yes, but I forget how to use it," "no," etc.

Here we are simulating the elements in the Lynch category scheme for the holdings-transaction reference interview.[18] The secondary slots deserve some amplification, since they are not so straightforward as in the previous cases. "User characteristics" indicates whether the user understands the names of the various components of a reference for the given bibliographic form. "Bibliographic details" includes the bibliographic label for each component of the reference; this is necessary only if the client does not know the bibliographic form. "Source of information" is a slot that need not be filled in unless prior and present action are extensive and unsuccessful. "Function" refers to whether only the item in question will do or whether something else on the same subject might be substituted. It really tries to determine whether the bibliographic request masks a subject request. This slot is required under the same conditions as "source of information." "Prior action" indicates the type of search that has already been undertaken to locate the item. Finally, "item previously used" indicates whether the client has used an item before. If not, the system may offer an instructional module.

LIBRARIAN AND CLIENT FRAMES

Depending upon the mode, there are frames for the characteristics of the librarian, the client or both. A partial list of the slots for many frames is as follows:

SLOT NAME	SLOT VALUES
player modelled	"client seen by libn,"
	"libn seen by client"
subject skills	"good," "fair," "poor"
library skills	"good," "fair," "poor"
wants transaction control	"yes," "not sure," "no"

In the consultation mode, where the system plays the role of librarian, a librarian frame is not used, since the characteristics of the simulated librarian are assumed fixed. A client frame is used, however, to capture the librarian's (i.e., the system's) perception or estimation of the client at the keyboard. This frame is as above, with the first slot value "client seen by libn." It allows the system to tailor its interface to the client.

In the simulation-based coach mode with the system as client, the system plays the roles of client and experienced coach/librarian. There, the frame above is used to allow the novice librarian at the keyboard to choose the client characteristics. A coach/librarian frame is not used since the characteristics of the coach are assumed to be fixed. In addition, there is a frame for the novice librarian as perceived by the client; the frame is as above, with the first slot value "libn seen by client." This allows the client to respond to different characteristics in novice librarians. There is also a different kind of frame (a student frame) that allows the performance of the novice to be tracked and evaluated by the coach, so that remedial action can be prescribed. This frame records fine details of the novice librarian's performance as perceived by the coach/librarian.

STRATEGY PRESCRIPTION RULES

1. For *directional* transactions, the rules are trivial. They essentially send the request straight to a database integrating the kinds of information usually found in certain library publications.

2. For *ready-reference* transactions, the rules are implementations of several of the search tactics described by Marcia Bates[19] in a classic paper on the subject. These REFSIM rules specify how to take the information gathered by the natural-language interface and

the frames and link it to a database of reference tools to determine appropriate reference tools.

The Bates *PATTERN* tactic involves using a search technique that the librarian's experience has shown frequently helps with the request in question. This tactic has been implemented in REFSIM as a large set of IF-THEN rules that comprise the vast majority of search rules in REFSIM. An example is: "IF request is for address of person AND IF person is alive, THEN recommend directories of living people." Another example is: "IF request is for address of person AND IF person is alive, THEN recommend using periodical indexes to find a recent article [which may give an address] by person." These PATTERN rules are meta-rules specifying general procedures. They link to categories of tools in the database of reference tools, and send it information gathered by the frames, which allows the selection of specific reference tools.

The Bates *STRETCH* tactic involves using a tool for a purpose for which it was not intended. This means that the tool could contain the desired information, but is an unusual source to consult for it. The STRETCH tactic, unlike the PATTERN tactic, is implemented in REFSIM as a *single* meta-rule that operates by going directly to the database of reference tools. The STRETCH tactic is to be used only if appropriate PATTERN tactics do not exist or are not useful. The meta-rule is:

> IF a reference tool satisfying the frames has the desired info-type (e.g., address) AND at least one of the given info-types (e.g., institute name), AND the reference tool was not already found using a PATTERN meta-rule,
> THEN consult the tool for desired information (AND browse it, IF the given info-type is not indexed).

The Bates *SCAFFOLD* tactic involves consulting tools that will not themselves give the answer, but will give additional information that can be taken to other tools that *will* give the answer. Like the STRETCH tactic, the SCAFFOLD tactic is implemented in REFSIM as a single meta-rule that operates directly on the reference-tool database. Because of the complexity of the process, it is expected that REFSIM will usually handle this tactic better than a human intermediary. The meta-rule is:

> IF reference tool Y satisfying the frames has the desired info-type, but does not have any of the given info-types,
> THEN find another reference tool, X, that *does* have one of the given info-types that is an indexed field in X, AND has another info-type, A, that is the same as an indexed field, B, in tool Y,
> AND use the value of the given info-type as input to tool X, and use the output from info-type A as input to info-type B in tool Y to obtain the desired output.

The Bates *WEIGH* tactic assigns a weight to most other tactics to indicate the effectiveness and efficiency of using those tactics to solve a problem. REFSIM implements this by combining the weight for the effectiveness of each meta-rule and weights for the completeness of the reference tool's coverage. Finally, the *SORT* tactic sorts the tactics in the optimum order for recommending to the library client. REFSIM uses the results of applying the WEIGH tactic to effect this.

3. For *substantive* transactions, there are, in addition to the Bates tactics mentioned earlier, special meta-rules for strategy like the following:

> IF acceptable answer is very brief information, THEN recommend dictionaries, encyclopedias and handbooks.

> IF acceptable answer is easy-to-find material, THEN recommend catalogue.

> IF acceptable answer is periodical articles, THEN recommend periodical indexes.

> IF motivation is term paper,
> THEN recommend periodical indexes and catalogue.

> IF motivation is writing thesis,
> THEN recommend theses indexes.

4. For *holdings* transactions there are meta-rules for deducing the bibliographic form of a reference and for identifying its components. An example is:

> IF there are two consecutive titles, AND the last part of the reference contains a sequence of numbers or dates,
> THEN the reference is probably a periodical article or a book chapter, AND the second title is the title that should be looked up.

It has been argued that, to represent knowledge about physical processes adequately, it is necessary to do so in more than one way, i.e. to have "multiple viewpoints."[20] The holdings transaction too requires multiple viewpoints for its knowledge representation. The previous paragraph discussed the representation of bibliographic knowledge from the viewpoint of *deducing* the form and components of an already constructed reference. It is also useful, especially in the Socratic tutor to be discussed later, to represent bibliographic expertise from the viewpoint of *constructing* references. Therefore, REFSIM also includes rules indicating how references in various bibliographic forms and styles are constructed from bibliographic components. An example is:

> IF bibliographic form is periodical article, AND bibliographic style is University of Chicago,
> THEN the component sequence is author-in-inverted-form + article-title-in-quotes + periodical-title-underlined + volume-number + date-in-brackets + colon + pagination.

There are also rules that use certain frame values (e.g., values for prior action, source of information, function) to prescribe action when simple prescriptions for finding items fail. For example, the action prescribed might involve verifying the reference in some bibliographic tool.

DATABASES OF REFERENCE TOOLS, ETC.

1. For *directional* transactions, there is a database integrating the kinds of information usually found in certain library publications. Examples of the types of information include services, programs, policies and locations in the library system.

2. For *ready-reference* transactions, a database of reference tools plays a central role in prescribing strategy. Every reference-tool record has the following multiply-recurring structure: bibl-reference, ref-info-type, ref-scope, ref-indexed, ref-weight. The first of these fields, bibl-reference, corresponds to the bibliographic description of the reference tool. The remaining fields correspond to a highly structured subject description of the reference tool.

To illustrate the structure, we will examine the record structure for "Encyclopedia of Associations":

    bibl-reference = "Encyclopedia of Associations. . . ."
    ref-info-type[1] = "geographical area"
      ref-scope[1] = "U.S."
      ref-indexed[1] = "yes"
      ref-weight[1] = 1 (the default)
    ref-info-type[2] = "association name"
      ref-scope[2] = ""(not restricted)
      ref-indexed[2] = "yes"
      ref-weight[2] = .98
    ref-info-type[3] = "address"
      ref-scope[3] = "" (not restricted)
      ref-indexed[3] = "no"
      ref-weight[3] = 1 (the default)
    ref-info-type[4] = "subject area"
      ref-scope[4] = "" (not restricted)
      ref-indexed[4] = "yes"
      ref-weight[4] = 1 (the default)

The greater part of the record structure (all fields but the first) is devoted to a description of the subject matter of the reference tool. As may be seen above, every ref-info-type, such as "geographical area," has associated with it three values: ref-scope, ref-indexed and ref-weight. The first of these, ref-scope, is in fact a *value* for the ref-info-type that indicates the breadth of scope of the ref-info-type for that tool. For example, "U.S." is the geographical scope of the "Encyclopedia of Associations." The second one, ref-indexed, indicates whether the ref-info-type is indexed in the tool. The final one, ref-weight, is a measure of the completeness of coverage of that ref-info-type in the tool. In our example above, we are saying that we believe that all geographical areas in the U.S., but only about 98% of all associations are covered in the tool.

The ref-scope fields mentioned above present an interesting problem, because one scope value can be nested inside another. For example, the geographical scope of a reference tool may be "Europe." A reference librarian would understand this scope to include the scope "France" as well. To ensure that a search for a tool with French coverage would also retrieve tools with European coverage, it is necessary to encode this kind of information about geographical hierarchies somewhere in the system. Clearly it would be tedious to handle the problem individually for each record. It makes more sense to record the hierarchical relationships between scope values in one place in the system. Consequently, *semantic nets* have been set up to link together the *values* that can be taken on by the ref-scope fields. The links between these scope values are the broader-than and narrower-than relationships typically used in thesauri. It should be noted that semantic nets are also used for other ref-scope fields like "subject area" and "date."

REFSIM also maintains a small database of sample values for slots in the reference interview frames. Examples are *personal name* = "Edward Frankland" and *subject area* = "chemistry." These are used in the simulation-based coaching ICAI mode. There is also a "student-bug" database, indicating tactics that are likely to be confused with one another.

3. For *substantive* transactions, the databases required are the same as for ready-reference transactions.

4. For *holdings* transactions, REFSIM has a small "student-bug" database, which points from a given bibliographic form to other forms with which students are likely to confuse it. There is

also a small database of sample bibliographic components (e.g., *author name* = "Smith, John R.").

CONSULTATION MODE (EXPERT SYSTEM MODE)

We will now examine an actual transaction, one in which a library client wants advice on searching for information. Before the transaction proper begins, the user specifies the mode of operation. Here the user chooses the consultation (advice-giving) mode. The system next conducts the reference interview with the client, and then prescribes strategy. Transcript 1 should be consulted for the sample transaction that we will be considering.

The client enters a request at the keyboard. The system's parser examines the request, finds the ready-reference phrase "biographical information," and classifies the request as a ready-reference question with type "biography." It then invokes the "biography" frame, which includes empty slots entitled *subject area*, *occupation* (work sector), *geographical area*, and *alive* (whether the subject is alive). The system proceeds to ask questions designed to find values for these empty slots. As can be seen from Transcript 1, it determines from the client that *alive* is dead, *subject area* is chemistry, *occupation* is academic, and *geographical area* is Britain.

Having completed the reference interview, the system performs an intermediate calculation, but does not display the results on the screen. In this calculation, the system searches for rules that satisfy the frame values that were determined in the reference interview. The rules that it finds suggest using the following classes of tools in this order:

— biographical dictionaries of dead people
— contemporary encyclopaedias
— modern encyclopaedias
— indexes to contemporary serials

The system then sends this information about classes of tools over to a database on reference tools. The system also sends over the complete frame information, in case it contains additional useful data (e.g., *subject area* and *geographical area*) for choosing among

> ## TRANSCRIPT 1
>
> ## CONSULTATION MODE
>
> ### Reference Interview
>
> *Client*: I'm looking for some biographical information on Edward Frankland.
> *System*: Is he still alive?
> *Client*: No.
> *System*: Do you know his field of work?
> *Client*: He was a chemist.
> *System*: Did he work in the industrial, government or academic sector?
> *Client*: Academic.
> *System*: Do you know where he lived?
> *Client*: In Britain.
>
> ### Search Strategy Prescription
>
> *System*: Use the tools below in the order given:
>
> 1. "Dictionary of Scientific Biography"
> 2. "Dictionary of National Biography"
> 3. "Encyclopaedia Britannica (old eds.)"
> 4. "Encyclopaedia Britannica (current eds.)"
> 5. Indexes to serial publications of the Royal Society of London (look for obituaries)
> 6. "Index to Biographical Fragments in Unspecialized Scientific Journals"

reference tools. As a result, the system identifies six tools, which it then recommends to the client.

SIMULATION-BASED COACH

One of the ICAI modes is a simulation-based coach, which simulates a library client and also a coach who teaches reference librarians. This mode bears some resemblance to the case-method dialogue approach used by Clancey in GUIDON.[21]

To begin, the person (say, a novice librarian) at the keyboard chooses the mode, here the simulation-based coach. The librarian then indicates the category of question for which training is required. The coach next invokes the appropriate frame and fills its slots with randomly chosen values. Then the system as client asks the preliminary question, to which the librarian responds by conducting the reference interview. When the librarian asks a question clearly intended to clarify some slot value of the frame, the system reveals the appropriate slot value, and adds to the librarian's score for the reference interview. This continues until the librarian terminates the interview.

Next, the system as coach uses its full set of slot values to calculate an ideal set of search tactics in optimum order. It then creates a new set of tactics, by adding inappropriate tactics and randomizing their order. It presents them to the librarian, asking that useful choices be made in optimum order. After the librarian responds, the coach compares its own prescriptions with those of the librarian. It indicates errors of omission, commission and ordering, and so assesses errors in understanding the *principles* of prescribing broad classes of reference tools. The process is then carried one step further—to the prescription of specific reference tools. There, the evaluation assesses errors in understanding the *scope* of particular reference tools.

After each question tried, the coach records errors in understanding, some concerning specific tools, others concerning general principles. With each new question, the coach looks for patterns in the librarian's history of errors, and then prescribes remedial action, either in the form of questions or review of material already covered.

SOCRATIC TUTOR

Another ICAI mode is a Socratic tutor mode similar to that used by Stevens, Collins and Goldin in WHY.[22,23] In this mode, the system simulates a tutor who teaches by revealing contradictions in the student's belief structures.

As before, the person sitting before the terminal chooses the mode, here the Socratic tutor mode. The person then indicates the category of question for which training is required. The coach then invokes the appropriate frame and fills its slots with randomly chosen values. It then calculates all appropriate tactics and specific tools resulting from the tactics and frame values. Next it chooses some tactic or tool as a testing point. It asks whether the tactic or tool in question is appropriate. The person answers. The tutor proceeds to ask questions to determine the underlying basis for the decision (even if the answer was correct). For example, if the person gives a necessary but insufficient condition for something to be true, the tutor provides a counter-example, and asks the person to identify the additional condition or conditions that are necessitated. As with the simulation-based coach, the tutor adds to the history of the student's errors, and uses it to choose remedial action.

CONCLUSIONS

REFSIM is a prototype system with the objective of using a simulation perspective to implement several recommendations made in an earlier paper. The implementation of those recommendations by REFSIM will now be summarized.

1. *User modelling*. The user model in the consultation mode tailors the interface to the client. In the ICAI modes, there are several user models. One user model tailors the interface to the user (the person being instructed). In addition, the simulation-based coach allows a novice librarian being instructed to alter the interface somewhat by choosing the characteristics of the client played by the system. The final ICAI user model is, properly speaking, a student model. It helps track the progress of the person being instructed and determines which material or questions to present.
2. *Determining acceptable answers*. REFSIM uses its frames to gather information on acceptable answers as laid out in the Lynch category schemes.
3. *Problem of prior action*. REFSIM also uses its frames to

gather information on prior action by the client as in the Lynch category schemes.
4. *Holdings transactions*. Following the example of Lynch, the holdings and substantive transactions are given balanced treatment in REFSIM. The holdings transactions are implemented using the Lynch category schemes.
5. *SCAFFOLD tactic*. The Bates SCAFFOLD tactic has been implemented in REFSIM by a meta-rule that operates on a database of reference tools. The record structure of the latter has been set up to facilitate the identification by the meta-rule of "scaffold" tools. REFSIM is expected to perform more efficiently in this task than most human intermediaries.
6. *WEIGH and SORT tactics*. The Bates tactics for evaluating and ranking the effectiveness of other search tactics are implemented using weights for effectiveness of meta-rule strategy and completeness of tool coverage.
7. *ICAI use of the knowledge base*. REFSIM puts considerable emphasis on the use of the expertise knowledge base to drive various ICAI modes for instructing library clients and librarians-in-training. Three modes of instruction are allowed, promising a powerful learning environment.
8. *Front end capabilities*. Since REFSIM separates its strategy meta-rules from its reference-tool database, it can act as a front end to any external bibliographic database with a compatible record structure.

In conclusion, the prototype system REFSIM implements some important features of the reference process that have not yet been well explored in knowledge-based reference systems. Probably the most striking of these features is the integration of consultation and instruction. By using techniques drawn from the promising new area of ICAI, REFSIM is able to use its knowledge base on the reference process for both purposes. Clearly, it is easier to justify the time-consuming construction of such a knowledge base, if the system will also alleviate the burden that instructional tasks can impose on a busy department. It is therefore expected that, as reference expert systems become more commonplace, so too will companion ICAI systems.

REFERENCES

1. Miller, William. (May 1984). What's wrong with reference: Coping with success and failure at the reference desk. *American Libraries, 15*, 303-306, 321-322.
2. Hernon, Peter et al. (May 1987). Library reference service: An unrecognized crisis—A symposium. *Journal of Academic Librarianship, 13*, 69-80.
3. Parrott, James R. (Spring 1988). Simulation of the reference process. *Reference Librarian, 21*, 189-207.
4. Parrott, James R. (1988). Implementation of reference models in expert systems. In Aluri, Rao & Riggs, Don (Eds.), *Expert systems in libraries*. Norwood, NJ: Ablex Pub. Corp. (in press).
5. Williams, Mitsuko, & Davis, Elisabeth B. (1982). Computer-assisted instruction: An overview. In Oberman, C. & Strauch, K. (Eds.), *Theories of bibliographic education*. New York: Bowker. pp.171-191.
6. Parrott, James R. (September 1986). Expert systems for reference work. *Microcomputers for Information Management, 3*, 155-171.
7. Slavens, Thomas P. (April 1970). *The development and testing of materials for computer-assisted instruction in the education of reference librarians. Final report*. Washington, D.C.: U.S. Department of Health, Education and Welfare, Office of Education, Bureau of Research. (ED 039 902) iv, 178p.
8. Starks, David D., Horn, Barbara J., & Slavens, Thomas P. (July-August 1972). Two modes of computer-assisted instruction in a library reference course. *Journal of the American Society for Information Science, 23*, 271-277.
9. Stabler, Karen Y. (Spring 1987). Introductory training of academic reference librarians: A survey. *RQ, 26*, 363-369.
10. Peachy, Darwin R., & McCalla, Gordon I. (January 1986). Using planning techniques in intelligent tutoring systems. *International Journal of Man-Machine Studies, 24*, 77-98.
11. Dede, Christopher. (April 1986). A review and synthesis of recent research in intelligent computer-assisted instruction. *International Journal of Man-Machine Studies, 24*, 329-353.
12. Harmon, Paul. (1987). Intelligent job aids: How AI will change training in the next five years. In Greg Kearsley (Ed.), *Artificial Intelligence and Instruction: Applications and Methods*. Reading, MA: Addison-Wesley. pp.165-190 (see especially p.170).
13. Clancey, William J., & Letsinger, R. (1981). NEOMYCIN: Reconfiguring a rule-based expert system for application to teaching. In *Proceedings of the 7th International Joint Conference on Artificial Intelligence, 1981*. pp.829-836.
14. Ibid.

15. Sleeman, Derek H., & Brown, John Seely. (1982). Introduction: Intelligent tutoring systems. In Sleeman, D. & Brown, J.S. (Eds.), *Intelligent tutoring systems*. London: Academic Press; 1982. pp.1-11.

16. Taylor, Robert S. (May 1968). Question negotiation and information seeking in libraries. *College and Research Libraries, 29*, 178-194.

17. Lynch, Mary Jo. (April 1978). Reference interviews in public libraries. *Library Quarterly, 48*, 119-142.

18. Ibid.

19. Bates, Marcia J. (July 1979). Information search tactics. *Journal of the American Society for Information Science, 30*, 205-214.

20. Stevens, Albert, Collins, Allan, & Goldin, Sarah E. (1979). Misconceptions in student's understanding. *International Journal of Man-Machine Studies, 11*, 145-156. Also reprinted in: Sleeman, D. & Brown, J.S. (Eds.), *Intelligent tutoring systems*. London: Academic Press; 1982. pp.13-24. (see especially p.24.)

21. Clancey, William J. (1979). Tutoring rules for guiding a case-method dialogue. *International Journal of Man-Machine Studies, 11*, 25-49. Also reprinted in: Sleeman, D. & Brown, J.S. (Eds.), *Intelligent tutoring systems*. London: Academic Press; 1982. pp.201-225.

22. Stevens, Albert, & Collins, Allan. (1977). The goal structure of a Socratic tutor. In *Proceedings of the Annual Conference of the Association for Computing Machinery, October 1977, Seattle*. pp.256-263.

23. Stevens, Collins and Goldin, 1979, op. cit.

Reference Expert Systems: Humanizing Depersonalized Service

Dana E. Smith

SUMMARY. The delivery of library reference service can be practically supplemented through the appropriate incorporation and use of software tools commonly referred to as expert systems. The level of support such systems can afford the reference service organization is dependent on the degree of complexity characteristic of the rule-based programming techniques used to develop a particular system and the size of its knowledge database. Since most expert systems are designed to simulate the process of problem-solving practiced by an expert in a given field, an expert system designed to fully emulate library reference work must have the potential to respond to a wide subject range of questions with varying degrees of response adequacy. The widespread development of expert systems with this type of potential is limited due to the tremendous personnel and hardware costs currently associated in the design and application of systems of this size. Most locations utilizing some form of reference expert system have applied a compromised, more cost-efficient approach in this area. The following describes a micro-computer-based reference expert-type system that has emerged due to this needed compromise.

WHAT IS AN EXPERT SYSTEM?

The British Computer Society's committee of specialists on expert systems has devised and approved a formal definition of what

---

The author is the Undergraduate Librarian, Purdue Undergraduate Library, Stewart Center, Purdue University Libraries, W. Lafayette, IN 47907.

© 1989 by The Haworth Press, Inc. All rights reserved.

constitutes an expert system. They have determined that

> an expert system is regarded as the embodiment within a computer of a knowledge-based component from an expert skill in such a form that the system can offer intelligent advice or take an intelligent decision about a processing function. A desirable additional characteristic, which many would consider fundamental, is the capability of the system, on demand, to justify its own line of reasoning in a manner directly intelligible to the enquirer. The style adopted to attain these characteristics is rule-based programming.[1]

To this extent, the distinguishing characteristics of an expert system, unlike conventional computer applications, are in the manner in which pertinent knowledge in the database is addressed and utilized.

Most conventional computer programs organize the pertinent knowledge in the database on two levels. In this respect, the pertinent knowledge or data and the method for manipulation of this data through the program application are integrated. In an expert system, knowledge is organized on three levels including the database, the knowledge-base, and the control structure to determine how to use the system's knowledge. If constructed properly, the interactive process or utilization of these three levels of knowledge will simulate the problem-solving process employed by human experts. The typical expert system will accomplish this feat through a developmental procedure of "if-then" relationships to construct rule networks determined by user input against the working memory of the system. It does this by using, firstly, a dialog module to elicit the nature of the problem from the user; secondly, a knowledge-base in the form of a set of rules of thumb that an expert would normally follow; and finally an inference engine that specifies how to apply the rules of thumb to the data gathered from the user in order to arrive at a solution.[2]

The application, use and performance of expert systems has received considerable attention in recent years within various specialized disciplines. Ultimate application and use of such systems is, conceivably, limitless. Expert systems have been successfully used to diagnose illness; locate precise drilling sites for oil and precious metals; offer chemical diagnosis; plan and design roads, buildings, bridges, and aircraft; and perform complex analyses for troubleshooting microcircuitry. In this respect, the application, use, and performance of an expert system is limited only by the degree of sophistication represented in the three levels of organized knowledge characteristic of the system. In short, if the global database or working memory of the system can adequately track input data for the current problem, and the knowledge-base can activate "if-then" rule networks with the input data, and the inference engine successfully organizes and controls the steps taken to solve the problem, then the system becomes a reliable, intelligent consultant.

EXPERT SYSTEMS IN REFERENCE WORK

The user-interactive expert system operates with conditions very similar to those found in the traditional reference interview and question negotiation process. In the simulation of this process, the expert system can be a valuable resource when applied to a situation in which a large number of possible alternatives must be investigated to answer a question. The system becomes even more valuable and efficient when the number of possible alternatives for answering a question is limited. The operational characteristics and potential application for expert systems of this nature should provide those engaged in the delivery of information service with practical advantages. For example, successful applications of this sort could allow reference personnel to refer certain types of inquiries to this alternative resource so they could concentrate their time on the more complex, resource-intensive reference questions determined as beyond the scope of the supporting computer system. This capability could lessen the need for professional service for routine inquiries, provide a reasonable alternative for service when reference personnel are not immediately available, and result in better overall service with fewer demands on all involved.

The ramifications for incorporation and use of such systems in the delivery of reference service can be an exciting and sobering prospect all at the same time. As a means for coping with the tremendous demands of the information explosion of this decade, expert system application is very intriguing. On the other hand, the essential criteria inherent in the development of expert systems for libraries presents some major obstacles.

DEVELOPING THE REFERENCE EXPERT SYSTEM

In the literature regarding the development of reference expert systems, it becomes quickly apparent that the final design is inextricably related to the personnel and financial resources available. No matter what the size or complexity of the final product, it is commonly recommended that staff identify what specific aspects of the reference process are readily and sensibly transferrable to an automated system. This recommendation is critical, since it is through this exercise that the nature and format of any further development will materialize. To accomplish this, an analysis of the tasks performed throughout the reference process is necessary. Once this analysis has been conducted, it will be much easier to decide what, if any, tasks can be transferred to another methodology, given the available resources.

In a typical reference transaction, the following actions could be partially or fully taken to answer a question:

1. Conduct the initial reference interview to determine the type and scope of the user's question.
2. Consider question solution possibilities against the range of reference resources pertinent to the type and scope of the user's question.
3. Identify appropriate reference resources and rank them for overall usefulness to satisfy the requirements of the user's specific inquiry.
4. Verify that initial reference interview question requirements have been addressed with the selected reference resource(s).
5. Renegotiate user's question and/or explain use of selected reference resource(s).

Clearly, the variables and range of actual tasks performed by the reference librarian in the process of finding factual information and/or conducting an extended literature search can become very involved. Like snowflakes, no two reference transactions are identical. In the process of providing reference service, reference librarians will construct their own unique agendas for satisfactorily answering a question, based on the realm of resource possibilities and their own level of experience and expertise. Those steps or tasks performed in the reference librarian's agenda for answering a question constitute those unique variables which need to be captured and simulated within the reference expert system design and operation. The relationship of these variables to the local expertise for successfully automating this process will determine to what extent potential reference expert system applications can be expected in a particular library.

Given these considerations, the factors limiting the prospect for development and application of a reference expert system for many libraries may seem insurmountable. Unfortunately, the majority of libraries do not have the necessary hardware and software programming support to simulate all the variables that could reasonably pertain to the interactive process for answering a reference question. In order to account for all the possible variables and simulate the expert-level decision-making process of a reference librarian, the completed reference expert system's knowledge-base could be very costly to produce and maintain, making this prospect out of reach for many library locations.

It may seem evident that the major obstacle to widespread development and use of reference expert systems has been the costs associated with the type and size requirements of the hardware and software needed to support such systems. It is likely, however, that future technological advances in this area will allow for fully integrated, all-encompassing reference expert systems to become more widespread as they become more financially feasible. The impact of such systems on the library profession and the overall nature of the delivery of reference service should prove to be very interesting. Whether this impact holds positive or negative implications for the profession is yet to be determined. Unfortunately, what appears to have already been determined is that library professionals will once again be relegated to a position wherein they must buy into rather than build into the potential developments in this area.

There is, however, a practical and economically prudent alternative. This alternative allows library professionals to develop their own site-specific requirements for expert system applications, gives the opportunity to realize the service advantages of this technology, and provides a location to experience the potential impact of such systems independent of externally motivated, controlling factors. This capability can also provide the library some leverage for a more proactive posture in its response to the heavy service demands of the information explosion of this decade. The process for development of this application is not difficult; it is flexible to meet the current and potential information needs of the library's end-users, and utilizes resources available in most libraries.

SITE-SPECIFIC REFERENCE EXPERT SYSTEM DEVELOPMENT

The widespread incorporation and use of microcomputer technology in libraries has provided the opportunity for a relatively inexpensive, flexible alternative on which to develop and apply useful reference expert systems. Microcomputers can be an effective compromise between the limitations of large-scale computer applications and the changing information needs of the end-user community. Microcomputers allow for programs to be customized, as determined by the local, unique service requirements and ultimate use of recorded data. Such microcomputer-assisted systems can directly support delivery of basic reference service, extend service when library personnel are not available, and provide management with useful data for overall library planning.

The use of microcomputers to support site-specific reference service objectives has been successfully incorporated in a small number of libraries. In 1983, the Purdue University Undergraduate Library introduced its Reference and Information Station for public use.

The development and ultimate use of this program was determined by a desire to acquire more information concerning the interaction of users with library collections and services, and to ease the demands for service at the Reference and Information Desk on routinely requested information. The initial design of the program was determined through an analysis of the type and nature of the questions presented at the reference desk. This analysis provided an understanding of the question content and method of interaction with available reference resources that were most often encountered by reference personnel. This analysis revealed that it was possible to reflect the most frequently requested general-interest topics of users with nine main categories. Once these nine had been identified, further question analysis showed the need for up to nine additional sub-categories, in which more specific information regarding the main categories was represented. In the nine sub-categories, an explanatory text screen was designed to allow for more elaborate descriptions, based on the user's specific menu selection process and area of inquiry. (In some cases, fewer than nine sub-categories were used.)

When all the main and sub-category descriptors had been determined, a program was written that would allow users to select any one of the main topics, select sub-category alternatives, and obtain the appropriate informational text screen. Through this menu process of prompts and responses, users are able to acquire information pertaining to specific questions they might have. Figure 1 represents the descriptors ultimately made available to users through the menu selection process. The program was written to guide the user to general information on library services, or, through the Reference and Index topics, to provide them with specific examples of library resources that could assist them in their introductory work in a particular subject area. The Reference and Index topic portions of the program provide detailed information regarding titles, call numbers, and locations of these materials depending on the user's subject interests. Presenting information in this format provides users an alternative resource by which to become aware of useful information in the area of their subject interest, receive information regarding library policies and procedures for certain service areas, or simply acquire directions to appropriate areas of the building.

This program capability is available at any time the library is open. It has served a useful purpose in providing extended reference service and has been a valuable resource in support of basic instruction in use of library materials. The "if-then" rule networks of the program are determined by the pre-described main and sub-category descriptors and are activated by the user's methodology of

Figure 1. represents the main category and corresponding sub-category selection possibilities provided users of the Purdue Undergraduate Library's Reference and Information Station. Each sub-category selected produces an appropriate informational text screen.

Directions	1. Bookstall	21. Catalogs (College)	
	2. Bookstorage	22. Reference Tools (College)	
	3. Copiers	23. Company Notebooks	Colleges
	4. Film Library	24. Reference Tools (Company)	Companies
	5. Group Study Rooms	25. Copiers	Copiers
	6. ISC	26. Placement Interview Schedule	
	7. Library Instruction Room		
	8. Newspapers	31. Catalogs	
	9. Periodical Room	32. Circulation/Scheduling	
		33. Equipment	
	11. Bookstall	34. Filmographies	Films, etc.
	12. College	35. ISC	
	13. Company	36. ISC Catalog	
	14. Film Library	37. Pick-up & Return	
Catalogs	15. ISC	38. Previewing	
	16. Reference	39. Reference	
	17. Serials/Periodicals		
	18. UGRL Books		
	19. Union		

Indexes
41. Mag Index/Readers' Guide
42. Newspapers
43. Biography
44. Business
45. Comm/Speeck
46. Education
47. Literature
48. Humanities/Social Sciences
49. Sciences/Sports

51. Back Issues
52. Indexes
53. Location
54. Microfilm
55. Newsbank
56. Wall Street Journal

Newspapers

Periodicals
61. Book Storage Unit
62. Catalogs
63. Locations
64. Microfilm
65. Periodical Room
66. Readers' Guide

Reference
71. Biographical Sources
72. Company Info
73. Dictionaries
74. Encyclopedias
75. Government Sources
76. Maps
77. Phone Numbers
78. Reference Catalog
79. Term Paper Topics

Reserves
81. Circulation
82. Company Notebooks
83. Exams
84. Lecture Notes
85. Policies
86. Reserve Books

menu selection. The network is supported by the principles found in the forward-chaining process characteristic of larger reference expert system designs, but on a smaller scale and in a less sophisticated manner. This procedure is somewhat enhanced by the insertion of an optional menu choice prior to or after each menu selection: the simple question, "Has your question been answered? (Y/N)." Depending on the response, the user will then be provided a further interactive opportunity: "Return to the Main Menu? (Y/N)," "Return to the Previous Menu? (Y/N)," or "Quit? (Y/N)."

In the final program design, it became apparent that not all subjects or general interests of users could be accommodated. An additional need was recognized for users to provide feedback to the microcomputer, and a way of doing this was developed and incorporated. If users did not find the appropriate information, or needed more information than was presented by the program, they could call a "suggestion box" feature to input their unique requirements, such as the nature of their question, a comment or suggestion, and their name, address, and phone number.

This information is recorded on a secure file maintained on the disk supporting the program in the microcomputer's drive. It can then be printed and/or reviewed on the screen by reference personnel at a designated time. Reference personnel may thus direct their attention to specific questions and consult with the individuals. This aspect of the program allows for questions to be entered at times when reference personnel are not available, such as nights and weekends, or when the Reference and Information Desk is closed. This feature also serves as a useful feedback mechanism regarding information requested but not found in the content of the program. This user-directed enhancement can be used by staff to determine areas for program content revision, and to monitor new subject areas of expressed interest. It provides an insight into the needs and interests of individuals who are willing to interact with this format, but are reluctant to pose questions at a reference desk for whatever reasons.

The program also incorporates a hidden statistical sub-routine, transparent to users, to provide library managers with data regarding the type and nature of user interaction with the program. This statistical subroutine accumulates data generated from the input selection and use of the program's menu alternatives to depict the pathway followed by the user through the program. This subroutine collects recorded use data to produce a report on which categories are most frequently requested, whether the user received satisfactory results from his menu selection, and at what point the user might have called the suggestion box while working with the program. The report that is generated allows the relative uses of each pathway to be assessed to determine which areas of the library are of most interest to users and whether the program content provided them with sufficient information to satisfy their needs—data useful in the library's planning process.

Information acquired regarding use within the main topic areas of Indexes, Periodicals, and Reference provides the ability to learn more about the user's specific subject interests. This information can be useful for planning special workshops in various subject disciplines. The workshops can be directed at reference personnel or incorporated as an area for special attention in the library's user instruction program. The accumulated data can also serve to determine which aspects of the collection are receiving heavy use. This information, in connection with data acquired from direct interaction with users, provides insights that can be used for collection analysis and development.

Monitoring the users' suggestions and questions in the suggestion box file provides another means of learning what information users most frequently or infrequently request. This can further assist in collection development or weeding projects. It helps to determine the subject areas (and corresponding instructors) of the library instruction program. Data acquired regarding use of other main and sub-category menu selections can be interpreted to ensure that building direction descriptions and library policies and procedures are adequately presented.

The program also has the ability to reveal on which day of the week the heaviest interaction with the program occurs. This information can assist in monitoring building and/or reference activity when the reference desk is closed, and provides an insight for possible staff scheduling adjustments. When the program is not in use, the screen "idles" with an eye-catching graphic display to attract users' attention and entice further involvement.

This program has proven to be a valuable alternative to individualized attention for routine inquiries. It affords a flexible, inexpensive alternative to meet demands for service when reference personnel are too busy or unavailable. There is, however, a major limitation to the application and use of this reference expert-like system design. The primary problem with this and other similar programs utilizing microcomputers is that they have been designed to accommodate unique, site-specific requirements in support of reference objectives. In this respect, they are not readily transferrable to other library locations. Like snowflakes, no two libraries are alike. The specific service objectives of each library, and the information requirements of its end-user community, make a local customizing capability imperative. Even though microcomputers support reference expert systems on a scale that is realistic for many libraries, the programming requirements necessary to develop even the most basic system may not be a readily available resource.

In consideration of this problem, the Reference and Information Station program design has recently been re-programmed to allow for site-specific, custom enhancement of all its operational characteristics. This can be accomplished at any location and does not require the developer of the final product to have any programming experience. The program has been written to run on both Apple and IBM microcomputers and compatibles requiring minimal memory and one disk drive. The software for customizing this application is essentially an authoring software, allowing the developers of the site-specific product to insert their own main and sub-category descriptors with a menu design and selection process of their own determination. The corresponding text screen to provide further elaboration on these categories is blank and can be filled in as necessary.

The program supplies the developer with up to 81 blank information screens that can be used in full or in part to custom-tailor main and sub-category topic directories. These categories can be designed in any configuration to assist users with reference, directional, and/or policy-related questions. The program routines perform the interactive process of chaining screens automatically. A screen editor function allows for easy development and/or revision of any part of the program content. Program main and sub-category descriptors and the information supplied on the corresponding text screens can be revised as needed to allow for changes in service or to accommodate newly perceived end-user requirements. This process can be accomplished without conducting a complete rewrite of the original program design.

The program also includes the capability for the aforementioned statistical sub-routine to be enacted. This routine can be turned on or off while the program is in operation, so that data can be recorded only at those times the library determines it to be necessary. The suggestion box feature of the program can also be turned on or off. This function to acquire user input is automatic and built in to the program's design. If enacted, the prompt for the user to call the suggestion box will appear at the bottom of each screen display; if not enacted, the prompt is not presented. When the final program outline is completed by the local developer, the program will automatically add the graphics screen to its operation to entice user interaction.

The program can assist in other applications due to its flexibility and the fact that development is not a one-time procedure. The actual source program can be used to design as many programs as may be necessary for a location. In this respect, the source program development disk serves as the foundation from which all further programming is created. The source program disk is not the public use program disk. A separate, locally created program disk serves this purpose, which allows a site to design as many operating programs as it might need. Specific point-of-use microcomputer stations can be created to describe certain resources in detail and/or make program content available to an expanded end-user community. This could be a desirable feature for a location wanting to experiment with CAI-type library instruction as an alternative means for supporting certain aspects of a library's instruction program.

Although this program's features and capabilities may not adhere to the precise definition of an expert system, it does allow a specific library to use microcomputers easily and inexpensively to assist in the delivery of reference service. Each program's content is limited only by the basic microcomputer configuration. Its application, however, is intended to utilize the expert input of its developer through flexible design and revision. To this extent, program application is restricted only by librarians' imagination and their site-specific service objectives.

REFERENCES

1. Naylor, Chris. "Build Your Own Expert System for the IBM-PC and Compatibles," *Sigma Press*, Wilmslow, England, c. 1987, pg. 1.
2. Parrott, James R. "Expert Systems for Reference Work," *Microcomputers for Information Management*, 3 (3): September 1986, pg. 155.

BIBLIOGRAPHY

Bivins, Kathleen T., and Eriksson, Lennart. "Reflink: A Microcomputer Information Retrieval and Evaluation System," *Information Processing & Management*, Vol. 18, No. 3, pp. 111-116, 1982.

Naylor, Chris. "Build Your Own Expert System for the IBM-PC and Compatibles," *Sigma Press*, Wilmslow, England, c. 1987.

Parrott, James R. "Expert Systems for Reference Work," *Microcomputers for Information Management*, 3 (3): pp. 155-171, September 1986.

Smith, Dana E., and Hutton, Steve M. "Back at 8:00 a.m . . . Microcomputer Library Reference Support Programs," *Collegiate Microcomputer*, Vol. II, No. 4, pp. 289-294, November 1984.

Yaghmai, N. Shahla, and Maxin, Jacqueline A. "Expert Systems: A Tutorial," *Journal of the American Society for Information Science*, 35 (5): pp. 297-305, September 1984.

POINTER vs. *Using Government Publications*: Where's the Advantage?

Karen F. Smith

SUMMARY. POINTER is a microcomputer program that simulates the advice of a government documents librarian by suggesting the use of particular reference books. *Using Government Publications* is a two volume work which identifies search strategies and sources of information for handling many specific topics and types of questions associated with federal documents. A comparison of these two reference aids reveals advantages and disadvantages of each as well as the difficulty of developing a conceptual framework for federal document research.

An expert system is a computer program that purports to simulate the reasoning or decision making process of a person who is knowledgeable in some field of human endeavor. POINTER is a computer program that simulates the advice of a government documents librarian by suggesting the use of particular reference books. To use a concrete example, if the user indicates that s/he is looking for a known item published before 1976 then POINTER will suggest using the *Cumulative Title Index to United States Public Documents, 1789-1976* to determine the Superintendent of Documents (SuDoc) classification number.

The author is Head of the Documents and Microforms Department of Lockwood Library, State University of New York at Buffalo, Buffalo, NY 14260.

THE DEVELOPMENT OF POINTER

The development of POINTER has been described elsewhere.[1] To summarize, POINTER was initiated with a Faculty/Librarian Cooperative Research Grant from the Council on Library Resources. The library was looking for an alternative way of providing reference assistance, because, at SUNY Buffalo, we are not able to staff the Documents Department reference desk with a librarian all the hours the library is open. The idea of a computerized system was intriguing because it could be used as a training tool and backup for student assistants and clerical staff as well as for direct patron use. It was thought that a computerized system would be flexible and direct as compared to a huge rack of guides and handouts which is the more traditional way libraries try to help patrons. And, despite an unknown incidence of computer phobia among the general population, we felt that students would be attracted to the new technology and that some might even feel less threatened approaching a computer with their questions than approaching a librarian.

How does one computerize the knowledge of a librarian? With POINTER it is done in BASIC and the structure of the program is derived from the types of questions that had been asked in the department and recorded during the previous year. The content and the delivery mechanism are separate design decisions. Either can be changed. For instance, the content of POINTER could be expanded and/or it could be fed into an expert system shell. The choice of BASIC means that other libraries do not need esoteric programming skills nor expensive software to adapt POINTER to their own situation.

POINTER was designed to be used in a dedicated microcomputer that would be placed on the service counter and constantly display a welcoming message. It would be the first thing a user would see upon entering the department. However, when we were finally able to bring POINTER out of the back room and into the public eye it had to share a public use microcomputer with the DISCLOSURE CD-ROM. The location is near the service counter but the availability of POINTER is not as immediately obvious to the person entering the department as had been envisioned. The menu the user sees provides three choices: POINTER for finding federal documents, a

New York State Document database, and DISCLOSURE for company information. This configuration has been available for the public to use since September, 1987.

Use of POINTER is low compared to use of DISCLOSURE but it is used. Occasionally we see people using reference books that they probably wouldn't have known about otherwise. Why isn't it used more? First, there has been no publicity except word of mouth during this test period. Second, we are no longer so desperately short staffed that users have nowhere else to turn. Third, the computer is being monopolized by users of DISCLOSURE. Fourth, it is difficult to grasp the concept of a computer reference program. If POINTER is not a database, what is it? If it doesn't answer questions, what does it do? To say that POINTER is like an expert system does not convey much information to the general user population.

WHAT POINTER DOES

POINTER does what a reference librarian does up to the point of recommending a particular reference book. Factors which contribute to the decision are made explicit in this computer program. These factors include the type of answer the person is looking for, what information the person already has, what time period is involved, etc. POINTER entices the user to reveal a type of information need by making choices from its menus. Then POINTER can advise on what reference books to use.

POINTER first leads the user through several screens that explain the importance of SuDoc classification numbers and how to identify them. When the user gets to the main menu s/he is confronted with four choices corresponding to the bold face headings in Figure 1. The user must mentally focus on a specific query and decide what type it is. Am I looking for a known item, information on a topic, or a map? Since many government documents do not have a title or have a title which is less important for searching purposes than the number assigned to them, known item queries are divided into two categories: title search and number search. Thus the basic choice at the main menu is between a known item search and a subject search.

The main menu includes maps even though maps are really a

subset of subject searching. It was expedient to place the choice there because the menu is short and because maps are a very distinctive format which are often housed in a separate location and accessed in special ways. The inclusion of maps on the "Type of Query" menu is an example of the conflicting influence of pure logic and pragmatism in the building of the POINTER system. It also illustrates the flexibility of POINTER to add new headings, since maps were not a choice in the original version.

A choice is made by typing a number from the menu and pressing ENTER. A new menu of choices then appears, possibly followed by other menus, and finally a list of reference books which will lead the user to the answer, appropriate sources, or SuDoc numbers. The list of reference books will vary depending on the starting point even when the object of the search is the same. For instance, laws are included under title search, number search, and subject search because the requirements of a user with a public law number differ from the requirements of a user who only knows the name of the law or what it is about. Figures 3 and 4 show examples of the output from POINTER.

Output is not automatically sent to a printer but can be printed using the Shift/PrintScreen key combination on the IBM PC. In general, POINTER is not an example of sophisticated programming. The ability to back up, display previous page, select more than one option, or abandon the search are not provided for. The program assumes that the user will deal with one question at a time and follow through to the end. If the user abandons the computer, the next person will have to answer a few questions to get back to the beginning. On the other hand, POINTER is quite reliable. It does not freeze up when it gets wrong input from the keyboard, but simply sends a helpful message to the screen so the user can try again. In answering a yes or no question the user may type YES, yes, Yes, Y, y, NO, no, No, N, or n.

SUBJECT SEARCHING IN POINTER

The types of subject searches listed in Figure 1 are illustrative of the difficulty a librarian has imposing a uniform scheme on government documents. It might be possible to force all the topics into a "branch of government" framework but that is not how we think. Very often it is some other aspect of the query that becomes of overriding importance like the fact that it is a census question or that a document from an early time period is needed. POINTER does not solve the dilemma of how best to conceptualize government document subject searching.

We shall now introduce a major alternative tool to which POINTER may be compared.

WHAT USING GOVERNMENT PUBLICATIONS *DOES*

Using Government Publications is a two volume work which presents search strategies and lists of sources for many specific topics and types of questions associated with federal documents. The authors are Jean L. Sears and Marilyn K. Moody.[2] *Using Government Publications* is the first work to address specific search strategies for finding material in government document collections. Bibliographic instruction writers often mention government documents as a separate step in the search process but fail to spell out how to proceed. Now Sears and Moody have paved the way.

Using Government Publications is organized into four basic sections: subject searching, agency searching, statistical searching, and special techniques. Known item searches are covered in a general chapter on search strategy included at the beginning of each volume. In all, there are 50 different chapters covering specific types of searches. Each chapter is arranged in a similar manner starting with a definition of the topic and a suggested search strategy, followed by lists of sources and narrative descriptions of sources, and ending with indexes to turn to for additional sources, names of online databases available, and related information including other chapters in the book and appropriate GPO Subject Bibliographies. Each chapter is self-contained. Titles are listed in order of importance or in logical progression and sources are repeated wherever relevant. This format lends itself to quick reference use.

PROBLEMS WITH THE INDEXING
OF USING GOVERNMENT PUBLICATIONS

Although *Using Government Publications* is designed with the hurried user in mind, its index is not. Index entries consist primarily of titles of sources and chapter titles. Thus *House Bills* and *Senate Bills* appear as titles but there is no entry under the generic word "Bills." The casual user might be misled into thinking that there is no discussion of bills in the text when, in fact, bills are covered as a special technique in the chapter on "Legislative History." There are no index entries for "Cost of Living" or "Inflation," both of which are implicit in the chapters on "Prices" and "Economic Indicators." Furthermore, getting to the relevant section of text is hampered by the fact that each volume of *Using Government Publications* is indexed separately. Thus the user must first of all decide which volume to look in. Would "Foreign Trade" be a subject search (vol. 1) or a statistics search (vol. 2)? Is finding regulations in the *Federal Register* a special technique (vol. 2) or an agency search (vol. 1)? Since the four basic sections of this work are not completely unambiguous categories, access to the text would be greatly facilitated if the number of entry terms in the index were increased and the two indexes were combined into one alphabet and repeated in each volume.

The four basic sections of *Using Government Publications* are not mutually exclusive because three of them—agency search, statistical search, and special techniques—can be considered simply extensions or elaborations of the subject search. The agency approach to information is, of course, fundamental for government documents. Agencies produce publications as an outgrowth or by-product of their functions and activities. The SuDoc classification, which groups documents by issuing agency rather than by subject, reinforces the primacy of the agency approach. So, when a particular agency is named or implied in a user's query, special strategies may be called into play, rather than following the ordinary subject search strategy. Likewise, when the user wants an answer in the form of numbers rather than words, special strategies geared to statistical searches can be called upon, which are more efficient than the ordinary subject search strategy. In fact many types of government documents—patents, for example—have their own set of specialized indexes and unique search procedures. However, all these queries start out as requests for information on a topic; they are seemingly subject searches.

CONCEPTUAL FRAMEWORK OF USING GOVERNMENT PUBLICATIONS

The distinction between subject, agency, statistical and special searches as used by Sears and Moody arises from the search strategy that is ultimately applied. These different search strategies are fully described in Chapter 2 of each volume but the user cannot be expected to know about them before choosing between volume one and volume two. Scanning the "Table of Contents" (see Figure 2 for an abbreviated version) is of some help in orienting the user, but even so the user might think directories, audiovisuals, and maps should be grouped with treaties, technical reports, and patents, which are format names, rather than with genealogy, agriculture, and education, which are topics. The user might think that elections is more of a statistical search than a subject search. The user might wonder why National Archives is treated as a special technique rather than as an agency search. These barriers to getting into *Using Government Publications* quickly are a minor matter that can be rectified in the next edition by redoing the index. However, the problem is symptomatic of a greater difficulty, that is, how to conceptualize the realm of government documents reference in such a way as to make it possible for the user to satisfy an information need without the intervention of a librarian.

POINT BY POINT COMPARISON OF THE TWO WORKS

Purpose

POINTER is designed for just one purpose: to get the user beyond the initial barrier of not knowing what to do next after successfully finding the Documents Department. *Using Government Publications* has several purposes other than the quick reference assistance use analyzed in this article. It can be used as a textbook or study guide, as a collection development tool for nondepository libraries, and as a point-of-use aid to demonstrate how complicated sources work.

Size

In terms of content, POINTER has approximately 130 screens of text, while *Using Government Publications* has over 400 printed pages, each of which is equivalent to at least four computer screens. In terms of physical space, POINTER requires a microcomputer and several square feet of space on a table, while *Using Government Publications* requires only two inches of shelf space or less than one square foot of table space if you leave it prominently displayed on the reference desk.

Cost

POINTER sells for $30. Additional expense is incurred in the form of staff time to customize the program and microcomputer equipment to run it. *Using Government Publications* costs $148 for the two volumes.

Inclusion of Material

POINTER is primarily a guide to reference books and not to sources of information, although a few of the actual sources may be included. For example, *American Statistics Index* is a reference book that leads to sources of statistics. The *Statistical Abstract* is a source for many figures but it can also be used as a reference tool to lead the user to more current or more detailed figures. *CPI Detailed Report* is a primary source. POINTER would include only the first two. *Using Government Publications* would include all three since it describes the most prominent sources or publications where information can be found on specific topics as well as the more general reference tools which can be used for finding additional information. Pertinent online databases are also mentioned in *Using Government Publications*, but not in POINTER. Both POINTER and *Using Government Publications* focus on official government publications, but each also includes major commercial reference tools which are essential for government documents reference work, such as *CCH Congressional Index*.

Presentation

POINTER presents the user with the title of a reference book, the call number, and the location in the library. Any library using POINTER would customize the call number and location statements in the program to fit its own local situation. *Using Government Publications* presents full bibliographic information for each source including the SuDoc number, which is very useful in a separate documents collection. It also includes descriptions of the content and explanations of how to use a particular source.

Organization

POINTER devotes nearly two thirds of its space to the intricacies of known-item searches. *Using Government Publications* covers known-item searches in two paragraphs. This is a major difference between the two works. When a person comes into the library looking for a specific item s/he should be able to find out whether the library does or does not own it. That is minimal level service which requires only a quick look in the card catalog or the serials list. But in the Documents Department where there is no overall catalog, the process is more complicated. POINTER goes to great lengths to make sure that the person who comes in looking for a House Report will be able to find it in the Serial Set, whether the librarian is around or not.

Using Government Publications devotes one third of its space to specific topics, whereas POINTER covers subject searching generically. *Using Government Publications* devotes another third of its space to statistics on specific topics where, again, POINTER handles statistical searches in a more general way. There are some sections in *Using Government Publications*, such as genealogy, patents, standards, and archival materials, that are lacking in POINTER. On the other hand, POINTER addresses biographical information and the Supreme Court, topics which are omitted from *Using Government Publications*. Figure 4 shows the output POINTER provides if you choose Subject Search/Judiciary Branch.

Although there is not one-to-one mapping between the organization and structure of POINTER and of *Using Government Publications*, the two works do cover many of the same topics. Thus, the agency search section in *Using Government Publications* corresponds roughly to the executive branch grouping in POINTER.

ADVANTAGES AND DISADVANTAGES

Because these two works, POINTER and *Using Government Publications*, are so dissimilar in format, it may be overlooked that they share a common purpose, which is to facilitate the use of government publications in libraries. Where is the advantage? *Using Government Publications* has the advantage of being in a format familiar to the user, although it suffers from being needlessly divided into two physical volumes with two separate indexes. Furthermore, *Using Government Publications* clearly has the advantage of being the more substantial of the two, with more than ten times the amount of text and ten to fifteen times the number of sources described.

POINTER, on the other hand, has some advantage for being able to zero in on the user's immediate need. It is easy to use and does not tax the user's patience with extra reading. POINTER has the advantage of being easily adapted to the circumstances of a particular library, which can customize the call numbers, location statements, and even the list of sources included in the program. POINTER is easily updated and is expandable. And it is less expensive.

POINTER is an ongoing experiment to see if reference expertise can be computerized. While far from perfect, it does prove that useful systems can be developed by working librarians, and it should encourage more librarians to try their hand at developing expert systems in difficult subject areas. The hard part is figuring out how to present the library's resources in the patron's terms rather than the librarian's. *Using Government Publications* struggles with this problem in delineating unique search strategies for the government documents domain. It is the closest thing we have to a standard work embodying the expert knowledge of government documents librarians. *Using Government Publications* could be used as the basis for the next generation of computerized government document reference systems.

REFERENCES

1. Smith, Karen F., Stuart C. Shapiro and Sandra Peters. "Final Report on the Development of a Computer Assisted Government Documents Reference Capability; First Phase" Supported by a Grant from the Council on Library Resources under the Faculty/Librarian Cooperative Research Program CLR 785-B. (Buffalo: State University of New York at Buffalo, November 1, 1984). Smith, Karen F. "Robot at the Reference Desk?" in *Energies for Transition*; Proceedings of the Fourth National Conference of the Association of College and Research Libraries, edited by Danuta A. Nitecki. (Chicago, ACRL, 1986), pp. 198-201. Reprinted: *College & Research Libraries*, 47 (September 1986) 486-490.

2. Sears, Jean L. and Marilyn K. Moody. *Using Government Publications*, Volume 1: Searching by Subjects and Agencies, Volume 2: Finding Statistics and Using Special Techniques. (Phoenix: Oryx Press, 1985-86).

FIGURE 1.
The Organization and Structure
of POINTER

INTRODUCTION

Title Search
  MONOGRAPH
  PERIODICAL
  SERIAL
  NUMBERED SERIES
  PUBLIC LAW
Number Search
  BILL
  PUBLIC LAW
  HOUSE OR SENATE REPORT OR DOCUMENT
  TECHNICAL REPORT
  PRESIDENTIAL EXECUTIVE ORDER
Subject Search
  BIOGRAPHICAL INFORMATION
  NUMERIC DATA
    1980 Census of Population and Housing
    Data prior to 1971

    Data after 1970
    Time series data
    Projections
NAMES, ADDRESSES, OR PHONE NUMBERS
GRANTS, FELLOWSHIPS, OR EMPLOYMENT OPPORTUNITIES
EXECUTIVE BRANCH
    Regulations
    Executive Orders/Presidential Statements
    Treaties
    Scientific or Technical Reports
    Periodical Articles
    General Information
LEGISLATIVE BRANCH
    Laws
    Debates
    Hearings
    Committee Prints
    Reports
    Documents
    Legislative History
    Bills/Proposed Legislation
JUDICIAL BRANCH
GENERAL INDEXES FOR SUBJECT SEARCHING
    1789-1892
    1893-1936
    1937-1946
    1947-1956
    1957-1966
    1967-1976
    1977-1982
    1983 to the present time
Maps

FIGURE 2.
The Structure
of *Using Government Publications*

INTRODUCTION

SEARCH STRATEGY AND GOVERNMENT DOCUMENTS
THE BASICS OF SEARCHING
The Subject Search
    FOREIGN POLICY
    FOREIGN COUNTRIES

OCCUPATIONS
FEDERAL GOVERNMENT JOBS
SELLING TO THE GOVERNMENT
BUSINESS AIDS
DIRECTORIES
TAX INFORMATION
TRAVEL INFORMATION
AUDIOVISUAL INFORMATION
COPYRIGHT INFORMATION
CLIMATE
ELECTIONS
MAPS
GENEALOGY
AGRICULTURE
EDUCATION
GEOLOGY
HEALTH
ENVIRONMENTAL AND NATURAL RESOURCES
The Agency Search
GOVERNMENT PROGRAMS AND GRANTS
REGULATIONS AND ADMINISTRATIVE ACTIONS
ADMINISTRATIVE DECISIONS
THE PRESIDENT
The Statistical Search
POPULATION STATISTICS
VITAL STATISTICS
ECONOMIC INDICATORS
BUSINESS AND INDUSTRY STATISTICS
INCOME
EARNINGS
EMPLOYMENT
PRICES
CONSUMER EXPENDITURES
FOREIGN TRADE STATISTICS
CRIME AND CRIMINAL JUSTICE STATISTICS
DEFENSE AND MILITARY STATISTICS
ENERGY STATISTICS
PROJECTIONS
Special Techniques
HISTORICAL SEARCHES
NATIONAL ARCHIVES
LEGISLATIVE HISTORY
BUDGET ANALYSIS
TREATIES

TECHNICAL REPORTS
PATENTS AND TRADEMARKS
STANDARDS AND SPECIFICATIONS
FOREIGN BROADCAST INFORMATION SERVICE REPORTS (JPRS/ FBIS)

FIGURE 3.
Sample Output from POINTER
Illustrating Referral to Reference Books
and Actual Sources

— REFERENCE TOOLS FOR SERIALS —

To find the SuDoc number for an annual report or other serial: USE THE FOLLOWING REFERENCE TOOLS:

Guide to U.S. Government Publications (Andriot)
   Doc Ref Z1223 Z7 A574
     located in the Documents and Microforms Reference Collection
Government Documents Catalog (MICRO MAX 800)
   Auto-graphics, Inc. rollfiche subscription
   located on the service counter

Here are the SuDoc numbers for a few popular serial titles . . .

Catalog of Federal Domestic Assistance PrEx 2.20:
Census of Manufactures C 3.24:
Census of Population C 3.223:
County Business Patterns C 3.204:
Crime in the United States J 1.14/7:
Economic Report of the President Pr Ex 40.9:
Handbook of Labor Statistics L 2.3/5:
Occupational Outlook Handbook L 2.3/4:
Statistical Abstract C 3.134: or Doc Ref HA202
U.S. Industrial Outlook C 61.34:
ZIP Code Directory P 1.10/8:

FIGURE 4.
Sample Output from POINTER
Illustrating Referral to Other Departments
and Libraries

— IF YOU WANT COURT CASES ON A SUBJECT —

The following source may prove useful for finding cites
to cases heard by the Supreme Court:

Guide to the U.S. Supreme Court (Congressional Quarterly)
Ref JK1571 C65 1979
located in the Reference collection on the 2nd floor

Opinions of the Supreme Court are printed in:
U.S. Reports (Decisions of the Supreme Court)
Ju 6.8: and Ju 6.8a:
located in the U.S. Documents collection

The best subject access to court cases is available at the
Law Library located in O'Brian Hall.

An Expert System for Microcomputers to Aid Selection of Online Databases

Rodes Trautman
Sara von Flittner

SUMMARY. An open-ended classification system for online databases was developed with nine attributes, each one of which has a controlled vocabulary schedule of categories. The first eight attributes involve miscellaneous coverage features and the ninth is a new subject classification using a three-level viewpoint schedule. Its categories were obtained by pooling and simplifying the subject indexes of three prominent database directories (Cuadra, KIPD, Williams), a gateway service (EasyNet), an online vendor's term frequency index (DIALINDEX), and an online strategy textbook (Hoover). This method of using published accounts captured the varying concepts deemed important by those already familiar with online database selection. Every category of each attribute was assigned a rank, which is a figure of its relative merit, albeit subjective, in terms of its generality. The classification system was used in creating a relational database of online databases that is the factual basis for retrieval.

A microcomputer program was written using the GURU (trademark) artificial intelligence development system. It consists of the internal database of all the attributes and ranks for the online databases considered and a script performance file that calls several modules. Each module has conventional context-sensitive help messages and rule-based expert system advice. The "user modeler" internal expert helps the users delimit their time, language, and geo-

---

The authors conducted this work at the Department of Library Science and Information Science, Åbo Academy, 20500 Turku, Finland, under a grant from the Academy of Finland. Current address of Rodes Trautman is Library Scientists, 7266 E. Camino Valle Verde, Tucson, AZ 85715; that of Sara von Flittner is Åbo Academy, 20500 Turku, Finland.

The authors are appreciative of the encouragement given by Mariam Ginman and the expert editing assistance of Phyllis Chen.

© 1989 by The Haworth Press, Inc. All rights reserved.

graphic coverage requirements and specify the extent and depth of coverage needed. The "question clarifier" internal expert helps users discover the underlying viewpoint of their need. The "searcher" internal expert gets four sets: one that the user asked for, and three more with successively broader viewpoints, including principal databases in the user's field of expertise. The "evaluator" internal expert analyzes the postings and guides the user, if requested, to the appropriate set to inspect. The inspection consists of reviewing uncontrolled textual descriptions that provide unique or special features of each database. The "ranker" internal expert provides an ordered list of those databases judged pertinent by the user.

Alternate methods of access to this expert system's knowledge are provided by the "browser" internal expert, which allows free-text search of text files and indexes. Users may contribute comments with the program's word processor and they may add their own data. Each session can be saved for continuing or restarting at a later time.

INTRODUCTION

Reference librarians had no problem with database selection a decade ago when only a small number of online databases existed. Today, even information specialists are interested in help because more than 4,000 online databases are already publicly available from dozens of international vendors (Cuadra, 1987). Even though Evans (1980) found that in each multiple database search, one file, termed a principal online database, generally gives a sufficient number of references, we believe that other databases may offer more pertinent information for a particular end-user. Furthermore, we believe that a wider selection of online databases would be used, by both professionals and end-users, if expert systems that give guidance were available.

The prototype system described in this paper is to be used offline to select a small group of likely databases for answering the actual research question online. This system could be installed in libraries to assist patrons in deciding which database to use later from their office or home computer. In libraries that offer end-user searching, the ordered database list would be obtained before the user logs on to a particular vendor to access the databases one by one. If the list happens to contain many databases from a vendor that supports simultaneous multiple database searching with a single command (e.g., ESA, 1987; Dialog, 1987), those databases could be used to specify the 10 to 20 files in the cluster. Even users not wanting to go online could use the system to find likely databases and then refer to the related print, microform, or CD-ROM counterpart in the library.

The system could also be used by a current awareness service to select a larger number of databases than three, which is the number commonly used for a customer profile. It might even be used by venture capitalists who want to produce a database and need to make sure that an equivalent one does not already exist. Such databases could represent new viewpoints or approaches as well as subjects. Finally, the system could be extremely useful in library schools and online training workshops.

BACKGROUND OF THE ONLINE INDUSTRY AND ARTIFICIAL INTELLIGENCE

Briefly, the online industry is characterized by dozens of vendors who provide access to thousands of databases developed by many producers (Glossbrenner, 1987). Proprietary retrieval software packages used by vendors have similar features but wide differences in syntax. Obtaining information online involves an interactive procedure in which the vendor reports the number of hits (postings) and waits for the user to decide whether the number is too small (especially if zero) or too large (say, for practical use). In the former situation, the user can broaden the search statement and try again. In the latter, the user can narrow the set by imposing additional coverage or conceptual limitations (facets). Then, after a set of reasonable size is obtained, the user must inspect some or all of the unit records for pertinency. To do so, the user usually looks at only a few of the many fields of data in each unit record.

Currently, database selection aids range from printed directories to online term frequency indexes. Problems with online aids are that (1) they are expensive to use, (2) some cover only one vendor, and (3) none offers advice. Our artificial intelligence system is intended to address these problems, being an offline selection aid that extends across all vendors and all subjects.

Artificial intelligence (Croft, 1987; Belkin et al., 1987; Croft &

Thompson, 1987) involves evolving programming concepts. In the branch called expert systems, current emphasis is on giving advice rather than merely listing things that meet certain criteria. The advice is supposed to result from an extremely user-friendly interaction in which the computer (i.e., the expert system) remembers details from a previous session, draws on the expertise of several human experts who are known for their ability to make decisions, and considers a large enough subject domain to be nontrivial. An appropriate domain would neither involve life-or-death situations, nor require a large amount of common sense or time to decide. However, the expert system should allow for change and be able to tell how it reached its conclusion. Knowledge engineering involves acquisition of the decision-making procedure of a human expert and coding it into a suitable software program.

PROJECT APPROACH

Our approach was to integrate producer, vendor, and knowledge engineer roles. That is, we not only generated a database of online databases, but also provided an expert system for access.

As a database producer, we had to decide:

1. What online databases should be included,
2. What fields would be useful,
3. Which fields should have descriptions using controlled vocabularies, and
4. Which fields should have free-text (uncontrolled) descriptions.

Reference details concerning these points are given in the Materials and Methods section. The development of controlled vocabularies for attributes of online databases, especially the viewpoint classification, is a major accomplishment of this work and tradeoffs involved are described in the Results section.

As a database vendor, we had to decide:

1. Whether to use a menu system or the common command language. We chose the former and give some screen displays in the Materials and Methods and Results sections.
2. How many modes of access we would support. We chose field searching in controlled vocabulary fields and display of uncontrolled free-text fields at appropriate places. Browsing of the free-text fields and our indexes is also permitted. It provides a modicum of "common sense" by allowing conventional character string access and lets the user find out what terms the program "knows." How these features are implemented is described in the Materials and Methods section.

As knowledge engineers, we had to decide:

1. How to extract knowledge from human experts proficient in selecting online databases. We chose those who have published and combined their suggestions for grouping into database families. We expect to include feedback from beta testing at a future time.
2. How to incorporate value judgments so that the system can give advice. We chose to provide a ranked list of appropriate online databases rather than a single recommendation. The methods developed for assigning the attribute ranks and for weighting the values to give one overall rank for each database is the second major accomplishment of this study; it is also described in the Results section.
3. Which artificial intelligence "shell" to use. We chose GURU (Micro Data Base Systems, Inc.; Holsapple & Whinston, 1986) because it combines standard functions (such as word processing, spreadsheet analysis, relational database management, telecommunications, and graphics) with rule-based expert system tools. We found its command language adequate to handle all the tasks currently specified for this project and powerful enough to allow incorporation of many more features envisioned for the future.

As producer, vendor, and knowledge engineers, we had to decide who the targeted audience would be. Some potential users of a "final" product are mentioned above.

MATERIALS AND METHODS

Knowledge Acquisition

There are a large number of journal articles relating to database selection (Hall, 1985, gives a bibliography of about 1,000 references specific to or about bibliographic databases). These journal articles reveal similarities and differences within a narrow group of related databases. In contrast, directories cover most databases, but with less discriminating detail. They have subject indexes of 500 to 2,000 terms, varying from specific words like "wine," with just four databases assigned, to broad terms like "economics," with hundreds. All these sources represent "experts" who have published about database selection. Our "knowledge acquisition" consisted of extracting from their printed record only the comments or parts pertaining to database selection itself, capturing all the different methods used by these experts:

> DIALINDEX categories (Dialog Information Services, Jan. 1987)
> EasyNet Database Directory (Oct. 1987)
> Directory of online databases (Cuadra, 8(1), 1987)
> Computer-readable databases (Williams, 2nd ed., 1985)
> Database directory (KIPD, 1985-86)
> Online search strategies (Hoover, 1982)

Online Databases Included

To avoid becoming embroiled in arguments about the definition of an online database, we selected vendors and included all of their database offerings. Thus, for us, an online database is whatever a particular vendor claims it to be. The domestic and international vendors we considered handle about a fifth of all the available databases and are:

> ADP Network Services
> BRS Information Technologies
> Data-Star
> Datasolve, Limited
> DataTimes

DIALOG Information Services, Inc.
G. Cam Serveur
NewsNet, Inc.
Pergamon ORBIT Infoline, Inc.
Telesystems/Questel, Inc.
VU/TEXT Information Services, Inc.
The H. W. Wilson Company
The Nordic databases
STN
ESA-QUEST
Finnish databases not included in the above

Standards

In coding online database attributes and constructing mnemonics we used the following international or readily available standards for:

Full database names
  Directory of online databases, Cuadra/Elsevier, vol.7, no.3 July 1986.

Abbreviated database names
  ISO 4, Documentation—Rules for the abbreviation of title words and titles of publications, developed by technical committee ISO/TC 46, Documentation, International Organization of Standardization, Geneva, 1984; and
  List of serial title word abbreviations. ISDS & ISO, Paris & Geneva, 1985.

Abbreviated geographic regions
  ISO 3166, Codes for the representation of names of countries. 2nd. ed., International Organization of Standardization, Geneva 1981,
  U.S. Postal Service two-capital-letter state codes, and
  Our own codes for groups of countries: #c cultural bloc; #e economic bloc; #g geographic bloc; #p political bloc, ## international.

Computers

IBM PC and MS-DOS compatible microcomputers were used. One computer with a 10mb fixed disk and full 640k primary memory was essential. Several other floppy disk systems were used simultaneously in the analysis and as multiple data entry stations in various parts of the project. Many productivity software programs, ranging from desktop organizers to programmable word processors, were used to manipulate and to both import and export text files between programs (Trautman, 1987).

Method of Programming

GURU (Micro Data Base Systems, Inc., P.O. Box 248, Lafayette, IN 47902) was selected as the artificial intelligence developmental "shell." Our program represents an application that can also be executed with a less expensive "run-time" version. The program consists of command files in the GURU procedural language, which is a very comprehensive and powerful computer language in its own right. The same command mode language is used across all of the individual modules and permits sharing of data. The current version of our program uses word processing, database management, and expert system modules. Eventually, we expect to incorporate existing business graphics, communications, spreadsheet, and natural language modules. The global arrays and other variables form the "blackboard," and the main procedural file constitutes the "scheduler" of current multi-expert systems (Croft, 1987). The integrated, synergistic GURU package (Holsapple & Whinston, 1986) obviates the language problem of communication among internal experts (Sparck Jones, Copenhagen, 1986).

The "scheduler" is a script performance file that has the main menu, Figure 1, and that calls the various performance files for each option. Each of these has (1) a menu display, (2) optional HELP display, and (3) optional ADVICE consultation. The consultations are rule-based expert systems in their own right that provide a "doctor-patient" interaction to help the user select an appropriate option. These internal experts are:

```
Step    WHAT DO YOU WANT ME, AS A COMPUTER, TO DO FOR YOU?
  1. CONTINUE from last session
       UPDATE your coverage restrictions -- NEW USERS pick this one

  2. ASK you about your current information need -- YOUR INQUIRY
       SHOW you what I know about specific databases -- FREE-TEXT BROWSE

  3. EXPLAIN how my program works
       LEARN from your comments or from supplementary data

  4. QUIT with optional saving of current session
```

Figure 1. The MAIN menu. Cursor movement ("arrow") keys move a highlight bar line-by-line through the options. You begin the session by picking one of the two options in Step 1. In Step 2, you learn something about online databases from the computer, normally by allowing the computer to probe about your information need, but alternatively, by allowing you to look up a specific database or to browse. Step 3 provides you an opportunity to find out how the computer reached decisions, especially useful if you disagree; even if you don't care to know, the computer (programmers) want your feedback and the second option in Step 3 puts you into the word processor for your comments or permits you to add your own records to the system. Step 4 ends the session. Any option may be selected at any time the MAIN menu is displayed.

1. The "user modeler," which determines the depth of interest, the time, language, and geographical coverage desired, and the user's viewpoint of the assorted kinds of information available online.
2. The "question clarifier," which narrows the user's need to a few of its 240 viewpoints.
3. The "searcher," which makes a Boolean search of an internal database that has nine coded characteristics for each of the online databases known to the program and then makes appropriate data available to the user and the "ranker" expert.
4. The "ranker," which presents the unique or "special features" information about each likely online database from a separate internal text database and asks for pertinence evaluation.
5. The "evaluator," which sums up the session with a ranked list of recommended databases.
6. The "browser," which provides the user with an alternative method of access, such as scanning of the internal files or getting statistics about them or the system.

RESULTS

Online Database Classification Concepts

An important result of this study is a coded file of online database attributes. Each attribute represents, in effect, a different classification scheme. Our problem was to integrate numerous schemes proposed by others in a manner that would exploit their suitability for (1) selecting online databases and (2) ranking them. Put negatively, a selection criterion is used to exclude from further consideration those online databases not useful for a specific user with a specific inquiry. In contrast, the rank assigned to an online database is an expression of its relative merit or value and is used to order after selection, excluding nothing.

We accepted nine attributes for classifying the "coverage" of an online database. The single-word descriptors for these attributes are: KIND, PERIOD, UPDATING, LANGUAGE, GEOGRAPHY, SOURCES, AUDIENCE, VOCABULARY, and VIEW-

POINT. Detailed schedules on disk are available from either author. In the next subsections, we give development details for several attributes—KIND, SOURCES, UPDATING, and VIEWPOINT—that caused us considerable difficulty. We first make some general design comments.

The schedule for each attribute consists of category descriptions, abbreviations (or mnemonics), selection codes, and ranks. Most categories are mutually exclusive. Hence, usually one category under each attribute will be selected during data entry as being most descriptive of the online database and then the corresponding mnemonics (where applicable), codes, and ranks will be entered into the unit record. All attributes must be considered for each online database.

The category mnemonics are codes that jog the memory, facilitate quality control of other coded data, and are used in brief screen displays. For an attribute category that has an unclear mnemonic string or none at all, the user may ask for a full description.

The category selection codes are controlled to make retrieval reliable and to reduce the size of files. In the prototype system, these codes are visible for debugging purposes, but in later versions, their display will be optional.

The category ranks are relative within an attribute. The single-digit values are subjective, but we followed these guidelines in assigning them:

1. The most common category in any attribute has a rank of 5,
2. Categories that are more international, broader, bigger, more generic, or more comprehensive in some other sense have a higher rank, and vice versa,
3. Categories that are not clearly hierarchical may have the same rank.

The overall rank for an online database is the weighted sum of its nine attribute ranks (i.e., the ranks of the selected categories). The default is to use equal weights, but the user has complete freedom to change these weights, and can even omit some attribute ranks in the computation. Users can also reverse the entire set of category ranks within any attribute so that what we considered to be of low merit can be changed to high. For example, we assign a higher rank to a full-text database than to one with references only. However, in a certain field, the reference databases might cover an enormous number of journals from around the world. The information specialist might therefore prefer to reverse the category ranks so that these reference databases have a higher rank than, say, a cover-to-cover full-text database of just one, though prestigious, journal. This reversal is done on retrieval, not in the internal database.

Factors Considered in Developing the KIND Attribute

Databases have been classified by others on the basis of mission (e.g., of an agency) or subject orientation (Hoover, 1982), and depth across disciplines of the source material (Karlsson, 1985). We merged the ideas of Hoover and Karlsson to arrive at four categories:

1. Multidisciplinary or multimission databases, which cover diverse fields, e.g., Scisearch, Dissertation Abstracts, and Environmental Bibliography,
2. Interdisciplinary or intermission databases, which cover interrelated fields, e.g., life sciences in BIOSIS, biosciences in Medline, and physics, electrical engineering, and computers in Inspec,
3. Single-discipline or single-mission databases, e.g., Zoological Record Online and Pollution Abstracts,
4. Subdiscipline or single-task databases, which cover only part of a discipline or represent a narrow task, e.g., Analytical Abstracts Online and Acid Rain.

We consider it unlikely for users to want to select on this basis, so only display the corresponding mnemonics of these categories during pertinency evaluation of online databases selected by other attributes. We do use these categories in figuring the rank for the KIND attribute, whose major contribution is from a second aspect, described next.

Online databases have also been classified according to the extent and format of the information included with schemes that are suitable for selection and ranking (Chung, 1986; Cuadra, 1987). Figure

2 shows the three formats of "directory," "bibliographic," and "numeric" across the top. Each of these has increasing extent levels, proceeding downwards, and all merge into the single "full text" format category at the bottom. "Full text" itself has several extent levels, leading to "executable full text," which includes downloadable software, for example. The dotted lines in Figure 2 show the traditional grouping into (1) "reference" databases, which refer users to the primary documents, persons, or organizations with the desired information, and (2) "source" databases, which give the complete information directly.

Table 1 gives our mnemonics, selection codes, and ranks for this composite kind of database attribute. The selection codes were chosen so that the internal "searcher" expert can issue a search statement with a relational operator. For example, to retrieve all online databases that have abstracts at least, the computer searches for "KIND GE 5." Planning selection codes so that relational operators can be used was also an important consideration for the attributes discussed below.

Factors Considered in Developing the SOURCES and UPDATING Attributes

Most database directories have such statements as "Sources include journal articles, symposia, and dissertations." We turned to the Library of Congress MARC schedules to see what kinds of sources have already been identified and coded, as our plan for developing the categories for each attribute was to incorporate, wherever possible, already existing standards or systems of classification. The MARC list was found to be adequate for our SOURCES attribute categories and is given in Table 2. Here we observe that a hierarchy doesn't seem appropriate; with this attribute we need an OR operator so that the user can select several different sources. The rank we assigned to each category is simply related to the number of sources specified by the producer.

For the UPDATING attribute, which refers to the frequency with which a producer updates an online database, the MARC schedule for the frequency of serials publication was tentatively adopted as the basis for the categories. However, use of a relational operator

```
          Reference                              Source

  DIRECTORY       BIBLIOGRAPHIC              NUMERIC

DIRECTORY with abstract  BIBLIOGRAPHIC with abstract    TEXTUAL-NUMERIC

                  BIBLIOGRAPHIC with summaries    NUMERIC with summaries

         SELECTIVE FULL TEXT
         COMPLETE FULL TEXT
         AUGMENTED FULL TEXT
         EXECUTABLE FULL TEXT
```

Figure 2. Online databases classified according to the extent and format of the information included (modified from Chung, 1986, and Cuadra, 1987).

Table 1. KIND: (1) MATERIAL as to nature and depth and (2) INFORMATION as to extent and format

MATERIAL			INFORMATION		
Category	Mnemonics	Rank*	Category	Mnemonics	Selection Rank*
Multidisciplinary or multimission	mu	+1	Directory " with abstract Bibliographic " with abstract " with summaries Numeric " with text " with summaries Full text, partial " , complete " , augmented " , executable	Dir Dir+A Bib Bib+A Bib+S Num Num+T Num+S FT FT+C FT+A SOFTW	0 4 3 5 1 4 4 5 6 6 2 4 5 5 6 6 7 7 7 7 8 8 9 8
Interdisciplinary or related missions	in	+0			
Single discipline or mission	si	-1			
Subdiscipline or single task	su	-2			

* The MATERIAL category rank is used only as a correction to the rank listed for EXTENT.

Table 2. SOURCES: types of materials covered, partially or cover-to-cover.

Category & Mnemonics	Selection*	Rank
Single source		4
Numerical data, statistics	#	
Journal articles, periodical articles	a	
Books, monographs	b	
Conference proceedings, symposia	c	
Dissertations, theses	d	
Governmental publications, legislation, legal documents	g	
Catalogs, organizations, biographical directories, handbooks	i	
Pamplets	p	
News, broadcasts	n	
Reviews	o	
Patents	p	
Reports, preprints, papers produced in research organizations	r	
Standards	s	
Translations		
Audiovisual and graphic material, maps	v	
Software	w	
Yearbooks, annual reports	y	
Two sources, e.g.	ab	5
Many, e.g.	abcp	6
Very broad assortment**, e.g.	abcprvy	7

* LC MARC schedule.
** Maximum of 12 sources.

for searching, as with the SOURCES attribute, doesn't quite work because the codes are usually the first letter of the terms and hence do not correspond to decreasing time intervals. As can be seen from Table 3, every updating frequency that has ever been used was assigned a unique letter in the MARC code. This is an example of "literary warrant" (Lancaster, 1986), in which storage of minutiae is paramount. But let's consider "user warrant." No user is likely to want only those databases that are updated precisely three times a year! We therefore abandoned the "standard" (i.e., the MARC

Table 3. UPDATING: frequency with which producer adds new material (lag between published date and entry date is not considered).

Category	Mnemonics	MARC* Selection	Rank
Closed	closed	n d	0
Occasionally, irregularly, or not applicable	unknown	u e	3
Triennially	triennial	h f	4
Biennially	biennial	g g	4
Annually	annual	a h	5
Semiannually	semiann	f i	5
Three times a year	3/year	t j	5
Quarterly	quarter	q k	5
Bimonthly	bimonth	b l	5
Monthly	monthly	m m	6
Semimonthly	semimon	s n	6
Biweekly	biweek	e o	6
Three times a month	3/month	j p	6
Weekly	weekly	w q	7
Semiweekly	semiwee	c r	7
Three times a week	3/week	i s	7
Daily	daily	d t	8
Instantly	instant	x u	8

* Library of Congress MARC codes for serials tend to be mnemonic, but do not permit relational operators.

code) and assigned letters sequentially so that a relational operator can be used. For example, to get all databases that are updated more than once a year, the computer should select for "UPDATING GT h."

Factors Considered in Developing the VIEWPOINT Attribute

The most challenging attribute we considered was the subject classification of online databases. No international standard exists, so we first considered general library classification schemes that cover all knowledge, as do online databases. The ensuing practical problem was how to assign categories when we had no personal experience with most of the thousands of online databases. We decided, instead, to analyze subject indexes of standard online database directories. The editors of the directories, experts in database selection, have assigned subject terms (descriptors) to the online databases. Each of these terms represents the name of a family for which its members are already listed. Table 4 gives the approximate number of online database families in six of the directories we considered.

We now had many terms, but how should they be presented to the user? The EasyNet opening menu gave us a clue: "Are you interested in people, places, organizations, or subjects?" This suggests that many information needs can be expressed other than by academic subjects. Our solution was to consider the possible underlying goal, prejudice, interest, theme, focus, or independent variable that the user might have when asking a question. We call examples of all of these by the generic term "viewpoints." As an aid to the user, we limited our categories in all levels to a number that could fit, together with brief explanations or examples, on a single 25-line screen. Ten first-level categories of viewpoints were adopted and have these brief names: TIME, FACTS, QUALITY OF LIFE, COMMUNICATIONS, COMMERCE, TECHNOLOGY, ADMINISTRATION, LIFE, ENVIRONMENT, and REALITY.

Figure 3 shows these ten first-level categories as they appear on the screen in our prototype version. A menu option form is used.

Table 4. Online database directories that were combined to develop viewpoint classification. Families are subject terms that have databases listed.

Code	Directory*	Approx. number of families
c	Cuadra	1500
e	EasyNet	800
w	Williams	550
k	KIPD	500
d	DIALINDEX	90
h	Hoover	15

* See References for complete citations.

Figure 3. Screen display of the ten first-level categories of the VIEWPOINT attribute (italics show optional HELP examples).

```
CAN YOU CHARACTERIZE YOUR INFORMATION NEED BY ONE OF THESE VIEWPOINTS?

A-- TIME            past (history), present (news) & future events
                    schedules, forecasts, investments, citations

B-- FACTS           organizations, people, places, products, terminology
                    library & museum holdings, funding research

C-- QUALITY OF LIFE culture, literature & leisure time activities
                    entertainment, build & run a home        -- ARTS & HUMANITIES

D-- COMMUNICATIONS  linguistics, education, publishing, computing
                    natural & machine languages, library     -- INFORMATION SCIENCE

E-- COMMERCE        domestic & international business & trade
                    banking, investment, consumer affairs    -- ECONOMICS
```

FIGURE 3. Screen Display (continued)

```
F--- TECHNOLOGY    manufacturing, producing, transporting products
                   construction, natural & synthetic materials      -- ENGINEERING

G--- ADMINISTRATION corporate & governmental management & human rights
                    labor, national & international law, patents    -- LAW

H--- LIFE          plants, animals & humans (sickness & health)
                   agriculture, human & veterinary medicine         -- BIOSCIENCES

I--- ENVIRONMENT   global view of our surroundings & survival
                   ecology, pollution, energy, space                -- EARTH SCIENCES

J--- REALITY       physical & philosophical nature of matter & thought
                   pure science, logic, philosophy                  -- INTERDISCIPLINARY FIELDS

            H E L P            A D V I C E
```

The screen begins with a heading line, and each category is followed by a few words suggesting its contents. Further explanation of the categories, shown in italics, can be obtained through the HELP option and expert consultation obtained through the ADVICE option.

Each of the first-level categories has a variable number of second-level categories that range roughly from specific to general in order to encourage the user to pick a narrower category first. An example of the LIFE second-level screen display is given in Figure 4, with the optional interlineation of HELP examples.

Application of the Viewpoint Classification to Subject Terms in Directories

We sorted and grouped repeatedly the thousands of terms from the directories listed in Table 4 into viewpoint categories, carrying along the number of online databases listed and the directory code for each. We found it valuable to further group the terms into a third level, using a subject term from the directories as the generic heading where possible. Sometimes, it was necessary to create a new umbrella term for the underlying concept. The result was a schedule for converting the directory terms to our categories. An example of one of the 1200+ lines of the alphabetical schedule is

"H5A Psychology(c10)(e9)(w61)(k19)(d10)."

Data entry using our viewpoint classification is now rather straightforward. For each online database, we take the subject terms that have been assigned in each directory and get the codes from the schedule. The original assignment, which was made in each of the directories, of individual databases to each term has been retained. (The terms "general" and "reference" in the directories were the only ones not used: databases so indexed were assigned more specific terms.)

Principal Databases

The subject indexing of the directories is often very narrow; consequently, the few databases listed are those to which the editor wishes to call attention. A serious concern is that there are major,

Figure 4. Screen display of the LIFE second-level categories of the VIEWPOINT attribute (italics show optional HELP examples).

```
H1? AGRICULTURE, food science & agribusiness
    forestry, pulp & paper, agricultural engineering

H2? VETERINARY MEDICINE, PLANT & ANIMAL sciences
    fisheries, crops, dairy science, fertilizers, pesticides

H3? SAFETY on & off the job
    emergencies, occupational medicine, traffic safety

H4? Human HEALTH CARE, NUTRITION, PUBLIC HEALTH & SOCIAL SERVICES
    nursing, hospitals, handicapped, food additives

H5? Families, PSYCHOLOGY, PSYCHIATRY & mental health
    human relations, group dynamics, behavioral & mental disorders
```

FIGURE 4. Screen Display (continued)

```
H6? Clinical medicine, DISEASES, PHARMACEUTICALS & drugs
    diagnosis, pathology, surgery & other therapies, toxicology

H7? PRECLINICAL MEDICINE & BIOLOGICAL specialties
    anatomy, biochemistry, genetics, immunology, microbiology

H0? BIOLOGY & MEDICINE, in general & interdisciplinary
    life sciences, biomedicine, medical industry, agriculture

H7? ALL these aspects of LIFE should have something of interest
    agriculture, human & veterinary medicine    -- BIOSCIENCES


        HELP                    ADVICE
```

comprehensive databases that also have a considerable amount of information on the same narrow topic. Such databases are called "principal databases" (Evans, 1980). We used our own judgment in assigning our viewpoint categories to these, introducing a special truncation code to indicate their broad coverage in either the second or third levels, or both.

The program retrieves four sets of online databases: (1) those that share the user-selected generic viewpoint (the ninth attribute), but are restricted to those that meet the user's requirements specified by the first eight attributes; (2) those that have the same viewpoint, but without the user's restrictions; (3) principal databases with the same viewpoint; and (4) principal databases with the next broader viewpoint. The postings are displayed first. The user can decide which set to inspect, whether to restart, or whether to ask the "evaluator" expert for advice.

Unique Features of Online Databases

For whatever set is selected, the program displays specific, uncontrolled text that pinpoints differences or special features that distinguish one member from another. In each screen display, the user may ask for more data in order to assign the online database into one of three categories: (1) pertinent, (2) not right, or (3) not now. The last category provides a list of those online databases that didn't meet the user's immediate information need, but awakens some other interest. The second category represents "false drops." These might be attributed to data entry coding errors. Alternatively, they could be "relevant" to the search statement, but not "pertinent" to the user's possibly subconscious information need (Fugman, 1985). The final display is a ranked list of the pertinent online databases with a few of the attribute mnemonics listed for each.

DISCUSSION

Advantages of Combining Conventional Database and Rule-Based Schemes

Our "database" is actually several relational database files about our subject: online databases. This internal database is the heart of our system and the rule-based internal experts provide user-friendly access to it. Consequently, we can take advantage of sophisticated database management techniques that have been developed over the years and can incorporate new artificial intelligence concepts as they emerge. Often, such a clear distinction between conventional database and rule-based schemes is not made. In fact, many expert systems have the underlying data completely embedded in the rule structure, with the term "knowledge base" used to denote the aggregate. Dividing the overall problem into parts and assigning each to an internal expert, besides clarifying our thinking, facilitates independent programming of the parts in as much detail as desired and independent updating as the project progresses.

Because the database underlies reasoning in the program, it was desirable to include fields and manipulations that have overtones of current artificial intelligence thinking, such as:

1. A value judgment (rank) for each attribute field and an overall ranking for each database formed by dynamically combining individual attribute ranks into a single value at the time of display. The user can modify this overall ranking algorithm by adjusting the weights assigned to the attribute ranks.
2. Coded records for speed and quality control, and free-text, variable-length records for uncontrolled keyword descriptions that might spark the user's imagination.
3. An ADVICE function, provided by consultation with one of the several internal expert systems, as well as a HELP function provided in a conventional, context-sensitive manner. The user can opt to select HELP or ADVICE, or neither, at several points during the session.
4. Browsing of indexes and internal text files, as well as alternative methods of subject classification.

These options all enable the user to exercise a modicum of common sense. Common sense has so far eluded programming and so is lacking in the current generation of artificial intelligence programs. We treat users as "subject specialists" who know when they are not getting the information they need and will pursue other options offered.

The complete viewpoint classification schedule is a composite index, by generic categories of user information needs, to those directories included. It shows at a glance how various editors differ in their assignment of subject terms. But this is the essence of the artificial intelligence approach. We wanted to capture the various ways in which different human experts view the problem. Our procedure captures the concepts deemed important by those already familiar with online databases. We want to facilitate new conceptual linkages in non-subject categories and interdisciplinary linkages in subject categories. Our ultimate goal is to get more online databases to be used—or at least to be considered.

Updating of Our Program

Our viewpoint classification can be updated by incorporating new families within an existing category, adding new categories in the existing three levels, or adding a fourth level. In general, deciding how much updating to allow in a controlled vocabulary is tricky because if there are too many changes, it is no longer controlled, and if too few changes are allowed, it quickly becomes obsolete. However, updating is relatively easy in our scheme because of its generic, rather than specific, nature.

The number of online databases is constantly changing, with more added every month than are dropped. How will our offline program be kept current? Floppy disk updates could be distributed or the existing communications module of GURU could be used for downloading updates. Each installation could even add updates along with its own private data. We prefer to delay an answer to this very serious question until the system is fully tested in the field.

Could Online Industry Changes Render Our Program Obsolete?

These are the categories of current online database selection aids, none of which are instantly updated:

1. Directories across all vendors and all kinds of databases: these are usually used offline, but several are now online,
2. Directories across the database offerings of a single vendor: these are normally used offline, but most vendors also have modified online versions,
3. Term frequency indexes across the database offerings of a single vendor: these must be used online, but some do permit complex search statements,
4. Menu systems on gateways across several vendors: these must be used online,
5. Menu systems in front-end software across a few vendors: these can be used either online or offline,
6. Literature reviews across databases in very restricted fields, and
7. Personal advice from an intermediary.

More sophisticated offline front-end software (Sormunen & Nurminen, 1987) can be expected to have the same problem we anticipate in updating. Even if online facilities from vendors are greatly expanded, we do not expect them to replace our program. Consider for a moment these limitations of term frequency indexes offered by some vendors (e.g., DIALINDEX, CROSS, DBI), which are used with very specific search statements to determine which databases have postings:

1. Only the database offerings of the connected vendor are provided,
2. The service is not free,
3. The databases do not have a common controlled vocabulary,
4. There will be a few postings on almost any topic with large databases,
5. The user still must decide whether a larger number of postings means better, and
6. Implied concepts (viewpoints) cannot be searched.

Cute versus Machinelike Messages

Should artificial intelligence programs represent humans as ideal problem solvers or, as they really are, problem generators? Should such programs represent humans as cool and logical or as subjective, arbitrary, and degradable under stress? Whether or not one believes computers can exhibit intelligence is irrelevant; what is important is that current concepts of artificial intelligence provide a fresh approach to programming. Instead of forcing a user to become a specialist in computer languages in order to communicate with a machine, enlightened software designers now make the interaction "user-friendly," cautiously cute, and they enable the machine to give their "advice" instead of just listing items that match specific attributes (Winograd & Flores, 1986).

Our screen design is quite common in menu systems, but our use of personal pronouns for the computer is not. We have experimented with suggesting that the user treat the program as a robot with an "alien intelligence," even though the intelligence is that of the programmers (Trautman & Gothberg, 1982; Smith, 1986). Whether this is cute or helpful in adjusting attitudes toward computer assistance is debatable. However, we illustrate by presenting the summary as though it were delivered by a talking robot.

SUMMARY

HELLO. I am an artificial intelligence, programmed to give advice on database selection. Would you entrust database selection to me as an alien intelligence? The answer is "no" if you are a master searcher for information from the many databases available online or on CD-ROMs. It is also "no" if you like to deal with a human intermediary who knows about certain subsets of these, who knows other human experts you can consult, or has a fair amount of subject knowledge in your speciality. I presume that your answer is "yes" and you are consulting me because you do not have the time to search through all that is written about the 4,000 publicly available databases.

I have heard that online databases defy classification, perhaps because they cover many, if not most, of the things you are concerned with at the office or at home. I don't believe that and so what we want to do together is to actually produce a list of online databases that should contain pertinent information for you.

Coming from another world, I expect an online database to render service. Which database to use will depend on what service you expect and on the underlying focus of your information need. Perhaps you don't think the way I do and won't recognize your focus among my viewpoints. If that is the case, then you may select a traditional—for you—academically oriented approach, or you may browse my indexes. You may even search all of my text files for any word or words using your Boolean logic.

You probably have some minimum requirements for what or how much information is acceptable. I caution you that I consider such restrictions handicaps and so I will tell you first only the numbers of databases that meet your need before and after imposing your limitations. Although I do have a pretty good idea of what some user stereotypes consider too many and too few, I would rather rely on your common sense about sizes of numbers to tell me which group to consider further.

Then I will show you the unique differences between the databases. You may look at as many as you wish from the top of a ranked list all the way to the bottom. None will be excluded, if you have the time to read the details about each.

I hope you will teach me about those databases unknown to me and I hope you will correct my erroneous information. For these tasks, I will let you use my word processor.

Acceptance, or at least recognition, of "artificial intelligences" requires an inquisitive attitude on your part. "Alien" is used advisedly to stress that you really don't know very much about my image of my environment and so you must try to find out if I know some things that you already know.

It is in this alien intelligence sense that my programmers have attempted to create an expert system for online database selection. If successful, their scheme could be extended to include other reference tools, such as monographs, microforms, or even to other inventory problems. They used a commercial program, "GURU," that integrates, in a synergistic way, many intellectual functions common to professionals.

To be worth the effort of knowledge engineers, a suitable expert system problem should not involve a life-or-death issue, it should not be trivial, there must be human experts who can be quizzed or who have written about their decision-making process, and decisions can't take more than a few hours. Experts disagree, so there has to be come means for resolving conflicting advice. I consider online database selection an appropriate problem. However, it is possible for a misguided device to misinterpret the inaccurate data at hand. Instead of artificial intelligence, that is what you call profound stupidity or natural ignorance.

REFERENCES

Belkin, Nicholas J., Borgman, Christine L., & Brooks, Helen M. et al. Distributed expert-based information systems: An interdisciplinary approach. *Information Processing & Management* 23 (5): 395-409, 1987.

Croft, W. B., ed. Artificial intelligence and information retrieval. Special issue. *Information Processing & Management* 23 (4); 1987.

Croft, W. B. & Thompson, R. H. I R: A new approach to the design of document retrieval systems. *Journal of the American Society for Information Science* 38 (3): 389-404; 1987.

Cuadra, Carlos, ed. *Directory of online databases*. New York: Cuadra/Elsevier; published quarterly.

Chung, Catherine, ed. *Directory of periodicals online: Indexed, abstracted & full-text*. Vol. 1: News, law & business. 2nd ed. Washington, D.C.: Federal Document Retrieval; 1986.

Dialog Information Services, Inc., 3460 Hillview Ave., Palo Alto, CA 94304. Announcing Dialog OneSearch(sm)! *Chronolog* 15 (10): 231, 233, 234-237; October 1987.

EasyNet, 134 N. Narberth Ave., Narberth, PA 19072 (division of Telebase Systems).

ESA. European Space Agency (ESA-ESRIN), Via Galileo Galilei, 00044 Frascati (Rome), Italy (Quest User Manual).

Evans, John Edward. Database selection in an academic library: Are those big multi-file searches really necessary? *Online* 4 (2): 35-43, 1980.

Fugman, Robert. The five-axiom theory of indexing and information supply. *Journal of the American Society for Information Science* 36(2): 116-129; March 1985.

Glossbrenner, Alfred. *How to look it up online: Get the information edge with your personal computer*. New York: St. Martin's Press; 1987.

Hall, James L. "Bibliography: Selected References on Online Bibliographic Databases," pp. 354-436 in *Online Bibliographic Databases*, 4th ed. London: Aslib, 1985.

Holsapple, Clyde W. & Whinston, Andrew B. *Manager's guide to expert systems using GURU*. Homewood, IL: Dow Jones-Irwin; 1986.

Hoover, Ryan E., ed. *Online search strategies*. White Plains, NY & London: Knowledge Industry Publications; 1982.

Karlsson, Ulla & Wallin, Marie. Att ska i databaser. Interaktiv informationsskning: metoder och mjligheter. Ballerup: Bibliotekkscentralens frlag: 24-25; 1985 (Nordinfo-publikation 8).

KIPD. *Database directory 1985-1986*. White Plains, NY & London: Knowledge Industry Publications.

Lancaster, F. W. *Vocabulary control for information retrieval*. 2nd ed. Arlington, VA.: Information Resources Press; 1986.

Micro Data Base Systems, Inc., P. O. Box 248, Lafayette, IN 47902.

Smith, Karen F. Robot at the reference desk? *College & Research Libraries* 47: 486-490; 1986.

Sormunen, Eero & Nurminen, Riitta. Search aid software packages and services. A survey prepared for Nordinfo, Helsinki; 1987 (Nordinfopublikation 11, IANI-rapport 1).

Sparck Jones, Karen. A problem in the construction of expert systems for document retrieval. Lecture at the Nordic meeting: AI and IR Interactions in Expert Systems and in Retrieval. The Royal School of Librarianship, Copenhagen, Denmark, 10-12 December 1986. (Nordinfo).

Trautman, Rodes. Sources and types of software. *Library Software Review* 6(3): 134-139; 1987.

Trautman, Rodes & Gothberg, Helen M. A reference tools database: A proposed application for a microcomputer at the reference desk. In: *Video to Online: Reference Services and the New Technology*. Edited by Bill Katz and Ruth A. Fraley. New York: The Haworth Press; 1982: 195-198.

Winograd, Terry & Flores, Fernando. *Understanding computers and cognition: A new foundation for design*. Norwood, NJ: Ablex; 1986.

Williams, Martha E., ed. *Computer-readable databases. A directory and data sourcebook*. Chicago: American Library Association; 1985.

For Product Safety Concerns and Information please contact our EU
representative GPSR@taylorandfrancis.com
Taylor & Francis Verlag GmbH, Kaufingerstraße 24, 80331 München, Germany

www.ingramcontent.com/pod-product-compliance
Lightning Source LLC
Chambersburg PA
CBHW071824300426
44116CB00009B/1426